THE PRINCETON REVIEW

High School
Biology Review

D1564151

THE PRINCETON REVIEW

High School
Biology
Review

BY KIM MAGLOIRE

RANDOM HOUSE, INC.
NEW YORK 1998
WWW.RANDOMHOUSE.COM

Princeton Review Publishing, L.L.C.
2315 Broadway, 3rd Floor
New York, NY 10024
E-mail: info@review.com

ISBN 0-375-75081-9

Editor: Rachel Warren
Production Editor: Jenn Nagaj, Silverchair Science + Communications
Designer: Illeny Maaza
Illustrations: Production Department of The Princeton Review

Manufactured in the United States of America

9 8 7 6 5 4 3 2

First Edition

ACKNOWLEDGMENTS

The author thanks the production staff of The Princeton Review. Special thanks go to Jennie Yoon, Melanie Sponholz, and Rachel Warren in the publishing department.

Heartfelt thanks go to my editor, Sean Barry, for his support and immense contribution to the manuscript.

Finally, I dedicate this book to my nephews, Sacha and Michael.

CONTENTS

PREFACE

Welcome to *High School Biology Review*. This book is designed to help high school students review and master the concepts learned in an introductory biology course. As you'll soon see, the majority of the book is devoted to a simple, straightforward review of the material introduced in a first-year biology course. At the end of each chapter you'll find quiz questions that you can use to identify the strengths and weaknesses in your understanding of the material. In addition, the last section of the book contains two practice exams, each with more than one hundred commonly asked biology questions.

Taken together, the review and the practice exams are a perfect study aid: Our review will bring you up to speed on your biology, and the questions and full-length exams provide excellent practice for those grueling midterm and final exams.

THE PRINCETON REVIEW APPROACH

The Princeton Review is the nation's fastest-growing educational publishing company. In addition to our well-known line of test review publications, our catalogue now includes a series of high school level, subject-based books, such as this one.

Rather than try to teach you everything there is to know about biology, we highlight and explain key concepts in a way that makes learning easy. There's no need for us to go into boring, drawn-out lectures. Rather, we jump right to the crucial topics, providing simple explanations of the most important points.

Here's a quick summary of what you'll find in these pages:

CONTENT

High School Biology Review contains a comprehensive review of the material covered in a standard introductory biology course. Consequently, *High School Biology Review* is the ideal supplement to your textbook and class notes: part study guide, part resource tool.

Because vocabulary is essential to the study of biology, special attention is given throughout the book to biological terms. In each chapter, important words are printed in bold type and fully explained.

As mentioned above, *High School Biology Review* also contains quiz questions at the end of each chapter and two full-length biology exams. Whereas the practice questions test your understanding of specific concepts presented in individual chapters, the two full-length exams offer a great way to test your mastery of the material.

LANGUAGE

One of the greatest difficulties students have with biology is the language. All those new terms! We simplify the learning process by presenting key terms and concepts in an accessible, easy-to-read manner.

ILLUSTRATIONS

High School Biology Review also contains dozens of illustrations and tables. These visual guides will help you grasp the concepts presented in each section.

LET'S GO!

Whether you're using this book to prepare for exams or simply to review your year of biology, it's bound to make your task a breeze. Without any further ado, let's leap into the world of biology . . .

CHAPTER 1

The Chemistry of Life

ELEMENTS

Although the countless substances in the universe are chemically diverse, they all have one thing in common: They are made up of **elements**. Elements are substances that cannot be broken down into simpler substances by chemical means. There are 92 such elements in nature.

To distinguish the elements from one another, scientists have come up with a shorthand using **chemical symbols**. In this system of notation, many elements are referenced by their first letters. For example, carbon is represented by the letter *C* and hydrogen by the letter *H*. Although these two examples seem simple and sensible, other symbols may strike you as a bit bizarre. Iron, for example, is represented by the symbol *Fe*. As strange as this might seem to us, it would seem sensible to the ancient Romans: The Latin word for iron is *ferrum*. In fact, many chemical symbols are drawn from the Latin and Greek names for specific elements.

Fortunately, you won't have to learn any dead languages to recognize the symbols for the elements. All you'll need is the periodic table of elements. If there's ever a doubt in your mind about a chemical symbol, just look it up in the periodic table.

Periodic Table of the Elements

1 H 1.0																	2 He 4.0
3 Li 6.9	4 Be 9.0											5 B 10.8	6 C 12.0	7 N 14.0	8 O 16.0	9 F 19.0	10 Ne 20.2
11 Na 23.0	12 Mg 24.3											13 Al 27.0	14 Si 28.1	15 P 31.0	16 S 32.1	17 Cl 35.5	18 Ar 39.9
19 K 39.1	20 Ca 40.1	21 Sc 45.0	22 Ti 47.9	23 V 50.9	24 Cr 52.0	25 Mn 54.9	26 Fe 55.8	27 Co 58.9	28 Ni 58.7	29 Cu 63.5	30 Zn 65.4	31 Ga 69.7	32 Ge 72.6	33 As 74.9	34 Se 79.0	35 Br 79.9	36 Kr 83.8
37 Rb 85.5	38 Sr 87.6	39 Y 88.9	40 Zr 91.2	41 Nb 92.9	42 Mo 95.9	43 Te (98)	44 Ru 101.1	45 Rh 102.9	46 Pd 106.4	47 Ag 107.9	48 Cd 112.4	49 In 114.8	50 Sn 118.7	51 Sb 121.8	52 Te 127.6	53 I 126.9	54 Xe 131.3
55 Cs 132.9	56 Ba 137.3	57 *La 138.9	72 Hf 178.5	73 Ta 180.9	74 W 183.9	75 Re 186.2	76 Os 190.2	77 Ir 192.2	78 Pt 195.1	79 Au 197.0	80 Hg 200.6	81 Tl 204.4	82 Pb 207.2	83 Bi 209.0	84 Po (209)	85 At (210)	86 Rn (222)
87 Fr (223)	88 Ra 226.0	89 †Ac 227.0	104 Unq (261)	105 Unp (262)	106 Unh (263)	107 Uns (262)	108 Uno (265)	109 Une (267)									

*Lanthanide Series:

58 Ce 140.1	59 Pr 140.9	60 Nd 144.2	61 Pm (145)	62 Sm 150.4	63 Eu 152.0	64 Gd 157.3	65 Tb 158.9	66 Dy 162.5	67 Ho 164.9	68 Er 167.3	69 Tm 168.9	70 Yb 173.0	71 Lu 175.0

†Actinide Series:

90 Th 232.0	91 Pa (231)	92 U 238.0	93 Np (237)	94 Pu (244)	95 Am (243)	96 Cm (247)	97 Bk (247)	98 Cf (251)	99 Es (252)	100 Fm (257)	101 Md (258)	102 No (259)	103 Lr (260)

ESSENTIAL ELEMENTS OF LIFE

Believe it or not, approximately 99% of living matter is made up of just six elements:

1. Sulfur

2. Phosphorus

3. Oxygen

4. Nitrogen

5. Carbon

6. Hydrogen

The three most common elements are nitrogen, carbon, and hydrogen. These three are particularly abundant in nature and are crucial to many biological processes.

WHAT ARE COMPOUNDS?

When two or more different elements combine in a fixed ratio they form a chemical **compound**. Because compounds are made up of elements, you might think that compounds would have the same properties as their constituent elements. Surprisingly, this is not always the case. A classic example of this is water.

Hydrogen and oxygen exist in nature as gases. Yet when they combine to form water, they turn into a liquid. This combination of hydrogen atoms and oxygen atoms is known as a **chemical reaction** and can be depicted as a **chemical equation** using the symbols discussed earlier:

$$2H_2 \, (g) + O_2 \, (g) \rightarrow 2H_2O \, (l)$$

In a chemical reaction, the starting materials or **reactants** are written on the left side of the equation, while the **products** of the reaction are written on the right side. In the reaction above, hydrogen and oxygen are the reactants, and water is the product. The lower-case letters beside the symbols for hydrogen, oxygen, and water indicate the states of the reactants and products. As mentioned above, hydrogen and oxygen come together as gases (g) to form liquid water (l).

CARBON: THE VERSATILE ATOM

Now that we've discussed compounds in general, let's talk about a special group of compounds. Most of the chemical compounds present in living organisms contain skeletons of carbon and hydrogen atoms. When a molecule contains both carbon and hydrogen, it is called *organic*. Most of the molecules essential for life are **organic compounds**.

In contrast, molecules that do not contain carbon atoms are called **inorganic compounds**. The most common inorganic compounds found in nature are **water** and **salts**. Water (H_2O) plays an important role in chemical reactions and accounts for nearly 70% of your body weight. Salts, such as NaCl, supply cells with the ions necessary for many chemical reactions.

To recap:

1. Organic compounds contain carbon and hydrogen atoms.

2. Inorganic compounds do not.

Now let's focus on four of the most important classes of organic compounds:

1. Carbohydrates

2. Amino acids

3. Lipids

4. Nucleic acids

CARBOHYDRATES

Carbohydrates are among the most important organic compounds. They serve many roles in living things, several of which are discussed in this chapter. Carbohydrates are made up of carbon, hydrogen, and oxygen, usually in a ratio of 1:2:1. Carbohydrates can be represented by the formula $C_nH_{2n}O_n$.

Carbohydrates are categorized as either **monosaccharides, disaccharides**, or **polysaccharides**. Don't let the long words fool you: *Saccharide* is just a fancy term for a sugar (just think of *saccharin*, the artificial sweetener found in diet soda). The prefixes *mono-, di-,* and *poly-* refer to the number of sugars in each molecule. *Mono-* means one, *di-* means two, and *poly-* means many. A monosaccharide is therefore a carbohydrate made up of only one type of sugar.

Monosaccharides: Simple Sugars

Monosaccharides, the simplest sugars, serve as an energy source for cells. The two most common monosaccharides are **glucose** and **fructose**.

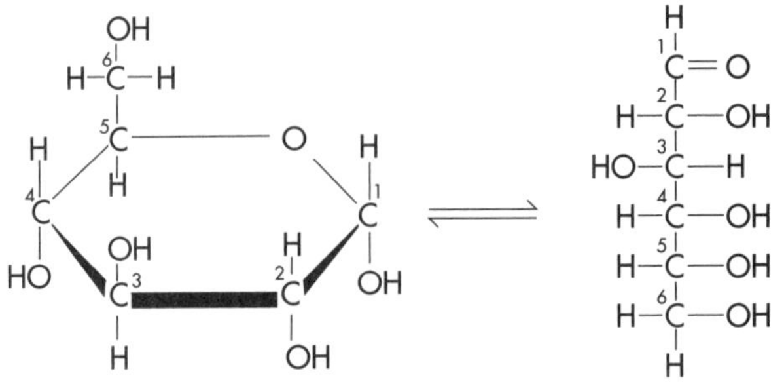

Ring form of glucose

Straight-chain
form of glucose

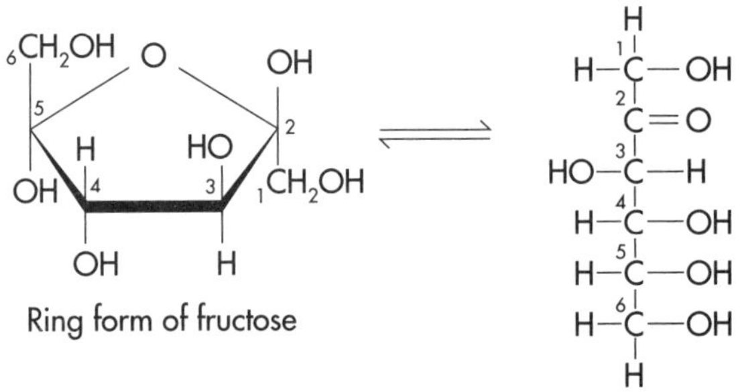

Ring form of fructose

Straight-chain
form of fructose

Both of these monosaccharides are six-carbon sugars that have the chemical formula $C_6H_{12}O_6$. Glucose, the most abundant monosaccharide, is the sugar most often found in living things. Plants produce glucose using the energy from sunlight (this process, *photosynthesis*, is discussed later), whereas animal cells break glucose apart, releasing the energy stored in its chemical bonds. Fructose, although similar to glucose, is not quite as common. It is found, among other places, in fruits.

How Do We Form a Disaccharide?

What happens when two monosaccharides are brought together? A hydrogen (—H) from one sugar molecule combines with a hydroxyl group (—OH) from another sugar molecule. What do H and OH add up to? Water (H_2O)! When these two sugar molecules combine, a molecule of water is removed. This process is called **dehydration synthesis**: *dehydration* for the removal of water and *synthesis* for the manufacturing of the new molecule. Through dehydration synthesis, the two monosaccharides are chemically linked, forming a **disaccharide**. Maltose is a common disaccharide formed by the combination of two molecules of glucose:

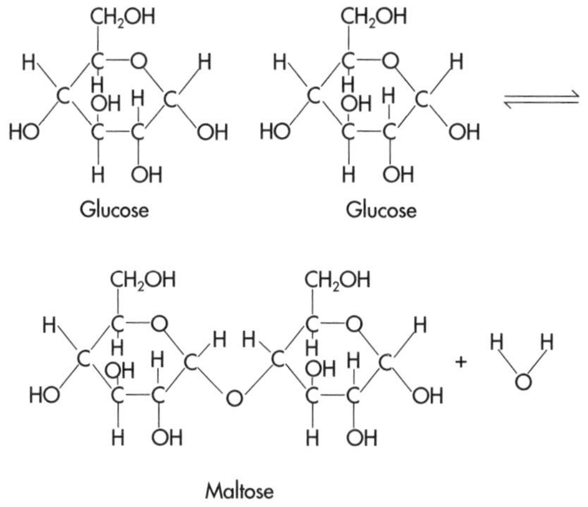

Glucose   Glucose

Maltose

Now, what if you want to break up the disaccharide and form two monosaccharides again? Just add the water molecule we took out when combining them. This process is called **hydrolysis**:

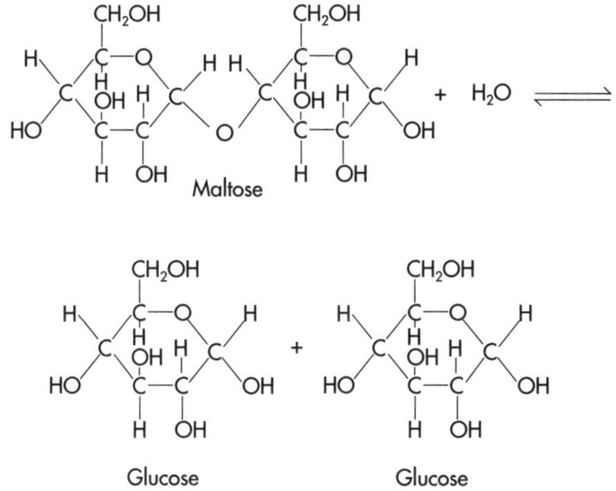

Maltose

Glucose   Glucose

Polysaccharides

Many biologically important carbohydrates are made up of repeated units of simple sugars. These chains of sugars are called **polysaccharides**. The most common polysaccharides you'll need to know for the test are **starch**, **cellulose**, and **glycogen**. Among other roles, polysaccharides serve as storage forms of sugar and lend structure to cells. Starch and glycogen, for example, are polysaccharides used for storage: Starch is found in plants, and glycogen is found in animals. Cellulose is found only in plants, enabling them to have rigid cell walls. These solid walls provide structural support, allowing plants to have sturdy trunks, branches, and stems.

AMINO ACIDS

Amino acids are organic molecules that serve as the building blocks of proteins. They contain carbon, hydrogen, oxygen, and nitrogen atoms. Every amino acid has four important parts: **an amino group** (—NH_2), a **carboxyl group** (—COOH), a **hydrogen,** and an **R group**. Here's a typical amino acid:

Amino acids differ only in the R group, which is also called the **side chain**. The best way to recognize an amino acid is to look for nitrogen— the letter N. Once you've found N, make sure it's part of an amino group (—NH_2) in the molecule, then look for the carboxyl molecule (—COOH). If you spot all of these together, odds are you're looking at an amino acid.

Polypeptides

When two amino acids join, they form a **dipeptide**. The carboxyl group of one amino acid combines with the amino group of another amino acid. Here's an example:

here's the peptide bond

This is the same process we saw earlier: dehydration synthesis. You may have figured that out already from the fact that a water molecule is removed in the formation of the bond. This bond between two amino acids has a special name: a **peptide bond**. When numerous amino acids are joined together, the resulting "string" is called a **polypeptide**. Once a polypeptide twists and folds on itself, it takes on a specific shape. The resulting molecule is called a **protein**.

There are 20 different amino acids commonly found in proteins. Amazingly, all the proteins in nature are made up of different arrangements of the same 20 amino acids.

LIPIDS

Like carbohydrates, **lipids** consist of carbon, hydrogen, and oxygen atoms, but not in the 1:2:1 ratio typical of carbohydrates. The most common examples of lipids are **fats**, **oils**, and **waxes**. A lipid consists of three fatty acids and one molecule of glycerol. A fancy name for lipids is *triglycerides*.

To make a lipid, each of the carboxyl groups (—COOH) of the fatty acids must react with one of the three hydroxyl groups (—OH) of the glycerol molecule. This happens through the removal of one molecule of water. Actually, a lipid requires the removal of *three* molecules of water. Once again, this is an example of dehydration synthesis.

Lipids function as structural components of cell membranes, as a source of insulation, and as a means of energy storage.

NUCLEIC ACIDS

The fourth class of organic compounds we need to look at includes the **nucleic acids**. Like proteins, nucleic acids contain carbon, hydrogen, oxygen, and nitrogen. Nucleic acids are molecules made up of simple units called *nucleotides*. Two kinds of nucleic acids you'll see later on are **deoxyribonucleic acid** (DNA) and **ribonucleic acid** (RNA). DNA is important because it contains genes, the hereditary "blueprints" of life. RNA is essential for protein synthesis. DNA and RNA will be covered in greater detail when we discuss modern genetics.

CHEMICAL REACTIONS

Now that we've introduced organic compounds, let's figure out how organisms use them. Organic compounds such as carbohydrates store energy in chemical bonds. Through a series of complicated steps and intermediaries, cells make use of this energy to perform the functions necessary for life.

Let's talk about chemical reactions. During the course of a reaction, the chemical bonds holding compounds together are either broken or formed. This process—taking molecules apart and reassembling them—requires energy. Here's something you need to remember: Every type of chemical reaction involves a change in energy.

WHAT ARE ENZYMES?

Chemical reactions don't occur haphazardly in the cell. Can you imagine what would happen if they did? The inside of the cell would be an explosive mess! To control the chemical reactions essential for life, cells rely on specialized protein molecules called **enzymes**. Enzymes are **organic catalysts**, which means they speed up the rate of a reaction without being changed themselves. In other words, they don't get used up in the process.

The Enzyme-Substrate Complex

The enzyme has a unique way of helping reactions along. The reactants in an enzyme-assisted reaction are known as **substrates**. During a reaction, the enzyme's job is to bring the substrates together. It accomplishes this by virtue of a special binding region on the enzyme known as an *active site*. When substrates are brought together at the active site they form a short-lived **enzyme-substrate complex**.

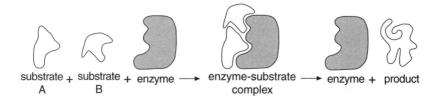

substrate + substrate + enzyme ⟶ enzyme-substrate ⟶ enzyme + product
   A   B   complex

Once the reaction has occurred, and the product is formed, the enzyme is released from the complex and restored to its original state. The enzyme is now free to repeat this process with another bunch of substrates.

How Do Enzymes and Substrates "Fit"?

Originally, scientists thought that enzymes and substrates came together the way a key fits into a lock. That is, that a given substrate fit into the active site of only one enzyme. This theory was known as the **lock-and-key theory**. Recently, however, scientists have discovered that enzymes and substrates don't fit together quite so perfectly. It appears that the enzyme's shape changes slightly to accommodate the substrates. This is called **induced fit**.

When discussing enzymes, we often talk about **enzyme specificity**. This means that enzymes are very picky: Each enzyme catalyzes only one reaction. For example, there is a specific enzyme that breaks down maltose into two glucose molecules. Because this is the only reaction this enzyme carries out, the enzyme is called *maltase*. Many enzymes are named this way, by replacing the suffix of the substrate with *-ase*.

Enzymes Don't Always Work Alone

Enzymes sometimes need a little help in catalyzing a reaction. This help is provided by a class of molecules known as **coenzymes**. Vitamins are examples of organic coenzymes. Other helpers are inorganic. For example, some cells use metal ions (Fe^{+2}) to get the job done. These inorganic elements are known as **cofactors**.

FACTORS AFFECTING REACTION RATES

Enzymatic reactions can be influenced by such factors as temperature, pH, and the relative amounts of enzyme and substrate.

Temperature

The rate of a reaction increases with an increase in temperature. This occurs because an increase in the temperature of a reaction increases the chance of collisions among the molecules. As more and more molecules collide, more enzyme-substrate complexes are formed, leading to an increase in the reaction rate. All enzymes operate at ideal or optimal temperatures. For most human enzymes, the optimal temperature is body temperature, 37°C.

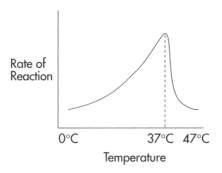

Rate of
Reaction

0°C   37°C 47°C

Temperature

As you can see from the chart above, although the reaction rate peaks at 37°C, it rapidly drops off above this optimal temperature. Excessively high temperatures make enzymes lose their shapes. When this occurs, an enzyme is said to be **denatured**. Denatured enzymes are no longer able to form active complexes with their substrates.

pH

Enzymes also function best at a particular pH. Chemical reactions are influenced by whether the solution in which they occur is **acidic, basic,** or **neutral**. The acidity or basicity of a solution can be measured using a **pH scale**.

The pH of a solution refers to the concentration of hydrogen ions (H^+). A solution with a high concentration of hydrogen ions is considered acidic, whereas one with a low concentration is considered basic.

When an acid is dissolved in solution, it fills the solution with free hydrogen ions. Lemon juice, cola, and coffee are all examples of acids. Bases, on the other hand, do not release hydrogen ions in solution. They release hydroxide ions (OH^-). Solutions with high concentrations of hydroxide ions are said to be **alkaline** (another term for basic). Soap is an example of a base.

The pH scale runs from 1 to 14. The midpoint, 7, is considered neutral pH. A solution with a pH below 7 is considered acidic, whereas one with a pH above 7 is considered basic. Because pH is a measure of the concentration of hydrogen ions, we can sum up the pH scale in this way:

1. An increase in hydrogen ions causes a decrease in the pH.

2. A decrease in hydrogen ions causes an increase in the pH.

The following scale illustrates the relative pHs of some common substances. Notice that stronger acids have lower pHs:

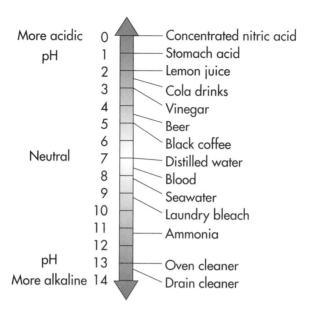

More acidic	0	— Concentrated nitric acid
pH	1	— Stomach acid
	2	— Lemon juice
	3	— Cola drinks
	4	— Vinegar
	5	— Beer
	6	— Black coffee
Neutral	7	— Distilled water
	8	— Blood
	9	— Seawater
	10	— Laundry bleach
	11	— Ammonia
	12	
pH	13	— Oven cleaner
More alkaline	14	— Drain cleaner

Returning to our discussion of enzymes, we said earlier that enzymes function best at a particular pH. Most enzymes function best in a neutral solution, that is, at a pH of around 7, as shown in the diagram below. However, there are other enzymes that function best in an acidic environment. For example, pepsin, a digestive enzyme found in the stomach, functions best at a pH of about 2.

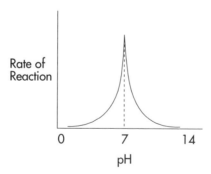

Note that enzymes are usually active over a *narrow* range of pH. Beyond or below this range, enzymes are denatured.

Concentration of Substrates

The rate of a reaction can also be affected by the amount of substrate available. If we were to take a fixed amount of a maltose-maltase solution and add more maltose, the reaction rate would increase. Take a look:

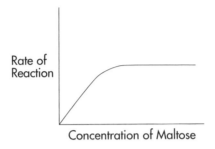

Concentration of Maltose

As the chart above shows, the reaction rate increases to a certain point, then levels off. At this point, the enzyme is said to be **saturated**. That is, there's too much maltose and too little maltase. No matter how much more maltose we add beyond this point, the rate of reaction will not increase.

CHAPTER 1 QUIZ

1. The diagram below represents three steps of a chemical reaction.

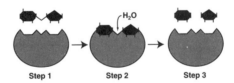

This diagram best illustrates the

(1) synthesis of a polypeptide

(2) emulsification of a fat

(3) synthesis of a polysaccharide

(4) hydrolysis of a carbohydrate

2. Maltose molecules are formed from glucose by the process of

(1) dipeptide synthesis

(2) intracellular digestion

(3) dehydration synthesis

(4) biological oxidation

3. The structural formula below represents urea.

$$\underset{H}{\overset{H}{\diagdown}}N-\overset{\overset{\displaystyle O}{\|}}{C}-N\underset{H}{\overset{H}{\diagup}}$$

This structural formula indicates that urea is

(1) an organic compound

(2) an inorganic compound

(3) a carbohydrate

(4) a nucleic acid

4. Which substances are inorganic compounds?

(1) water and salts

(2) proteins and carbohydrates

(3) fats and oils

(4) enzymes and nucleic acids

5. Which chemical formula represents a carbohydrate?

(1) CH_4 (3) CO_2

(2) $C_6H_{12}O_6$ (4) $C_3H_7O_2N$

6. Which compounds represent the building blocks of a lipid?

(1) a water molecule and a fatty acid

(2) a glycerol molecule and a fatty acid

(3) an amino acid and a water molecule

(4) a carboxyl group and an amino group

7. Which of the following is a true statement about the relationship between pH and enzyme action?

(1) All enzymes work best at a neutral pH.

(2) Adding more acid does not affect the rate activity of an enzyme.

(3) Enzymes function only in a pH range of 4.0–5.5.

(4) The activity of an enzyme is affected by pH.

2

The Cell: Life's Basic Building Block

All living things are composed of **cells**. Biologists have spelled out the importance of cells in a theory known as the *cell theory*. According to the cell theory, the cell is the basic unit of structure and function for all living things, from the smallest to the largest. It is the smallest unit of living material that can carry out all the activities necessary for life. Consequently, the cell is the basic building block of all complex organisms.

WHAT MAKES UP A CELL?

Our knowledge of cells goes as far back as the seventeenth century, when Anton van Leeuwenhoek first peered through a microscope. However, it wasn't until this century and the development of the electron microscope that biologists were able to figure out what actually happens inside a cell. From our studies of the inner workings of a cell, we now know that cells come in two distinct types: **eukaryotic** and **prokaryotic**. In this chapter, we'll be discussing mainly eukaryotic cells.

Eukaryotic cells are filled with a jelly-like fluid known as **cytoplasm**. In this cytoplasm are tiny structures called **organelles** (literally "little organs"), as well as a membrane-bound structure known as a **nucleus**. Whereas the organelles enable the cell to carry out all the functions necessary for life, the nucleus serves as the cell's command center, directing all the activities within the cell. As is discussed later, the nucleus also plays an important role in reproduction. Fungi, protists, plants, and animals are all made up of eukaryotic cells.

Prokaryotic cells, which are both smaller and more ancient than eukaryotic cells, lack a nucleus and many of the membrane-bound organelles that are examined in this chapter.

ORGANELLES: THE CELL'S MACHINERY

You can think of a eukaryotic cell as a microscopic factory filled with specialized organelles, each of which handles some part of the business of life. Let's take a tour of a eukaryotic cell and look at the structure and function of the cell's principal organelles. Here's a picture of a typical cell along with its organelles:

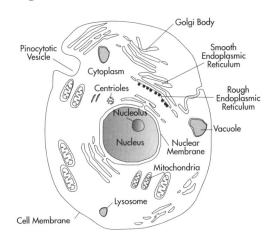

Plasma Membrane

Our first stop is the **plasma membrane**. You'll notice from the diagram above that the cell has an outer envelope. This envelope is known as the plasma membrane. Although the plasma membrane appears to be a simple, thin layer that surrounds the cell, it's actually a complex structure made up of proteins and two layers of phospholipids:

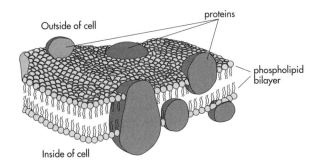

Notice that the proteins float throughout the double-lipid layer like icebergs. You'll also notice that the round "heads" of the lipids face out, one layer toward the outside of the cell, and the other toward the inside of the cell; while the "tails" of the lipids point in, toward the middle of the membrane. This arrangement of lipids and proteins is known as the **fluid-mosaic model**.

The plasma membrane and its arrangement are important because they allow the cell to regulate the movement of substances into and out of the cytoplasm. The membrane is *semipermeable,* meaning that only certain substances move across it.

The Nucleus

The next stop is the **nucleus**. The nucleus, which is usually the largest organelle, is the command center of the cell. As mentioned above, the nucleus not only directs the inner workings of the cell, but also enables the cell to reproduce. It is here that the cell's DNA is located, bunched into large structures called *chromosomes.* As you probably already know, DNA contains the "software" that runs the cell and allows it to make copies of itself.

The most visible structure within the nucleus is the nucleolus, which makes ribosomes.

Ribosomes

Ribosomes are the sites of protein synthesis. Their job is to manufacture the proteins required by the cell. Ribosomes are round structures composed of RNA and proteins. They float freely throughout the cell or are attached to another structure called the *endoplasmic reticulum* (ER).

Endoplasmic Reticulum

Not all proteins are made on freely floating ribosomes. In fact, some are synthesized by ribosomes attached to the surface of the **endoplasmic reticulum**. The ER is a continuous channel extending throughout the cytoplasm. When the ER is "studded" with ribosomes, it's called the *rough ER* (RER). Proteins made on the RER are "earmarked" to be exported out of the cell. When the ER lacks ribosomes, it's called the *smooth ER* (SER).

Golgi Bodies

The **Golgi bodies** are flattened sacs that participate in the processing of proteins. These structures pick up where the ER leaves off. Once the RER has done its part in synthesizing proteins, the Golgi bodies modify, process, and sort the products. They package and distribute proteins that are subsequently sent out of the cell.

Mitochondria

Another bunch of important organelles are the **mitochondria.** The mitochondria are often referred to as the "powerhouses" of the cell. They're responsible for converting the potential energy packed in organic molecules into a form of energy the cell can use. The most common energy source used by the cell is **adenosine triphosphate (ATP)**. From each molecule of glucose a cell takes in, it can produce 36 ATPs. We'll see exactly how this is done a little later.

The mitochondria are usually easy to spot. They have a unique oblong shape (something like pudgy little footballs) and distinct inner and outer membranes.

Lysosomes
Throughout the cell are small membrane-bound structures called **lysosomes**. These tiny sacs release digestive enzymes when they fuse with worn-out organelles or debris. Lysosomes are the cell's clean-up crew.

Centrioles
The centrioles are small, paired cylindrical structures that hang out near the nucleus. The role of centrioles is to assist in cellular division. When the cell is ready to divide, the centrioles produce spindle fibers that serve to separate chromosomes and move them to opposite ends of the cell. Although centrioles are common in animal cells, they are not found in plant cells.

Vacuoles
In Latin, the term *vacuole* means empty cavity. But vacuoles are far from empty. They enable the cell to store water, food, wastes, salts, and pigments.

Cilia and Flagella
Some cells have whip-like structures called **flagella** or hair-like structures called **cilia** on their surfaces. These structures are often associated with two particularly well-known microscopic organisms, *Euglena*, which has a flagellum, and *Paramecium*, which is covered in cilia.

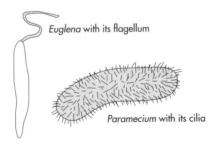

Euglena with its flagellum

Paramecium with its cilia

Cilia and flagella enable these unicellular organisms to move about in their watery environments.

PLANT CELLS AND ANIMAL CELLS
Plant cells contain most of the same organelles and structures found in animal cells. However, plant cells also contain a **cell wall** (made of cellu-

lose) and **chloroplasts** (structures involved in photosynthesis). Chloroplasts contain chlorophyll, the light-capturing pigment that gives plants their characteristic green color. Another difference between plant cells and animal cells is that most of the space within a plant cell is taken up by a single huge vacuole. In mature plants, this vacuole contains the cell sap.

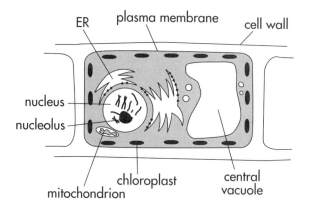

To help you remember some of the basic differences among prokaryotes, plant cells, and animal cells, we've put together this simple table:

STRUCTURAL DIFFERENCES AMONG CELL TYPES			
Structure	**Prokaryote**	**Plant Cell**	**Animal Cell**
Cell Wall	Yes	Yes	No
Plasma Membrane	Yes	Yes	Yes
Organelles	No	No	Yes
Nucleus	No	No	Yes
Centrioles	No	No	Yes

CHAPTER 2 QUIZ

1.   Which of the following is *not* characteristic of an animal cell?

(1) It contains ribosomes.

(2) It has a membrane-bound nucleus.

(3) It contains a cell membrane.

(4) It contains chloroplasts.

2. Which of the following organelles is a continuous channel associated with protein synthesis?

    (1) ribosomes

    (2) Golgi bodies

    (3) rough endoplasmic reticulum

    (4) mitochondria

3. A major difference between plant cells and animal cells is that plant cells have

    (1) a plasma membrane

    (2) mitochondria

    (3) a cell wall

    (4) vacuoles

4. Which of the following is a feature of prokaryotic cells?

    (1) They lack a plasma membrane.

    (2) They contain organelles.

    (3) They lack DNA.

    (4) They lack a membrane-bound nucleus.

Directions for 5–7: For each statement in questions 5 through 7, select the organelle, chosen from the list below, that is best described by that statement.

    Organelles

    (1) nucleus

    (2) lysosomes

    (3) centrioles

    (4) vacuoles

5. A large membrane-bound, fluid-containing sac

6. Paired organelles that migrate to opposite poles of a dividing eukaryotic cell

7. An organelle that contains hydrolytic enzymes

3

Cellular Respiration

ADENOSINE TRIPHOSPHATE (ATP)

Nearly everything the cell does requires energy. But where does the cell get the energy it needs? In nature, there are some organisms that make their own food, and others that need to acquire it from their environments. Members of the first group are called **producers** or **autotrophs**, whereas those in the second group are known as **consumers** or **heterotrophs**. As we'll soon see, these two different groups have evolved very different strategies for acquiring their nutrition. However, they do have one thing in common: All living things, whether autotroph or heterotroph, use adenosine triphosphate (ATP) as a major energy source.

ATP can be thought of as the cell's energy currency. Cells use ATP because of its unique structure. This structure makes ATP perfect for the storage and release of energy. The diagram below depicts a typical ATP molecule:

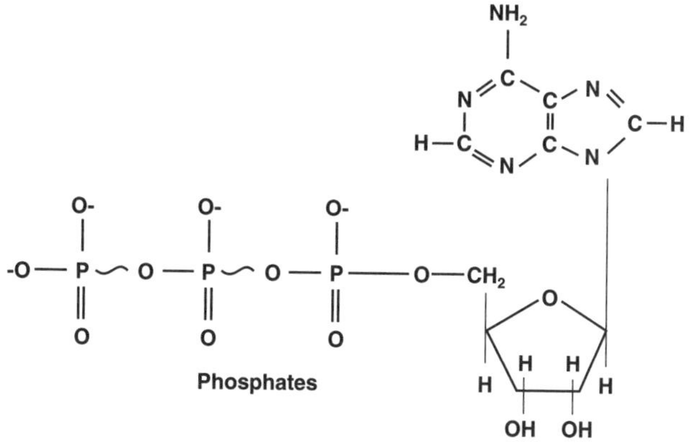

Adenosine triphosphate (ATP)

In the diagram above, squiggly lines connect the phosphate groups to the adenosine. Each of these represents a high-energy bond. When a cell needs energy, it takes a molecule of ATP and splits the third phosphate through the addition of a molecule of water, or **hydrolysis** (remember that one?). This release of inorganic phosphate, P_i, leaves the cell with a molecule of adenosine diphosphate (ADP) and energy.

$$ATP \rightarrow ADP + P_i + energy$$

The energy released from this reaction can be put to whatever use the cell pleases. When the cell wants to store energy, it merely goes in the other direction. The cell attaches another P_i to the ADP molecule via dehydration synthesis, resulting in the formation of another energy-packed molecule of ATP.

CELLULAR RESPIRATION

ATP is produced in a process known as **cellular respiration**. In cellular respiration, nutrients are broken down to release the energy contained in their bonds. This energy is then used to produce ATP. You'll recall that many organic molecules are important to cells because they are energy rich. This is where that energy comes into play. In the shorthand reaction, cellular respiration looks something like this:

$$C_6H_{12}O_6 + 6O_2 + 6H_2O \rightarrow 6CO_2 + 12H_2O + ATP$$
glucose

Notice that we've taken sugar and combined it with oxygen and water to produce carbon dioxide, water, and energy in the form of our old friend, ATP. However, as you probably already know, the actual picture of cellular respiration is far more complicated.

Generally speaking, we can break cellular respiration down to two different approaches: **aerobic respiration** and **anaerobic respiration**. If oxygen is present, ATP is produced via aerobic respiration. If oxygen isn't present, cells turn to anaerobic respiration. However, because anaerobic respiration is far less efficient than aerobic respiration, most organisms rely on aerobic respiration for their energy needs. Let's start, then, by taking a look at aerobic respiration, the more important of the two processes.

AEROBIC RESPIRATION

Aerobic respiration consists of two major stages: (1) **glycolysis** and (2) **oxidation of glucose**. Although there are many smaller parts of each of these stages, we only look at the general outline of the two. For practical purposes, that's all you'll need to know for the time being. If you're curious about the enzymes and intermediaries involved at each step, consult your biology textbook. For now, let's begin where the cell begins, with glycolysis.

Stage 1: Glycolysis

The first stage is **glycolysis**, which takes place in the cytoplasm of the cell. Glycolysis involves the splitting up (*-lysis*) of a molecule of glucose (*glyco*). Glucose, as we already saw, is a six-carbon molecule. In glycolysis, glucose is split into two three-carbon molecules. These three-carbon molecules are known as **pyruvic acid**:

$$C\text{-}C\text{-}C\text{-}C\text{-}C\text{-}C + 2 \text{ ATP} \rightarrow C\text{-}C\text{-}C + C\text{-}C\text{-}C + 4 \text{ ATP}$$
$$\text{glucose} \qquad \rightarrow \qquad \text{pyruvic acid}$$

Notice that we must invest two ATPs to split glucose and make four ATPs. It's sort of like the expression, "you have to spend a little money to make money." To make four ATPs, we had to invest two. Our net profit? Two ATPs. Though this may not seem like a lot, keep in mind that this is only the first stage of cellular respiration.

Keep in mind that glycolysis is an *anaerobic* process. It occurs in all living cells and requires no oxygen. The products of glycolysis, the two molecules of pyruvic acid, can be used in aerobic respiration (if oxygen is present) or anaerobic respiration (if oxygen is absent). Let's see what happens when oxygen is present.

Stage 2: Oxidation Of Glucose

When oxygen is present, pyruvic acid moves to the mitochondria. Through a complicated series of steps involving many enzymes and intermediate molecules, pyruvic acid is converted to 34 ATPs, water, and carbon dioxide. We can sum up this process as follows:

$$2 \{C\text{-}C\text{-}C\} + 6O_2 \rightarrow 34 \text{ ATP} + 6CO_2 + 6H_2O$$
$$\text{pyruvic acid}$$

You may have already seen this stage in a more complicated fashion in your textbook. Oxidation of glucose, as mentioned above, involves many intermediate steps, including the **formation of acetyl CoA, the Krebs cycle**, and **oxidative phosphorylation**. These steps describe in detail how the carbons in glucose are broken down to CO_2 and ATP. Don't worry about all the details of these steps. The most important thing to keep in mind about the oxidation of glucose is the outcome: From two molecules of pyruvic acid, the cell produces 34 ATPs. Recall from our discussion of glycolysis that the cell already produced two ATPs. The net result of aerobic respiration can be summed up this way:

Aerobic respiration:

Glycolysis	Occurs in the cytoplasm	Produces net: 2 ATP (gross 4 ATP)
Oxidation	Occurs in the mitochondria	Produces net: 34 ATP
		Net: 36 ATP

WHAT ABOUT ANAEROBIC RESPIRATION?

Some organisms can't undergo aerobic respiration. They're anaerobic. They can't use oxygen to make ATP. How do anaerobic organisms get energy? Because glycolysis is an anaerobic process, they can make two ATP from this stage. However, instead of continuing on to stage two of aerobic respiration, these organisms carry out a process called **fermentation**. Under anaerobic conditions, pyruvic acid is converted to either lactic acid or ethyl alcohol (or **ethanol**) and carbon dioxide.

Unfortunately, anaerobic respiration is not very efficient. It only produces two ATP for each molecule of glucose broken down. As you can see from the chart below, there are two basic end products in anaerobic respiration:

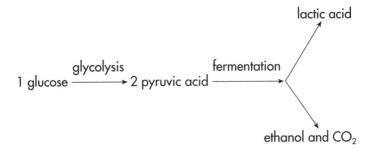

What types of organisms undergo fermentation? Yeast cells and some bacteria. Whereas yeast cells always produce ethanol and carbon dioxide, some bacteria produce lactic acid as a result of fermentation.

Your Muscle Cells Can Ferment

Did you know that your muscle cells ferment? It's true. Although we're aerobic organisms by nature, we can actually carry out fermentation in our muscle cells. Have you ever had a cramp? If so, that cramp was the consequence of anaerobic respiration.

When you exercise, your muscles require a lot of energy. To get this energy, they convert enormous amounts of glucose to ATP. But as you continue to exercise, your body doesn't get enough oxygen to keep up with the demand in your muscles. What do your muscle cells do? They switch over to anaerobic respiration. Pyruvic acid produced from glycolysis is converted to lactic acid. This lactic acid causes the pain in your muscles.

CHAPTER 3 QUIZ

1. According to the summary equations below, what is the net gain of ATP molecules from the complete oxidation of one glucose molecule?

    A. 1 glucose + 2 ATP $\xrightarrow{\text{enzymes}}$ 2 pyruvic acid + 4 ATP

    B. 2 pyruvic acid + oxygen $\xrightarrow{\text{enzymes}}$ carbon dioxide + water + 34 ATP

    (1) 34

    (2) 36

    (3) 38

    (4) 40

2. Two species of bacteria produce different respiratory end products. Species A always produces ATP, CO_2, and H_2O. Species B always produces ATP, ethyl alcohol, and CO_2. Which conclusion can correctly be drawn from this information?

    (1) Only species A is aerobic.

    (2) Only species B is aerobic.

    (3) Species A and species B are both anaerobic.

    (4) Species A and species B are both aerobic.

3.   What is a direct result of aerobic respiration?

(1) The potential energy of glucose is transferred to ATP molecules.

(2) The enzymes for aerobic respiration are produced by lysosomes.

(3) Lactic acid is produced in muscle tissue.

(4) Alcohol is produced by yeast and bacteria.

Directions for 4–7: For each statement in questions 4 through 7, select the term chosen from the list below that is best described by that statement.

Cellular respiration

(1) pyruvic acid

(2) lactic acid

(3) alcoholic fermentation

(4) water

4.   The end product of glycolysis

5.   A method of anaerobic respiration

6.   A molecule that is produced during the oxidation of glucose

7.   A substance that accumulates during strenuous muscle exertion

Photosynthesis

Plants and algae seem to have it pretty easy. No running about chasing prey, no long lunch lines. As producers, all they have to do is bask in the sun, churning out the glucose necessary for life. To make this glucose, plants perform a process called *photosynthesis*. Here's an overview of photosynthesis:

$$\text{sunlight} + 6CO_2 + 12H_2O \rightarrow C_6H_{12}O_6 + 6O_2 + 6H_2O$$

You'll notice from this equation that carbon dioxide and water are the raw materials plants use in manufacturing glucose or fructose. But there's much more to photosynthesis than the simple reaction shown above. You'll soon see that this beautifully orchestrated process occurs thanks to a host of special enzymes and pigments. Before we turn to the stages in photosynthesis, let's talk about where photosynthesis occurs.

ANATOMY OF A LEAF

Photosynthesis takes place in the leaves of plants. Here's a cross-sectional view of a typical leaf:

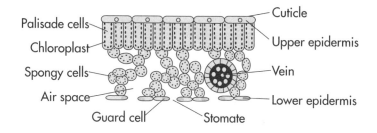

If you look closely at a leaf, the first thing you'll notice is a waxy covering called the **cuticle**. The cuticle is produced by the upper epidermis to protect the leaf from water loss through evaporation. Just below the upper epidermis are the tightly packed cells of the **palisade layer**. These cells contain lots of chloroplasts and are therefore the primary sites of photosynthesis.

Now let's take a peek at an individual chloroplast. If you were to peel back the membrane of a chloroplast, you would find a fluid-filled region called the **stroma**. Inside the stroma, there are structures called **grana**. As you can tell from the diagram below, the grana look like stacks of coins.

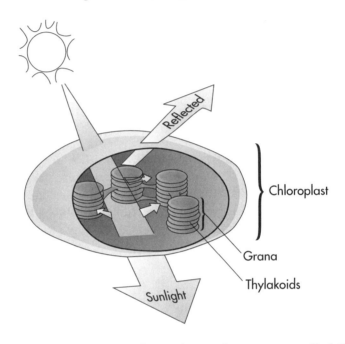

The many disk-like structures that make up the grana are called **thylakoids**. These thylakoids contain chlorophyll, the pigment that drives photosynthesis. Chlorophyll also gives plants their characteristic green color. It does this by absorbing the red and blue spectra from sunlight and reflecting back the green.

Now let's talk about the other structures in the leaf that are not immediately involved in photosynthesis. Just below the palisade layer, you'll find irregular-shaped cells in the **spongy layer**. The conducting tissues are found in this layer of the leaf. These tissues include the xylem and phloem. At the **lower epidermis** are tiny openings called **stomates**, which allow for gas exchange. Surrounding each stomate are **guard cells** that control the opening and closing of each stomate.

A CLOSER LOOK AT PHOTOSYNTHESIS

There are two stages in photosynthesis: the **light reaction** and the **dark reaction**.

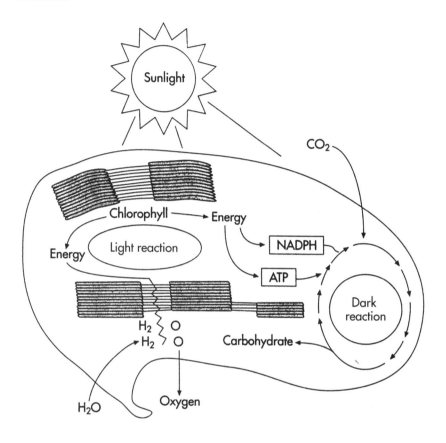

THE LIGHT REACTION

Photosynthesis begins when **photons** (energy packets) of sunlight strike a leaf, activating chlorophyll and other light-absorbing pigments by exciting their electrons. The excited electrons are passed down to a series of electron carriers, ending in the production of ATP and the reduced form of nicotinamide-adenine dinucleotide phosphate (NADPH).

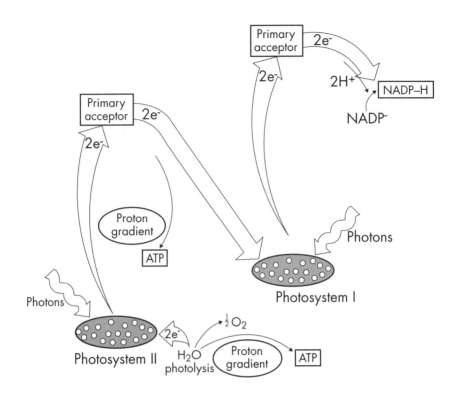

When chlorophyll absorbs light, it also splits water (H_2O) into hydrogen ions, oxygen, and electrons. This process is called **photolysis** ("splitting with light"). The light reaction requires three things: light, CO_2, and H_2O. Using just these three simple ingredients, plants produce hydrogen atoms, oxygen gas (O_2), and oodles of energy (in the form of ATP).

THE DARK REACTION

Now let's turn to the dark reaction. The dark reaction uses the products of the light reaction—ATP and hydrogen atoms—to make glucose. We now have energy to make glucose, but what do plants use as their carbon source? CO_2, of course. Carbon dioxide is first converted into an unstable three-carbon compound called **phosphoglyceraldehyde** (**PGAL**). PGAL is then used to make glucose. The dark reaction is also called the **carbon fixation reaction** and occurs in the stroma of the chloroplasts.

CHAPTER 4 QUIZ

1. A wet-mount slide of photosynthetic protists was prepared and then exposed to light that had been broken up into a spectrum. When viewing this preparation through the microscope, a student would most likely observe that most of the protists had clustered in the regions of

    (1) yellow and blue light

    (2) orange and green light

    (3) green and yellow light

    (4) red and blue light

2. Which of the following plant structures regulates the opening of the stomates?

    (1) guard cells

    (2) thylakoids

    (3) grana

    (4) stroma

3. Which of the following equations represents the overall reaction for photosynthesis?

    (1) $6O_2 + 12H_2O \rightarrow C_6H_{12}O_6 + 6O_2 + 6H_2O$

    (2) $C_6H_{12}O_6 + 6O_2 + 6H_2O \rightarrow 6CO_2 + 12H_2O$

    (3) $6CO_2 + 12H_2O \xrightarrow{\text{sunlight}} C_6H_{12}O_6 + 6O_2 + 6H_2O$

    (4) $6O_2 + 12H_2O \xrightarrow{\text{sunlight}} C_6H_{12}O_6 + 6O_2 + 6H_2O$

Directions for 4–6: For each phrase in questions 4 through 6, select the photosynthetic reactions, chosen from the list below, that are best described by that statement.

   Photosynthetic reactions

   (1) Photochemical reactions only

   (2) Carbon-fixation reactions only

   (3) Both photochemical and carbon fixation reactions

4. The reaction in which photolysis occurs

5. The reactions in which the radioactive isotope carbon-14 can be used to trace the chemical pathway of the carbon in carbon dioxide

6. The reactions that involve the electron carriers

5

Plants

The plant kingdom is incredibly vast. As you already know, plants are found everywhere, from the tropical seas to the Arctic tundra. There are more than 260,000 species of flowering plants alone! Here's what we know about plants so far:

- They are multicellular, eukaryotic organisms.
- They have a cell wall made of cellulose.
- They are photosynthetic: They convert light energy to chemical energy.

PLANT CLASSIFICATION

Now let's discuss the classification system of plants. Here's a simple flow chart of the different subdivisions of plants:

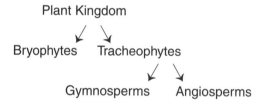

All plants fall into two major categories or phyla: **bryophytes** and **tracheophytes**. Bryophytes are primitive plants that lack true stems, roots, and leaves. Tracheophytes are more advanced plants that have specialized conducting and vascular tissues, the xylem and phloem we saw briefly in chapter 4.

BRYOPHYTES

Bryophytes are the simplest plants and are characterized by their lack of true stems, roots, and leaves. Common bryophytes include mosses and liverworts. The absence of specialized transport systems means these plants are unable to store water for times of drought. Consequently, bryophytes have a hard time surviving far from a water source. Moreover, these primitive plants need water for reproduction. Without an abundant supply of water, reproduction is nearly impossible for them: There's no way for the sperm to reach the egg.

TRACHEOPHYTES

The other phylum, tracheophytes, is far more numerous. Plants that belong to this phylum contain vascular tissues and are found all over the globe. Vascular tissues make it possible for tracheophytes to thrive on land by helping them transport and store water and nutrients. As seen earlier, these plants contain two types of vascular tissues: **phloem** and **xylem**. Phloem carry nutrients, such as glucose, throughout the plant. Xylem are tissues that conduct water and minerals up the plant from its roots.

Water enters the plant through the roots. How does water move up through a plant? There are two forces at work: **cohesion** and **adhesion**.

- Water molecules have a strong tendency to stick together. That is, water exhibits **cohesive forces**. When water molecules evaporate from a leaf, they "tug" on nearby water molecules further down the vessel, pulling them up the stem.

- Water molecules also tend to stick to other substances. This is known as **adhesion**. If you've ever tried to separate two glass slides stuck together by a film of water, you know how strong this force can be. It's tough to separate the slides because the water sticks to the glass.

Both of these forces, cohesion and adhesion, account for the ability of water to rise in the thin vessels of plants.

Roots have special features in their outer layer called **root hairs**, which increase the surface area for absorption of materials. Roots are also important because they anchor the plant.

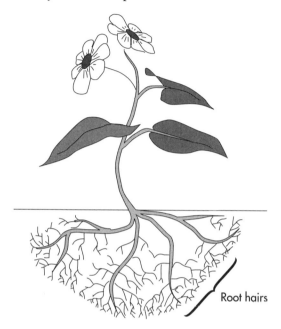

Root hairs

FLOWERING PLANTS

When it comes to plant structures, few are as marvelous or as important to the study of biology as the flower. From an evolutionary standpoint, the flower is a remarkable example of successful adaptation.

Flowering plants have several important parts. Among these are the **stamen, pistil, sepals,** and **petals**:

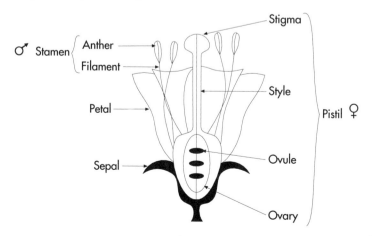

The male parts are collectively called the *stamen,* and the female parts are called the *pistil.* The sepals are the green leaf-like structures that cover and protect the flower. The petals are usually brightly colored to attract potential pollinators.

THE STAMEN

The stamen consists of the **anther** and the **filament**. The anther is the structure that produces pollen grains. These pollen grains are the plant's male gametophytes or sperm cells. Pollen grains are produced by the millions and tossed into the air. The filament is the thin stalk that holds up the anther.

THE PISTIL

The pistil includes three structures: the stigma, style, and ovary. The stigma is the sticky portion of the pistil that captures the pollen grains. The style is the tube-like structure that connects the stigma to the ovary. The ovary is where fertilization occurs. Within the ovary are the ovules that contain the plant's equivalent of the female gametophytes. The ovary is very familiar to you, no doubt: In a fertilized plant it develops into the fruit. Apples, pears, and oranges are all fertilized ovaries of flowering plants. The female gametes of plants undergo meiosis to produce eight female nuclei, including one monoploid egg and two polar nuclei.

Some flowers can pollinate themselves. This is called **self-pollination**. Other flowers are fertilized solely by pollen grains from other plants. This is called **cross-pollination**. The primary agents of cross-pollination are insects, birds, water, and wind.

DOUBLE FERTILIZATION

Now that we've seen both the male and female organs in plants, let's take a look at how they reproduce. Flowering plants carry out a process called **double fertilization**. When a pollen grain lands on the stigma, it germinates and grows a thin pollen tube down the style. The pollen grain divides into two sperm nuclei that descend the pollen tube into the ovary. One sperm nucleus (1n) fuses with an egg nucleus (1n) to form a zygote (2n). This zygote eventually forms a plant. The other sperm nucleus (1n) fuses with two polar nuclei (2n) in the ovary to form the **endosperm** (3n), food for the plant embryo. So double fertilization produces two things: a plant and food for the plant.

Let's review the steps involved in double fertilization:

- Grains of pollen fall onto the stigma. The pollen grains grow down the style into the ovary.

- The monoploid nucleus divides into two sperm nuclei that meet up with the female gametes in the ovule.

- One sperm nucleus unites with an egg nucleus and eventually develops into an embryo.

- The other sperm nucleus unites with two polar nuclei and develops into food for the developing plant.

EMBRYONIC DEVELOPMENT

As the embryo germinates, different parts of the plant begin to develop. The **cotyledons** are the first leaves of the embryo. They temporarily store all the nutrients for the plant. The **hypocotyl** is the stem below the cotyledons. This portion becomes the roots of the plant. The **epicotyl** is the part at the tip of the plant. This portion becomes the stems and leaves.

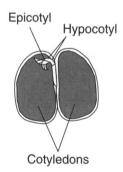

Epicotyl
Hypocotyl
Cotyledons

PLANT GROWTH

How do plants grow? Plants have undifferentiated, actively dividing cells called **meristems**. There are two types of meristems: **apical meristem** and **lateral meristem**. The apical meristem is the region of active cell division at the tip of a plant's root and stem. These dividing cells increase the length of a plant.

Lateral meristems are dividing cells that give girth, or width, to a plant. They're responsible for annual growth in stems and roots in such woody plants as trees. These dividing cells are located on the sides of stems and roots. Another name for the lateral meristem is **cambium**.

TROPISMS

Plants need light. This is pretty easy to prove: Just stick a houseplant in a closet for a week and see what happens (preferably not one of your mother's favorites). Unfortunately for the plant, it is rooted in its pot and cannot move to an area where there is more light. As a result, it will die.

Although you wouldn't think so from your houseplant's reaction, plants do in fact move. Not enough to escape from the closet, but enough to ensure that they get a maximum of sunlight. Notice that all the plants in your house tip toward the windows. This movement toward the light is known as **phototropism**. As you also know, plants generally grow up and down: The branches grow upward, while the roots grow downward into the soil, seeking water. This tendency to grow toward or away from the earth is called **gravitropism**.

A tropism is a turning response to a stimulus. There are three basic tropisms in plants. They're easy to remember, because their prefixes indicate the stimuli to which plants react:

- **Phototropism** refers to how plants respond to sunlight. Plants always bend toward light.

- **Gravitropism** refers to how plants respond to gravity. Stems exhibit negative gravitropism (i.e., they grow up, away from the pull of gravity), and roots exhibit positive gravitropism (i.e., they grow downward into the earth).

- **Thigmotropism** refers to how plants respond to touch. For example, ivy grows about a post or trellis.

These responses are initiated by hormones. The major plant hormones are known as **auxins**. Auxins promote growth on one side of the plant. For example, in phototropism, the side of the plant that faces away from the sunlight grows faster thanks to the plant's auxins, making the plant bend towards the light. (Imagine yourself on crutches. If your left crutch was longer than your right, you would wind up tipping to the right. This is precisely how a plant tips toward the sun: It makes its "left" side, or side facing away from the sun, longer.)

Generally speaking, auxins are found in the tip of the plant, because this is where most growth occurs. Auxins are also involved in cell elongation and fruit development.

Other plant hormones that influence the growth and development of plants are **gibberellins**, **cytokinins**, **ethylenes**, and **abscisic acid**.

CHAPTER 5 QUIZ

Two plants were observed to have the characteristics indicated in the chart below. An X indicates that the characteristic was present.

Specimen	Multicellular	Photosynthetic	Vascular tissue	Roots	Stems	Leaves
Plant A	X	X				
Plant B	X	X	X	X	X	X

1. According to the chart, which statement about these plants is correct?

    (1) Plant A is a tracheophyte, and plant B is a bryophyte.

    (2) Plant A has xylem and phloem, but plant B does not.

    (3) Plant A could be a pine tree, and plant B could be a moss.

    (4) Plant A is a bryophyte, and plant B is a tracheophyte.

2. When a geranium plant is placed in a horizontal position, auxins accumulate on the side of the stem closest to the ground. As a result, what will most likely occur in the stem of the geranium?

    (1) Stomates will close.

    (2) Leaves will develop.

    (3) Cells will grow unequally.

    (4) Cell growth will stop.

3. The function of the cotyledon in a seed is to

    (1) form the upper portion of the plant

    (2) form the lower portion of the plant

    (3) protect the ovary from drying out

    (4) provide nutrients for the germinating plant

Base your answers to questions 4 and 5 on the diagram below of a flower and on your knowledge of biology.

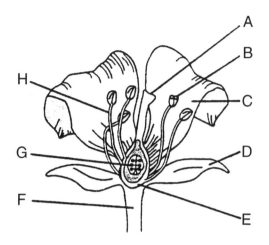

4.   Which structures form the stamen?

(1) A and F

(2) B and H

(3) C and D

(4) E and G

5.   During pollination, pollen is transferred from

(1) B to A

(2) C to D

(3) B to G

(4) F to H

6.   In the branch of a cherry tree, gases are exchanged between the environment and the cells through

(1) lenticels

(2) cambium

(3) xylem

(4) phloem

7. Growth in higher plants most often takes place in regions of undifferentiated tissue known as

   (1) meristems

   (2) lenticels

   (3) palisade layers

   (4) vascular tissues

6

Life Functions

All organisms must perform certain activities to survive. These activities are known as *life functions*. The principal life functions are as follows:

- Nutrition
- Respiration
- Transport
- Excretion
- Regulation
- Locomotion
- Growth
- Reproduction

This chapter deals with each of these functions in turn, with the exception of growth and reproduction, which are covered in chapter 7. Naturally, different organisms have evolved different ways of meeting the challenges of staying alive. For each life function, we'll look at the principal ways in which organisms as varied as *Amoeba* and *Homo sapiens* carry out these various activities.

Let's start our overview with the life function of nutrition.

NUTRITION

All organisms need nutrients to survive. But where do the nutrients come from? The answer to this question varies widely, depending on whether the organism is an autotroph or a heterotroph. As you may recall, autotrophs make their own food through photosynthesis, drawing almost all of the building blocks from their immediate environments. Heterotrophs, on the other hand, can't make their own food. They must find their energy sources in the outside world.

When we say **ingestion**, we're talking about the taking in of food from the environment. Food particles, once taken in, are broken down into simpler compounds. This process is called **digestion**. Digested molecules are then absorbed by the cells. Cells use these molecules to carry out their many activities. Undigested food particles must be eliminated from the body. This process is known as **egestion**. In fact, everything we'll discuss concerning nutrition boils down to two simple questions: How do organisms acquire what they need to survive, and what do they do with it once they get it?

UNICELLULAR ANIMALS

Single-celled organisms, such as protists, are able to absorb materials directly across their cell membranes. In some cases, these single-celled creatures rely on specialized structures. *Paramecium*, for example, uses its cilia to move food into an opening called an **oral groove**. Once the food has been digested, wastes are then excreted through the **anal pore**. *Amoeba*, on the other hand, surrounds its food with flexible extensions of its body known as **pseudopodia**. These tiny "arms" reach out, close around a chunk of food, and reunite, forming a **food vacuole**, which acts like a tiny stomach: Digestive enzymes are added, and the food is broken down. The vacuole then recombines with the cell membrane, squirting the waste products out into the environment. This process is called **phagocytosis**.

Pseudopodia

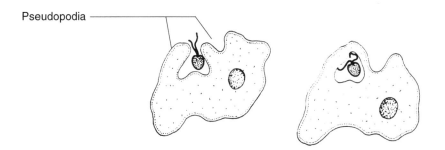

SIMPLE ANIMALS

More complex organisms don't have it quite so easy. Because most cannot simply absorb food across their cell membranes, multicellular organisms have evolved a variety of ways of obtaining their nutrients. In the simplest cases, a single cavity serves as both the digestive and the respiratory system. This type of system is known as a **gastrovascular cavity**.

The hydra is an example of an organism relying on such a system:

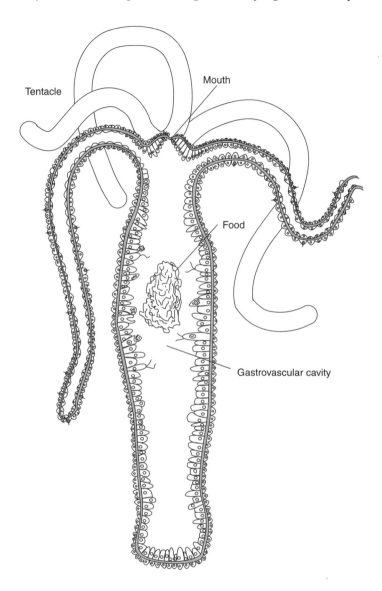

The hydra sweeps food into its mouth using its tentacles. Special digestive cells then release digestive enzymes into the gastrovascular cavity. Food is dissolved and the nutrients pass directly into the cells lining the cavity. Interestingly, the same opening is used both for nutrition and for excretion: Wastes pass out through the mouth as well. As unappetizing as that may seem, it works pretty well for such simple multicellular creatures as the hydra.

COMPLEX ANIMALS

More complex animals have evolved a proper digestive tract. In these organisms, food is digested through extracellular digestion. That is, food is digested in specialized cavities, then transported to the cells. For example, earthworms pass their food through specialized regions of the gut: the **mouth**, **esophagus**, **crop** (a storage organ), **gizzard** (a grinding organ), **intestine**, and **anus**.

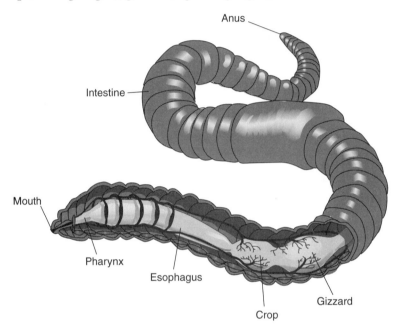

Once food has passed through all these portions of the earthworm's gut, it is thoroughly digested. Grasshoppers, which are arthropods, have a similar digestive system:

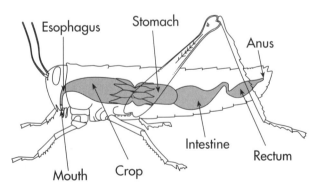

In addition to the organs pictured above, grasshoppers also have **salivary glands** (which secrete saliva) and **gastric caeca** (which contain digestive enzymes). These specialized organs enable the grasshopper to digest its food more effectively.

Different animals have different digestive systems (cows, for example, have four stomachs!). Few, however, are as elegant or as well understood as the human digestive system.

HUMAN DIGESTIVE SYSTEM

The human digestive tract consists of the **mouth, esophagus, small intestine, large intestine**, and **accessory organs**.

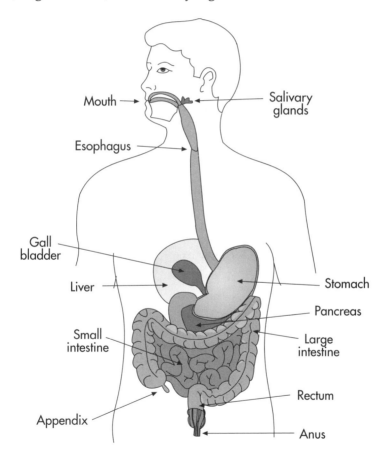

Three groups of molecules must be broken down by the digestive tract: **starch, proteins**, and **fats**.

The Mouth

The first stop in the digestive process is the mouth or **oral cavity**. When food enters the mouth, the teeth chew away, softening and breaking up food. Chewing is a form of mechanical digestion. As you know from any mouth-watering experience, the mouth also has **saliva** in it. Saliva, which is secreted by the **salivary glands**, contains an important enzyme known as **salivary amylase**. Salivary amylase begins the chemical digestion of starches into maltose. This explains why a cracker melts in your mouth, whereas a piece of steak does not: Crackers are made mostly of starches.

Once chewed, the food moves into a tube called the **esophagus**. Food moves through the esophagus in a wavelike motion known as **peristalsis**.

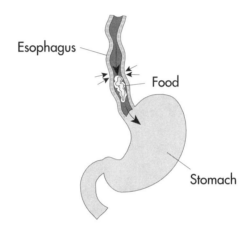

Peristalsis

The waves of contraction push the food toward the stomach.

The Stomach

Once food has been munched, it moves from the esophagus to the stomach. The stomach is a thick, muscular sac that serves three main functions:

1. Temporarily stores the ingested food

2. Partially digests proteins

3. Kills bacteria

The stomach secretes gastric juices that contain digestive enzymes and hydrochloric acid (HCl). One of the most important enzymes is **pepsin**. Pepsin breaks down polypeptides or proteins by splitting the peptide bonds between amino acids. (Remember our discussion of peptide bonds? How about our discussion of the naming of enzymes? *Pep*sin gets its name from the *pep*tide bonds it breaks apart.)

Pepsin works best in an acidic environment. When HCl is secreted, it lowers the pH of the stomach and activates pepsin. The stomach also secretes mucus that coats the stomach lining, protecting it from its own acidic juices. HCl also kills bacteria.

Once pepsin has done its thing, this mushy food is ready to enter the small intestine. At this point, because the food is no longer really food but rather a ball of partly digested mush, biologists give it a new name: **chyme**. The chyme then travels into the small intestine, which, you'll soon learn, isn't really that small.

The Small Intestine

The **small intestine** may seem like a silly name for this part of the body. After all, an average man's small intestine is about 23 feet long! The *long* intestine would seem to make more sense. However, this organ earns its name not from its length, but from its width: The small intestine is only about 1 inch in diameter. As you've probably already figured out, the large intestine, which we'll look at in just a bit, is much thicker.

All three food groups are completely digested in the small intestine. Although the walls of the small intestine produce enzymes known as **proteases** that help breakdown proteins and dipeptides, the main digestive enzymes are produced in the **pancreas**.

The Pancreas

The pancreas releases enzymes into the small intestine, among them **protease**, **lipase**, and **amylase**. Protease breaks proteins and dipeptides into amino acids. Lipase breaks down lipids into fatty acids and glycerol, while amylase breaks down starch into simple sugars.

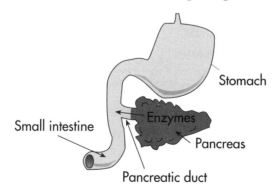

These enzymes are dumped into the small intestine via the **pancreatic duct**.

By the way, there is another substance that works in the small intestine. This substance is called **bile**. Bile is not a digestive enzyme. It's actually an **emulsifier**, meaning it mechanically cuts up fats into smaller fat droplets. This process makes the fat goblets more accessible to pancreatic lipase.

Here's something you should keep in mind:

- Bile is made in the liver and stored in the gall bladder.

Once food is broken down, it is absorbed by tiny, finger-like projections called **villi**. Villi are folds that increase the surface area of the small intestine for food absorption. They are so numerous that if you were to stretch out the villi of your small intestine, they would cover an area the size of several classrooms!

Within each villus is a capillary that absorbs the digested nutrients and sends them into the bloodstream, where individual cells eventually pick them up.

The Large Intestine

The last stop is the large intestine. It is much shorter and thicker than the small intestine. The large intestine has an easy job: It reabsorbs water and salts. The large intestine also harbors useful bacteria. These bacteria break down undigested food and in the process provide us with certain essential vitamins, such as Vitamin K. The leftover undigested food, called **feces**, then moves out of the large intestine and into the rectum.

Digestive Disorders

What happens when there's a malfunctioning of the digestive system? Any of several disorders may develop. Here's a list of the most common digestive disorders.

- Constipation: The feces in the large intestine become so hard that the body is unable to eliminate them.
- Diarrhea: The large intestine fails to absorb water properly, resulting in a loose, watery stool (feces).
- Ulcers: The mucosal lining of the stomach wears through, resulting in extreme pain.
- Appendicitis: An infection leads to the inflammation of the appendix. Although the appendix is a vestigial organ

(i.e., it once served a purpose, but is no longer used for anything, like wisdom teeth), appendicitis is extremely dangerous if not properly treated.

- Gallstones: A hardened cholesterol mass sticks in the gall bladder, producing excruciating pain.

RESPIRATION

All cells need oxygen to survive. Once they've gotten their oxygen, they then need to get rid of the waste products resulting from their use of it. As we saw in chapter 3, CO_2 is one of the by-products of cellular respiration. Because high levels of CO_2 can be just as deadly as a total lack of oxygen, you can imagine how crucial it is for the body to rid itself of gaseous wastes!

Respiration, then, involves the way in which organisms solve both these problems: the acquisition of oxygen and other gases and the excretion of gaseous wastes.

MICROORGANISMS

For microorganisms, no special structures are needed. As with nutrition, respiration takes place in unicellular organisms in a very simple way: Gases diffuse directly across the cell membrane. When CO_2 builds up in the cytoplasm as a result of cellular respiration, it automatically passes outside the cell to a region of lower concentration. Similarly, lower levels of oxygen inside the cell result in the diffusion of O_2 directly into the cell. It's that easy. (Diffusion is discussed in greater depth in the section on transport.)

PLANTS

As we move into the multicellular organisms, respiration becomes a bit more complicated. Let's start by taking a look at plants.

Plants have special structures called **stomates** and **lenticels** that allow for gas exchange. Stomates are pores found in the leaves, and lenticels are pores found in woody stems. Most of the gas exchange occurs in the stomates. Oxygen passes into these openings, while CO_2 passes out. Gas exchange among plants also occurs via simple diffusion.

ANIMALS

As we've already seen, unicellular organisms exchange gases by simple diffusion. Many smaller, multicellular organisms can do the same. The hydra, for example, is only two cell layers thick. This enables all of its cells to exchange gases directly with the environment, whether through the exterior layer of the hydra or into the gastrovascular cavity we saw earlier.

With more complex multicellular organisms, however, not all cells are in direct contact with the environment. These organisms must find other ways of getting oxygen into their system. Some animals, such as earthworms, can breathe directly through their moist skin. Oxygen, once taken in, enters the earthworm's circulatory system and is distributed to those cells not near the outside environment.

Other organisms, such as grasshoppers, have hard, chitinous shells that make it impossible for them to exchange gases directly with their environments. All insects have such a covering. Grasshoppers and other insects solve this problem by breathing through special tubes called **tracheal tubes**. Air enters these tubes through tiny openings called **spiracles**. Once oxygen passes through the spiracles into the tracheal tubes, it can be transported throughout the grasshopper's body.

Vertebrates rely on two different types of respiratory structures: **gills** (found in fish and amphibians) and **lungs**. Gills are found only in creatures that live in watery environments. They work in much the same way as an earthworm's skin: They allow gases to diffuse directly into and out of the environment. However, unlike an earthworm's skin, gills are highly specialized organs that have evolved solely for the purpose of respiration. Have you ever wondered why no land animals have gills?

Because gills work by simple diffusion, they have to be in contact with their environments. On land, gills dry out very quickly. As they dry out, gas exchange becomes more and more difficult. Have you ever seen a fish on dry land? Fish can survive for some time in an empty fishing bucket—certainly longer than we would survive under water! Fish don't die immediately, because they're still able to breathe on land (unlike us in water): Oxygen and carbon dioxide continue to diffuse into their blood via the gills, even in the bottom of the bucket. Eventually, however, the fish's gills dry out and, well . . . you know the rest.

Interestingly, lungs can be thought of as little more than internal gills. By internalizing the organs used for gas exchange, organisms made the transition from a watery or **aqueous environment** to a land or **terrestrial environment** possible. To understand how lungs work, let's take a look at the human respiratory system.

HUMAN RESPIRATORY SYSTEM
When we breathe, air enters through the **nose** or **mouth**:

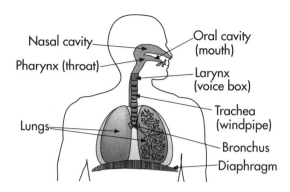

Nasal cavity

Pharynx (throat)

Lungs

Oral cavity (mouth)

Larynx (voice box)

Trachea (windpipe)

Bronchus

Diaphragm

The nose cleans, warms, and moistens the incoming air and passes it through the **pharynx** and **larynx**. Next, air enters the **trachea**, a tube lined with rings of cartilage. The cartilage enables the trachea to remain open as air rushes in.

A special flap called the **epiglottis** covers the trachea and prevents food from entering it. If food does enter the trachea, or windpipe, breathing becomes impossible. This is precisely what happens when someone is choking. The Heimlich maneuver, in which a second person forcibly squeezes the choking person's stomach, is a first-aid technique used to help someone in this predicament. By squeezing a choking person's stomach, you force air upwards, expelling the stuck piece of food—another good reason to finish chewing and swallowing before you open your mouth!

The trachea branches into two tubes: the **left** and **right bronchus**, which service the lungs. In the lungs, the passageways break down into smaller tubes known as **bronchioles**. Each bronchiole ends in a tiny air sac known as an **alveolus**. These sacs enable the lungs to have an enormous surface area. If you were to lay out all your alveoli, they would cover an area equivalent to that of a high school basketball court. Let's take a look at one of these tiny air sacs:

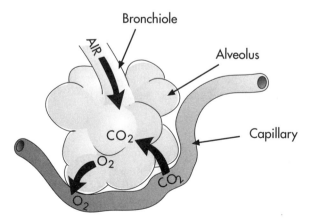

Bronchiole

AIR

Alveolus

CO_2

O_2

Capillary

CO_2

O_2

You'll notice that alongside the alveolus (singular of *alveoli*) is a **capillary**. Oxygen and carbon dioxide diffuse across the membrane of both the alveolus and capillary. Every time you inhale, you send oxygen to the alveoli. The alveoli then dump the oxygen into the capillaries. The capillaries, on the other hand, have lots of carbon dioxide. They, in turn, dump carbon dioxide into the alveoli. When you exhale, you expel the carbon dioxide dumped into your lungs. Gas exchange occurs via passive diffusion.

Carbon dioxide can travel in many forms in the body. Most of the carbon dioxide enters red blood cells and combines with water to form bicarbonate ions. Other times carbon dioxide combines with hemoglobin, a protein in red blood cells that usually carries oxygen. Carbon dioxide is then transported by the hemoglobin to the lungs.

The Mechanics of Breathing

What happens to your body when you take a deep breath? Your ribcage expands and your diaphragm contracts. This action increases the volume of the lungs and allows air to rush in. This process of taking in oxygen is called **inspiration**. When you breathe out and let carbon dioxide out of your lungs, that's called **expiration**. Getting back to the Heimlich maneuver . . . When the second person squeezes the first, he is not actually squeezing the stomach but rather the diaphragm! This is what forces the air back up the lungs and trachea, freeing the lodged food.

Respiratory Disorders

Following are some respiratory disorders you should be familiar with:

- Asthma: an allergic reaction in which the bronchi are constricted. Asthma usually results in wheezing and difficulty in breathing.

- Bronchitis: an inflammation of the bronchi resulting in a severe cough.

- Emphysema: a swelling or inflammation of air passages due to a loss of elasticity in the alveoli. This disease is common among individuals who smoke (although the cigarette companies would like you to believe there's absolutely no connection between the two).

TRANSPORT

We've already discussed how organisms acquire nutrients and essential gases. But how exactly do they distribute them throughout their bodies? In other words, how do organisms get all their nutrients *into* cells?

As we've already seen, this is no problem for such simple organisms as protists. Single-celled organisms in a watery environment have no trouble moving materials directly across their membranes. Even simple multicellular organisms, such as the hydra, manage to do the same. But what about complex organisms like ourselves?

TRANSPORT: THE TRAFFIC ACROSS MEMBRANES

Before we discuss transport, let's review the cell membrane. You'll recall from our discussion in chapter 2 that cells possess a plasma membrane. This plasma membrane is **selectively permeable**. This means that certain substances such as water and lipids move freely across the membrane, while others are kept out. The substances that move freely across the membrane do so by **passive transport**.

We already saw passive transport in the section on respiration. Basically, whenever there's a higher concentration of substance outside the cell than inside the cell, the substance moves into the cell. It's like riding a bicycle downhill. Just like your bike, the substance outside the cell "goes with the natural flow." In the case of the diagram below, the "natural flow" is toward the interior of the cell:

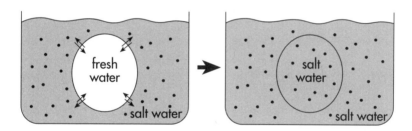

Passive transport is also known as **diffusion**. We often refer to this diffusion of substances from a region of higher concentration to one of lower concentration as *moving along a concentration gradient*. Keep in mind that this type of transport does not require energy.

One last thing: When we speak of the diffusion of liquids such as water, we call it **osmosis**.

ACTIVE TRANSPORT

Suppose the cell wants to move a substance in the *opposite* direction, from a region of lower concentration to one of higher concentration. To do this, the cell is going to need energy. This time it's like riding a bicycle uphill: It takes a lot more work. Movement against the natural flow is called **active transport**.

Where does the cell get this energy? From adenosine triphosphate (ATP), of course! ATP molecules are used to activate the specialized proteins embedded in the plasma membrane (remember the fluid-mosaic model?). These specialized proteins allow the cell to bring substances into and out of the cell against the gradient. A classic example of such a mechanism is the sodium-potassium pump. This particular form of active transport is extremely important to organisms. Without the sodium-potassium pump, we'd be senseless lumps of flesh. Among other things, this marvelous adaptation is what allows our nerves "to fire," enabling us to react, think, and feel.

ENDOCYTOSIS

What happens when the particles that want to enter a cell are just too large? The cell takes in the particles by forming a pocket from the cell membrane. This process is called **endocytosis**. The pocket pinches in and eventually forms either a vacuole or vesicle.

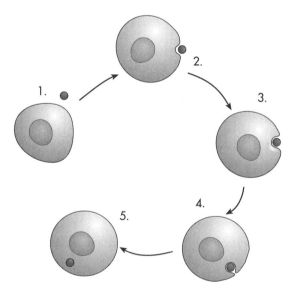

Two types of endocytosis exist: **pinocytosis** and **phagocytosis**. In pinocytosis, the cell ingests fluids ("cell-drinking"). In phagocytosis, the cell ingests large particles ("cell-eating"). You'll recall from our discussion of nutrition that *Amoeba* accomplishes this thanks to its pseudopodia.

Now that we've looked at some of the ways organisms move substances across the plasma membrane, let's jump to more complex means of transport.

ANIMALS

Larger organisms can't use the same strategies as their smaller counterparts to supply all their cells with the necessary materials. Too many cells are not in contact with the environment. These organisms therefore need special systems to accomplish internal transport. There are two types of circulatory systems: an **open circulatory system** and a **closed circulatory system**. In an open circulatory system, blood is carried along by open-ended blood vessels that spill blood into the body cavity. In grasshoppers, for example, blood vessels from the heart open into large spaces known as **sinuses**. Blood is pumped by the **heart**, also known as the **dorsal aorta**.

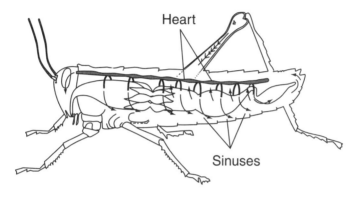

Other organisms have a closed circulatory system. That is, blood flows continuously through a network of blood vessels. Earthworms have a closed circulatory system.

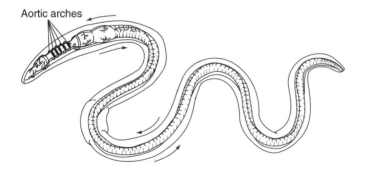

Closed circulatory system of an earthworm

As you can see from the diagram above, earthworms have five **aortic arches** that pump blood throughout the body. Now that we've looked at a couple of invertebrate circulatory systems, let's move on to the human circulatory system.

HUMAN CIRCULATORY SYSTEM

As you already know, the heart is the body's pump. If you stop to think about it, the heart's work is pretty amazing. In your lifetime, your heart will beat more than two billion times, pumping about 180 million liters of blood!

The heart is divided into four chambers, two on the left and two on the right. The four chambers of the heart are the **right atrium**, the **right ventricle**, the **left atrium**, and the **left ventricle**. Let's take a look at the heart:

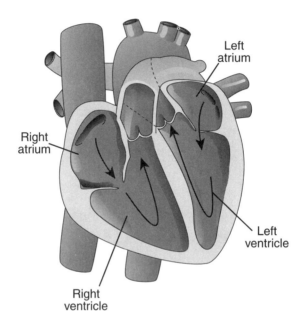

As you can tell from the arrows, the heart pumps blood in a continuous circuit. Let's take a closer look at how the blood travels through the heart. Because blood makes a complete circuit in the body, it doesn't matter where we begin to trace its flow. Let's begin at the left atrium. Blood flows from the left atrium to the left ventricle, then out the aorta toward the body. It then returns via the right atrium, flows into the right ventricle, and leaves again via the pulmonary arteries.

Let's go back for a moment to the point in the circulatory system where the blood exits the left ventricle. When blood leaves the left ventricle it starts its long tour of the body. This is called the **systemic circulation**.

Systemic Circulation

Blood leaves the heart through a huge blood vessel called the **aorta**. The aorta is the largest artery in the body. The aorta carries blood away from the heart, quickly branching out into smaller vessels called **arteries**. Arteries always carry blood away from the heart. Just remember: *A* stands for *a*way from the heart. Arteries are thick-walled, elastic vessels. Their strength and elasticity make it possible for them to manage the high-pressure flow as blood is pumped away from the heart.

The arteries lead into even smaller vessels called **arterioles** and finally into the smallest vessels called **capillaries**, which are tiny tubes no more than a single cell thick.

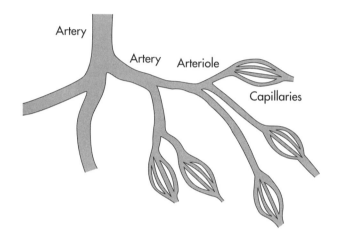

There are thousands and thousands of capillaries in the body. In fact, some estimate that the capillary routes in your bloodstream are as much as 100 km long! These vessels are so tiny that red blood cells must "squeeze" through them single file. Capillaries intermingle with the tissues, allowing for the exchange of nutrients, gases, and wastes. Oxygen and nutrients leave the capillaries and enter the tissues; carbon dioxide and wastes leave the tissues and enter the capillaries.

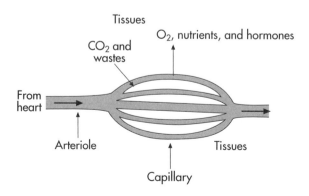

Back to the Heart

After touring the body, the blood has very little oxygen left. Most of its oxygen has passed through the capillary walls to the body's cells. Because the blood is now depleted of oxygen, it is said to be **deoxygenated**. To get a fresh supply of oxygen, the blood now needs to go to—where else?—the lungs.

However, the blood doesn't go directly to the lungs. It must first return to the heart. As the blood returns to the heart the vessels get bigger and bigger:

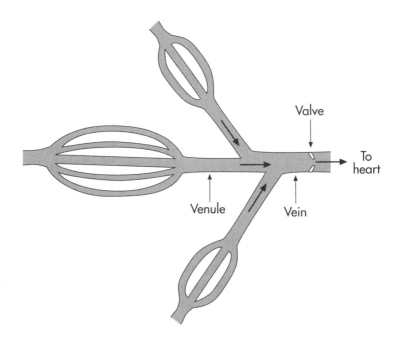

From the capillaries, blood travels through vessels called **venules**, then into larger vessels called **veins**. Veins always carry blood toward the heart. Veins are thin-walled vessels with valves that prevent the backward flow of blood. The deoxygenated blood finally reaches the heart, entering by the **right atrium.**

The blood is then pumped from the right atrium to the right ventricle. From the right ventricle, blood shoots out again into the body, but this time toward the lungs. This is called **pulmonary circulation.**

Pulmonary Circulation

Blood leaves the right ventricle through a large artery known as the **pulmonary artery**. Remember what we said about arteries? Blood vessels that leave the heart are always called **arteries**. The pulmonary artery then branches into right and left pulmonary arteries, which lead to the lungs.

These arteries then become smaller vessels called **arterioles** and finally **capillaries**.

We mentioned above that the blood arriving in the right atrium is deoxygenated, having donated its oxygen to the body. When it leaves the right ventricle, it heads toward the lungs to pick up fresh oxygen and dump its load of carbon dioxide. Does this sound vaguely familiar? It should. This is the gas exchange we discussed above, when we looked at the respiratory system. Keep in mind that the tiny capillaries in the lungs are wrapped around alveoli, or small air sacs.

At the alveoli, the blood picks up the oxygen the body needs. We now say that the blood is **oxygenated**. It then returns to the heart via the **pulmonary veins** and enters the left atrium:

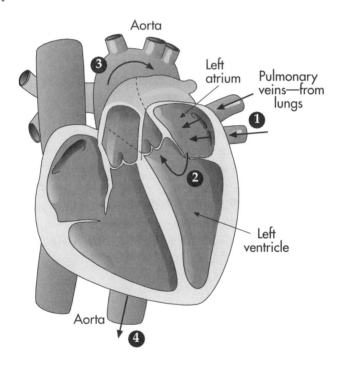

Once the blood moves to the left ventricle, it's ready to start its circuit all over again.

Contents of the Blood

Blood consists of two things:

1. Fluid (called **plasma**)

2. Cells suspended in the fluid

Blood doesn't just carry oxygen and carbon dioxide throughout the body. It also carries three types of cells: **red blood cells**, **white blood cells**, and **platelets**. Red blood cells are the oxygen-carrying cells in the body. They contain hemoglobin, a specialized protein that transports oxygen and carbon dioxide.

Blood also contains two types of white blood cells: **phagocytes** and **lymphocytes**. Phagocytes fight infection by destroying bacteria invading the body. The other class of white blood cells, lymphocytes, are specialized cells that are part of the immune system. They produce **antibodies** (an immune substance) when they come in contact with foreign proteins called **antigens**. The role of antibodies is to bind antigens and trigger the immune system to prepare for an attack. Where does all this stuff originate?

- All of the blood cells are made in the bone marrow. The bone marrow is located in the center of bones.

Blood Types

Blood comes in four different types: **A**, **B**, **AB**, and **O**. Blood types are important. If a patient is given the wrong type of blood in a transfusion, it can be fatal! Why? Because blood cells clump when exposed to the wrong blood type. For example, if you have blood type A, and you receive a blood transfusion of blood type B, your blood will clump as the body produces antibodies that bind to the surface of the foreign blood. For this reason, it's very important for doctors and nurses to know a patient's blood type before giving a transfusion.

As you'd expect, there are seldom problems with an individual receiving blood of his or her own type. In addition, there are two unique properties of blood types:

- Type **O** blood is the universal donor.
- Type **AB** is the universal recipient.

This means that anyone can receive a blood transfusion of type O blood, which produces no immune response, and those with type AB blood can receive any kind of blood.

IMMUNE SYSTEM

In addition to the circulatory system, we have another system called the **immune system**. The immune system is the body's defense system. We've already talked about phagocytes and lymphocytes, specialized white blood cells involved in the body's immune response. As we saw, lymphocytes trigger an immune response when they detect an antigen, or foreign invader. In addition to these cells, the immune system includes a network of **lymph vessels** that run along the same basic routes as the blood vessels:

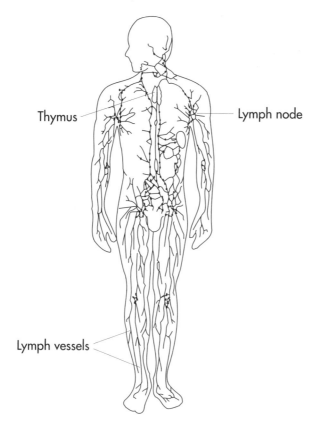

Thymus

Lymph node

Lymph vessels

Lymph vessels transport a clear watery fluid called **lymph** throughout the body's tissues. Sometimes a lymph vessel forms a **lymph node**, a bulge found along the course of a lymph vessel. Lymph nodes contain heaps of lymphocytes.

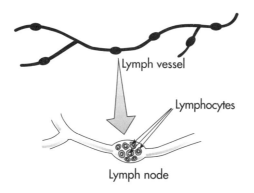

Lymph vessel

Lymphocytes

Lymph node

When your body is infected, your lymph nodes swell as they churn out lymphocytes. This is what your doctor is checking for when she feels the sides of your throat: She's feeling to see if your lymph nodes are swollen.

One final point about the immune system. The immune system can provide **immunity** to certain diseases. For example, if you had chicken pox when you were a kid, you'll never get it again. This is because the body has learned to recognize the virus that causes chicken pox. The first time your body was infected, it took the immune system a while to generate the right antibodies and tackle the invader. However, now that your body has been exposed, the immune system's response is incalculably faster: The moment it detects the presence of chicken pox, it "remembers" the virus and sends out the appropriate antibodies. This speedy response, and the protection it offers the body, is known as *immunity*.

Allergies

There are times, however, when the immune system doesn't function perfectly. In some cases, such common substances as dust and pollen can trigger an immune response. When your body treats harmless substances as dangerous invaders, it's called an **allergy**. Many people have allergies to specific foods or drugs. In these cases, the mere presence of the substance is enough to induce a runny nose or eyes, asthma, and sneezing. All of these responses are typical immune responses, which explains why the symptoms of allergies are identical to the symptoms of a cold: The body is reacting the same way in both cases.

CARDIOVASCULAR AND BLOOD DISORDERS

Here are some common cardiovascular and blood disorders you should be familiar with:

Cardiovascular disorders

- High blood pressure: The arteries have become narrowed, reducing the flow of blood to the heart. If left untreated, this condition can cause damage to the heart muscles and blood vessels. The primary cause of narrowed blood vessels is a buildup of fatty deposits or "plaque" on the walls of the arteries.

- Angina pectoris: This is an intense pain in the chest related to reduced coronary circulation. The heart doesn't get enough oxygen because of the blocked arteries.

- Coronary thrombosis: The arteries of the heart are so severely blocked that it causes a heart attack.

Blood disorders

- Anemia: This is a condition in which the blood doesn't carry enough oxygen because the number of healthy red blood cells is below normal.

- Leukemia: This is a blood disease in which production of immature white blood cells is uncontrolled. Leukemia is a type of cancer.

EXCRETION

As you already know, all organisms must get rid of wastes. Waste products include carbon dioxide, salts, and nitrogenous wastes. Simple organisms, such as protists and hydra, get rid of toxic wastes though simple diffusion: Wastes are released either directly into the environment or, in the case of the hydra, into a simple gastrovascular cavity and then into the environment.

The cells of more complex, multicellular organisms, however, are not directly in contact with their environments. Consequently, these organisms had to develop ways of getting rid of wastes. This issue is especially important because nitrogenous wastes—products containing nitrogen and produced in abundance during the breakdown of amino acids—are highly toxic to the body.

EARTHWORMS

Earthworms have **nephridia** as their excretory organs. These branched tubes concentrate the wastes and open to the outside of the body through tiny pores.

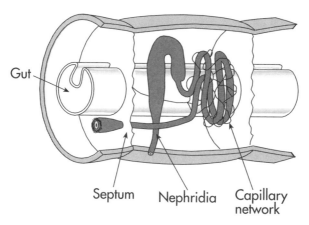

Gut

Septum   Nephridia   Capillary network

INSECTS

The excretory organs in insects are called **Malpighian tubules**. These tubules concentrate the waste and empty into the intestine. The major waste product, **uric acid**, is excreted as a dry pellet.

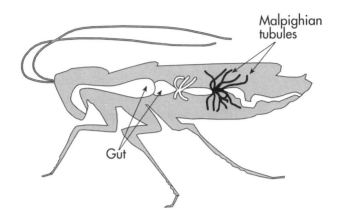

HUMAN EXCRETORY SYSTEM

In humans, the organ that regulates excretion is the **kidney**. The kidneys are shaped just like the bean—ergo "kidney bean"—and are found above the waist. Although the kidneys look rather unassuming, they are fantastically complicated structures made up of millions of tiny units called **nephrons**.

Nephrons

Nephrons are the functional units of the kidney. A nephron consists of several regions. Here's what a nephron looks like under a microscope:

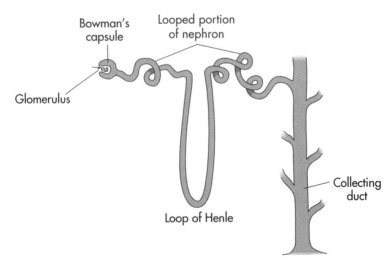

How does a nephron work? Let's trace the flow of blood in a nephron. Blood vessels from the aorta lead to the kidney and branch into tiny balls of capillaries called the **glomerulus**. The glomerulus sits within a cup-shaped structure called the **Bowman's capsule**. Blood is filtered as it passes by the Bowman's capsule. Small substances, such as ions, water, glucose, and amino acids, easily pass through the capillary walls into the porous surface of the Bowman's capsule. This fluid collected here is called a **filtrate**.

The filtrate travels along the entire nephron. The filtrate passes through the looped portion of the nephron and finally into the collecting duct. As the filtrate moves through the nephron, glucose, amino acids, and salts are retained by the body. The rest of the fluid is concentrated into urine.

The concentrated urine moves from the **kidney**, into the **ureter**, then into the **bladder**, and finally out through the **urethra**, a tiny tube leading from the bladder to the outside of the body.

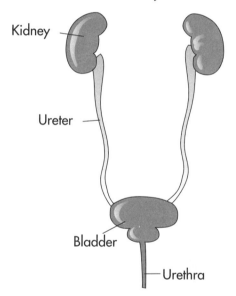

Kidney

Ureter

Bladder

Urethra

Skin

The **skin** is another important organ that helps us get rid of wastes. Believe it or not, your skin is an organ. In fact, it's the largest organ in the body! Your skin contains more than two million sweat glands that secrete water and ions in warm weather. Sweat glands not only help to maintain an optimal salt balance in your body but also help maintain body temperature.

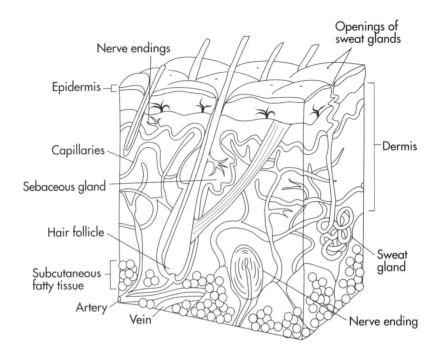

Nerve endings

Openings of
sweat glands

Epidermis

Dermis

Capillaries

Sebaceous gland

Hair follicle

Sweat
gland

Subcutaneous
fatty tissue

Artery

Vein

Nerve ending

The skin has three layers: the **epidermis**, **dermis**, and the **subcutaneous tissue**. Sweat glands are found in the dermis layer along with blood vessels, nerves, and oil (sebaceous) glands.

Lungs and Liver

The lungs and liver also get rid of wastes. Carbon dioxide is mainly excreted by the lungs. The liver is responsible for converting amino acids to urea. This is known as **deamination**.

DISORDERS OF THE EXCRETORY SYSTEM

Following are some common disorders associated with the excretory system:

- Kidney failure: a condition in which the kidney fails to function properly.

- Gout: a condition associated with excessive uric acid in the blood. The acid hardens and deposits into the joints of the body, resulting in great pain and decreased mobility. Interestingly, gout is not unique to human beings. In fact, even the dinosaurs had gout. Sue, a fossilized Tyrannosaurus Rex found in the Black Hills of South Dakota, apparently suffered from this painful disorder.

REGULATION

All organisms must be able to react to changes in their environments. As a result, organisms have evolved systems that enable them to pick up cues from the outside world. The task of coordinating and processing this information falls to the **nervous system** (nerve control) and **endocrine system** (chemical control). Let's start our discussion of regulation by taking a look at the nervous system.

NERVOUS SYSTEM

The basic unit of structure and function in the nervous system is a **neuron**. Neurons are specialized cells that pick up and transmit messages throughout the body. Neurons consist of a **cyton** (the cell body), **dendrites**, and an **axon**:

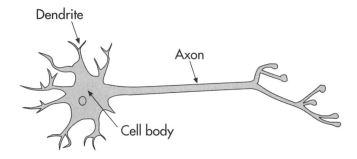

The cyton contains the nucleus and all the usual organelles found in the cytoplasm. The dendrites are short extensions of the cell body that receive the stimuli. The axon is a long, slender extension of the cell body that transmits an impulse from the cell body to another neuron. An axon can be very long. For example, giraffes have single axons that span the entire length of their necks.

At the end of the axon are thin fibers known as **terminal branches** that release a chemical substance called a **neurotransmitter**. Neurotransmitters enable messages to be passed from one neuron to another. When a message arrives at a neuron's dendrites, it passes through the dendrites to the cell body, then down the axon to the terminal branches.

When an impulse reaches the end of an axon, it triggers the release of a neurotransmitter into the space between the first cell's axon and the next cell's dendrites. This space is called a **synapse**. The neurotransmitter "swims" to the other side and binds to receptors on the dendrites of the next neuron. Now the impulse moves along the second neuron from dendrites to axon. It's the neurotransmitter that triggers the passing of the signal to the second neuron. There are a lot of neurotransmitters, but the one we need to know is called **acetylcholine**. Acetylcholine is the chemical "messenger" responsible for muscle contractions, among other things.

ANIMALS

Now that we've taken a look at the neuron, let's discuss the different types of nervous systems found in various organisms. The simplest arrangement is no more than a web of undifferentiated neurons. This is known as a **nerve net**. The hydra has such a nervous system, in which the neurons receive stimuli and transmit impulses in all directions.

As animals became more complex, some of the neurons gathered into what are known as **ganglia**. Ganglia are found in all higher organisms, including humans. In more primitive creatures, the ganglia can be thought of as rudimentary brains. In earthworms, for example, ganglia bunch together to form a simple **two-lobed brain**. Other ganglia form smaller bunches running the length of the animal. In the earthworm, this stringy mass of bunched nerve cells is known as the **ventral nerve cord**.

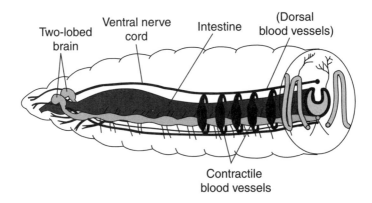

The grasshopper has a nervous system very similar to the earthworm's.

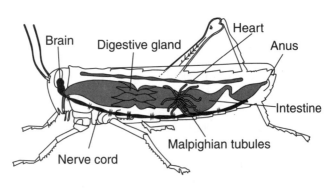

HUMAN NERVOUS SYSTEM

Neurons

Types of Neurons

Neurons in humans, which are highly specialized, fall into three groups: **sensory neurons**, **motor (effector) neurons**, and **interneurons**. These three different types of neurons play separate roles in the transmission of a nervous impulse. Consider the sense of touch, for example. As your fingers come in contact with this page, sensory neurons pick up impulses and bring them to the body. These sensory neurons are also called **receptors**. Once the receptors have picked up information from the environment (about the texture of the page, for example), this signal is sent to the interneurons. Interneurons act as links between sensory neurons and motor neurons and are often found in the brain or spinal cord. Once the brain has processed the signal, it can send another signal out to the motor neurons. The motor neuron in turn transmits an impulse to the muscles in the hand, "telling" it to flip the page. Motor neurons are also called **effectors**.

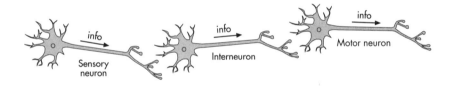

How Neurons Communicate

Before we talk about the events related to the transmission of a nerve impulse, let's review how neurons interact. There are literally billions of neurons running throughout the body, firing all the time. More often than not, several neurons are interconnected. This means that one neuron has its dendrites next to the axons of several other neurons. In this way, the dendrites of the first cell can pick up the impulses sent from the axons of several other cells. The second neuron, in turn, can then send the impulse to its cell body and down its axon, passing it on to other cells.

An example of this is the **reflex arc**. When the doctor taps your knee with a hammer, he provokes a reflex arc. In this type of neuronal communication, sensory neurons pick up an impulse and send it to the motor neurons, which in turn make the muscle contract.

Schwann's Cells

Sometimes a neuron has supporting cells that wrap around its axon like plastic insulation around an electric wire. These cells are called **Schwann's cells**. Schwann's cells produce a structure called a **myelin sheath** that insulates the axon.

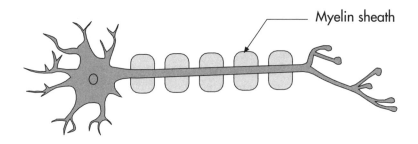
Myelin sheath

The myelin sheath enables the neuron to speed up its transmission of the impulse. It manages this by letting the impulse jump from node to node (the block-shaped chunks in the illustration above). This speeding up of the impulse allows the organism to react much more quickly to its environment.

Parts of the Nervous System

The nervous system can be divided into two parts: the **central nervous system** and the **peripheral nervous system**.

All of the neurons within the brain and spinal cord make up the central nervous system.

The brain can also be divided into three parts. The **cerebrum** controls all voluntary activities and receives and interprets sensory information. It is the largest part of the brain. The **cerebellum** coordinates muscle activity and controls balance. The **medulla** controls involuntary actions such as peristalsis and the beating of the heart.

The **spinal cord** extends from the base of the brain to the vertebrae. It has two functions: (1) to transmit impulses to and from the brain and (2) to control reflex activities.

All of the other neurons lying outside the brain and the spinal cord—in our skin, our organs, and our blood vessels—are collectively part of the **peripheral nervous system**. Although both of these systems are interwoven, we still use the terms *central* and *peripheral*.

The peripheral nervous system is further broken down into the **somatic nervous system** and the **autonomic nervous system**. The somatic nervous system is the part that controls voluntary activities. For example, the movement of your eyes across the page as you read this line is under the control of your somatic nervous system. The **autonomic nervous system** is that part that controls involuntary actions. Your heartbeat and your digestive system are the domain of the autonomic nervous system.

The interesting thing about these two systems is that they sometimes overlap. For example, you can control your breathing if you choose to. Yet when you sleep, you no longer need to think about it: Your somatic system hands control of your respiration over to the autonomic system.

How can you remember all this? The flow chart below provides a nice overview of the different parts of the nervous system:

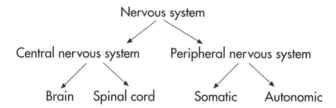

Disorders of the Nervous System

Following is a list of some common disorders associated with the nervous system:

- Meningitis: a disease in which the connective tissue covering the brain (meninges) is infected and inflamed.

- Cerebral palsy: a group of motor disorders that results in loss of muscle control due to damage to the motor areas of the brain.

- Stroke: a disease in which the brain tissue is destroyed because the blood vessels lack oxygen.

- Polio: a viral disease that results from the destruction of motor neurons in the spinal nerves and leads to paralysis.

That should do it for the nervous system. Now let's look at the endocrine system. As mentioned above, the endocrine system is the other major system involved in maintaining the body's internal balance, or **homeostasis**.

ENDOCRINE SYSTEM

The **endocrine system** is closely tied to the nervous system. Many organisms depend on the signals provided by the nervous system to release certain chemical messengers called **hormones**. The hormones are produced by the endocrine system and serve to maintain the internal balance of the body. Hormones are produced in one part of the body and act on a gland in a distant part of the body.

The specialized organs responsible for the production of hormones are called **endocrine glands**. Endocrine glands release hormones directly into the bloodstream, where they are then carried throughout the body. Take a look at the endocrine glands in the human body:

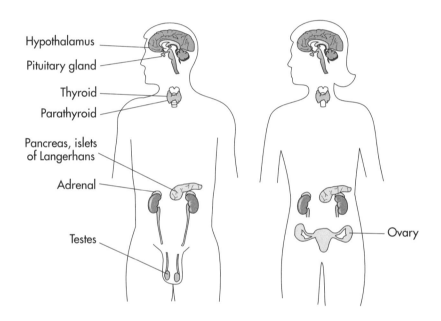

Hypothalamus
Pituitary gland
Thyroid
Parathyroid
Pancreas, islets of Langerhans
Adrenal
Testes
Ovary

Negative Feedback

Before we launch into a review of the different hormones in the body, let's talk about how hormones work. Although hormones flow in your blood, they only affect specific cells. The cells that a hormone affects are known as the **target cells**. Suppose, for example, that gland X makes hormone Y. Hormone Y, in turn, has some effect on organ Z. We would then say that organ Z is the target organ of hormone Y.

Hormones are also regulated by a **negative feedback system**. That is, an excess of the hormone temporarily shuts down production. For example, when hormone Y reaches a peak level in the bloodstream, the organ secreting the hormone, gland X, is temporarily inhibited from producing hormone Y. Once the levels of hormone Y decline, the gland resumes production of the hormone.

The Pituitary: The Master Gland

Let's start by discussing the **pituitary**. The anterior pituitary is called the *master gland* because it releases many hormones that reach other glands and stimulate them to secrete their hormones. We could therefore say that the anterior pituitary has many target organs. The pituitary secretes several hormones:

1. **Follicle-stimulating hormone** (FSH), which stimulates the follicle to grow. This is an important stage in the female menstrual cycle. (We'll see FSH again in chapter 7.)

2. **Luteinizing hormone** (LH), which causes the release of the ovum during the menstrual cycle.

3. **Growth-stimulating hormone** (GH), which stimulates growth throughout the body.

4. **Thyroid-stimulating hormone** (TSH), which stimulates the thyroid to secrete its hormone.

Hypothalamus

The pituitary works in tandem with a part of the brain called the **hypothalamus**. The pituitary sits just below the hypothalamus:

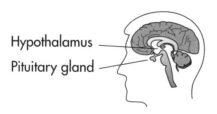

Hypothalamus
Pituitary gland

The hypothalamus secretes substances that can stimulate or inhibit the actions of the pituitary.

Pancreas

We already know that the pancreas produces enzymes that it releases into the small intestine. The pancreas also secretes two hormones, **glucagon** and **insulin**. These pancreatic hormones are produced in a special cluster of cells within the pancreas called the **islet of Langerhans**. The target organs for these hormones are the liver and muscle cells. Glucagon, for example, stimulates the liver to convert **glycogen** (the stored form of glucose) into glucose. Glucagon therefore increases the levels of glucose in the blood. Insulin has the opposite effect: It stimulates the uptake of glucose and its conversion to glycogen. Insulin therefore *lowers* the levels of glucose in the blood.

When a person's body cannot properly regulate its blood sugar, that person is said to be **diabetic**. Diabetes, though relatively easy to control, is a potentially life-threatening disorder if left untreated. Millions of Americans suffer from diabetes.

Adrenal Glands

The adrenal glands are actually two endocrine glands. One is called the **adrenal medulla** (the inner region) and the other is called the **adrenal cortex** (the outer region). Although they are part of the same organ, these two endocrine glands work independently of one another.

Adrenal Cortex

The adrenal cortex releases steroid hormones that do two things: (1) They increase the blood's concentration of glucose by promoting the conversion of amino acids and fatty acids to glucose, and (2) they help the body retain salt and water in the kidneys.

Adrenal Medulla

The other adrenal gland, the **adrenal medulla,** is often referred to as the *emergency gland*. It releases hormones involved in the fight-or-flight response. These hormones "kick in" under stress. They increase your heart rate, metabolic rate, and blood pressure, giving you a quick boost of energy.

Thyroid Gland

The thyroid gland is located in the neck and is the target organ of the TSH released by the pituitary.

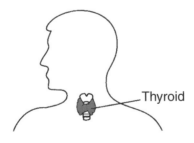

When the thyroid is stimulated by TSH, it releases the hormone **thyroxin**. Thyroxin regulates the metabolic rate in most body tissues.

Parathyroid Glands

The parathyroids are four little pea-shaped organs that sit on your thyroid. The parathyroids secrete the hormone **parathormone**. Parathormone regulates your blood calcium levels. If your body needs more calcium, parathormone triggers the bones to release the calcium stored inside them. Excess calcium triggers the parathyroid to stop releasing parathormone (remember that negative feedback?). This, in turn, allows the bones to uptake and store this excess calcium.

Sex Hormones

Three hormones that are involved in reproduction are **estrogen**, **progesterone**, and **testosterone**. Estrogen and progesterone are hormones released by the ovaries. Both hormones regulate the menstrual cycle. Estrogen also promotes female secondary sex characteristics. Testosterone is the male hormone that promotes the production of sperm. It also promotes male secondary sex characteristics. We'll take a closer look at these hormones in chapter 7.

Endocrine Disorders

The following are some principal disorders associated with the endocrine system:

- Goiter: a condition in which the thyroid gland is enlarged because it doesn't produce enough thyroxin.

- Diabetes: as stated above, a condition in which blood sugar levels are not properly regulated by the body. It is usually due to a problem with the body's ability to produce the hormone insulin.

LOCOMOTION

Most organisms have the ability to move from one place to another. In biological terms, this ability to get around is called **locomotion**. Locomotion is important to organisms because it confers four basic advantages. It makes it easier to

1. Reproduce

2. Get food

3. Avoid predators

4. Find shelter

Needless to say, all four of these increase an organism's chance for survival.

ONE-CELLED ORGANISMS

Unicellular organisms, such as protists, use specialized structures to move about. As we saw earlier, *Amoeba* uses its pseudopodia, *Euglena* its whip-like flagella, and *Paramecium* its cilia. Although there are other means of locomotion among microorganisms, these three solutions are among the most common.

EARTHWORMS

Some organisms have **muscles** that are responsible for locomotion. Earthworms have muscles that contract and relax to make the body move. They also contain short bristles called **setae** that grip the soil as the earthworm inches forward.

GRASSHOPPERS

Other organisms have a supporting skeletal system. Some animals wear their support on the outside. They have an **exoskeleton**—a hard covering or shell. Grasshoppers, for example, have an exoskeleton made of chitin. By attaching their muscles to the exoskeletons, insects such as the grasshopper provide themselves with a sturdy, effective means of locomotion. Moreover, insects have both jointed appendages specially adapted for moving about on land and wings that enable them to fly.

Interestingly enough, wings in insects have nothing whatsoever to do with wings in birds or mammals, other than the fact that wings enable all three to become airborne. What do we mean when we say that they have nothing to do with one another? Biologically speaking, we mean that wings in insects, birds, and bats evolved independently of one another: Each group evolved wings on its own and did not inherit them from a common ancestor. We'll come back to this concept in chapter 10.

VERTEBRATES

All **vertebrates** (animals with backbones) possess an **endoskeleton**: Their entire skeleton is on the inside. Just think of your own backbone or spine and you'll get the point. In addition to ourselves, fish, amphibians, reptiles, birds, and all other mammals are considered vertebrates and therefore have endoskeletons.

HUMAN SKELETAL SYSTEM

In humans, the supporting skeleton is made of **cartilage** and **bone**. Cartilage is a flexible connective tissue found in the embryonic stages of all vertebrates. It is later replaced by bone, except in areas such as your external ear and the tip of your nose.

Bones and Joints

Bone is a hard connective tissue that provides support for the body. It is made up of calcium and collagen. Bones are held together by **joints**, like the ball-and-socket joints in your shoulder. The joints are held together by tough connective tissues called **ligaments**. Just remember that ligaments attach bone to bone. Bones not only serve as support but, together with muscles, also help us move about. The connective tissues that attach muscles to bones are called **tendons**.

Muscles

There are three kinds of muscles: **skeletal**, **smooth (visceral)**, and **cardiac**. Skeletal muscles control voluntary movements. You'll notice that they have stripes called **striations** and are filled with multinucleated cells.

Smooth muscles are found throughout the body—in the walls of blood vessels, the digestive tracts, and internal organs. They are long and tapered, and each cell has one nucleus. Smooth muscles are responsible for involuntary movements. Compared to those of skeletal muscles, the contractions of smooth muscles are slow.

Cardiac muscles are found in the heart. They have characteristics of both smooth and skeletal muscles. Cardiac muscles are striated, just like skeletal muscles. They are under involuntary control, like smooth muscles. Contractions in cardiac muscle are spontaneous and automatic. This simply means that the heart can beat on its own. Both the smooth muscle and cardiac muscle get their nerve supply from the autonomic nervous system.

One last thing you should remember about muscle contractions: They are energy dependent. A muscle contraction requires energy in the form of ATP.

Here is a chart to help you compare the types of muscle tissues:

Types of Muscle Tissues			
	Skeletal	Smooth	Cardiac
Location	Attached to skeleton	Wall of digestive tract, inside the blood vessels	Wall of heart
Type of control	Voluntary	Involuntary	Involuntary
Striations	Yes	No	No
Multinucleated	Yes	No	No
Speed of contraction	Rapid	Slowest	Intermediate

Diseases of the Locomotive System

Here are some common diseases that can affect locomotion among humans:

- Arthritis: an inflammation of the joints.
- Tendonitis: an inflammation of the tendons. This disorder is common among athletes.

CHAPTER 6 QUIZ

1. Which sequence represents the direction of flow of carbon dioxide as it passes out of the respiratory system into the external environment?

   (1) alveoli → trachea → bronchioles → bronchi → pharynx → nasal cavity

   (2) alveoli → bronchi → pharynx → bronchioles → trachea → nasal cavity

   (3) alveoli → pharynx → trachea → bronchioles → bronchi → nasal cavity

   (4) alveoli → bronchioles → bronchi → trachea → pharynx → nasal cavity

Directions for 2–4: For each phrase in questions 2 through 4, select the malfunction, chosen from the list below, that is best described by that statement.

Malfunctions

(1) polio

(2) stroke

(3) meningitis

(4) cerebral palsy

2. A congenital disease characterized by abnormal motor functions

3. A clot in a cerebral blood vessel that can result in brain damage

4. Inflammation of the membrane surrounding the brain and spinal cord

5. Short-tailed shrews and ruby-throated hummingbirds have high metabolic rates. As a result, these animals

    (1) use energy rapidly
    (2) need very little food
    (3) have very few predators
    (4) hibernate in hot weather

6. Which activity would not be carried out by an organism to maintain a stable internal environment?

    (1) removal of metabolic waste products
    (2) transport of organic and inorganic compounds
    (3) production of offspring by the organism
    (4) regulation of physiologic processes

7. The diagram below represents a protist.

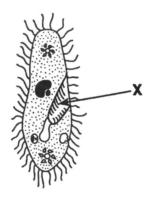

    Structure X is most directly involved in the process of

    (1) extracellular digestion
    (2) enzymatic hydrolysis
    (3) ingestion
    (4) transpiration

8. In an amoeba, which process is best represented by the arrows shown in the diagram below?

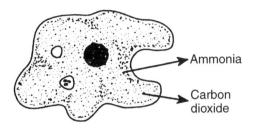

(1) absorption by active transport

(2) excretion by diffusion

(3) respiratory gas exchange

(4) egestion of digestive end products

9. Tendons are best described as

(1) tissue that is found between bones and that protects them from damage

(2) cords that connect bone to bone and that stretch at the point of attachment

(3) striated tissues that provide a wide range of motion

(4) fibrous cords that connect muscles to bones

10. Which statement describes a relationship between the human cells illustrated in the diagrams below?

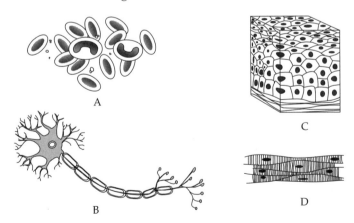

(1) B may cause D to contract.

(2) A is produced by D.

(3) C transports oxygen to A.

(4) B is used to repair C.

11. In plants, glucose is converted to cellulose, and in human muscle cells, glucose is converted to glycogen. These processes are examples of which life activity?

(1) regulation

(2) respiration

(3) synthesis

(4) excretion

12. One way in which the intake of oxygen is similar in the hydra and the earthworm is that both organisms

(1) absorb oxygen through a system of tubes

(2) use cilia to absorb oxygen

(3) use capillaries to transport oxygen

(4) absorb oxygen through their external surfaces

13. The life function of transport in the grasshopper involves

(1) an internal gas exchange surface and alveoli

(2) an open circulatory system and tracheal tubes

(3) moist outer skin and hemoglobin

(4) a dry external body surface and hemoglobin

14. Which process is correctly paired with its major waste product?

(1) respiration: oxygen

(2) protein synthesis: amino acids

(3) dehydration synthesis: water

(4) hydrolysis: carbon dioxide

15. The diagram below represents a growth response in a plant:

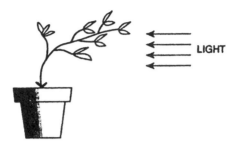

This growth response was most likely due to the effect of light on

(1) acetylcholine

(2) minerals

(3) auxin distribution

(4) vascular tissue

16. The diagram below shows a longitudinal section of the human heart:

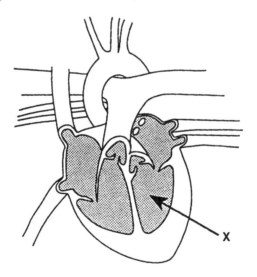

The structure labeled X is known as

(1) a ventricle

(2) an atrium

(3) a valve

(4) the aorta

17. A hawk sees a field mouse, which it then captures for food. In this activity, the eyes of the hawk function as

(1) effectors

(2) receptors

(3) stimuli

(4) neurotransmitters

18. Methyl cellulose is a chemical that slows the movement of paramecia on a slide. This chemical most likely interferes with the movement of

(1) pseudopodia

(2) flagella

(3) setae

(4) cilia

19. Which adaptation found within the human respiratory system filters, warms, and moistens the air before it enters the lungs?

(1) clusters of alveoli

(2) rings of cartilage

(3) involuntary smooth muscle

(4) ciliated mucous membranes

20. Food is usually kept from entering the trachea by the

(1) diaphragm

(2) epiglottis

(3) villi

(4) ribs

21. The nephrons and alveoli of humans are most similar in function to the

(1) nephridia and skin of earthworms

(2) Malpighian tubules and muscles of grasshoppers

(3) nerve nets and gastrovascular cavities of hydras

(4) cilia and pseudopodia of protozoa

22. Which part of the human central nervous system is correctly paired with its function?

(1) spinal cord: coordinates learning activities

(2) cerebellum: serves as the center of reflex

(3) cerebrum: serves as the center of memory and reasoning

(4) medulla: maintains muscular coordination

Reproduction

With regard to living things, *reproduction* refers to the ability to grow and produce offspring. This chapter takes a look at both asexual and sexual reproduction. Because reproduction begins on a cellular level, let's start with the cell's own means of reproduction, mitosis.

MITOSIS

Every second, thousands of cells are reproducing throughout our bodies. Cells are able to make identical copies of themselves at an amazing rate thanks to a means of asexual reproduction known as **mitosis**.

All living things undergo mitosis. Bacteria, for example, are particularly good at it. How good? Imagine taking a single bacterium and placing it in a medium at 37°C with unlimited food resources. Within 24 hours, that single bacterium would reproduce so many times that its offspring would cover an area the size of New York City. Fortunately, nature would never allow this to happen. Growth is kept in check by many things, including predation and limited food resources.

THE NITTY GRITTY OF MITOSIS

Mitosis is an extremely important process. During mitosis, two things occur: (1) The cell duplicates its genetic material and (2) splits in half, forming equal "daughter" cells. At the outset of mitosis, the cell's chromosomes duplicate themselves:

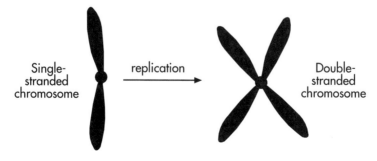

Single-stranded chromosome → replication → Double-stranded chromosome

You'll notice that the original chromosome and its duplicate are still linked, like Siamese twins. These identical chromosomes are now called **sister chromatids**. The chromatids are held together by a round structure called the **centromere**:

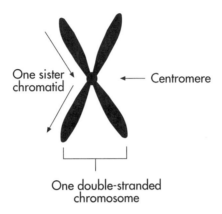

One sister chromatid

Centromere

One double-stranded chromosome

This duplication of the chromosomes indicates that the cell has already begun mitosis. Let's discuss the different stages of this crucial process.

STAGES OF MITOSIS
Mitosis consists of a sequence of four basic stages: **prophase**, **metaphase**, **anaphase**, and **telophase**.

Prophase
In prophase, the chromosomes thicken and become visible:

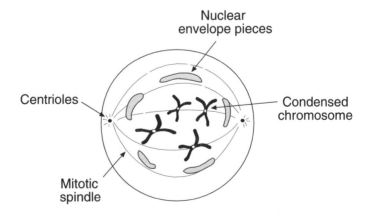

Nuclear envelope pieces

Centrioles

Condensed chromosome

Mitotic spindle

One of the first signs of prophase is the disintegration of the nuclear membrane. Now the cell has more room to sort out the chromosomes. During prophase, paired structures called **centrioles** start to move away from each other, toward opposite ends of the cell. The centrioles spin out a system of microtubules known as the **spindle fibers**, which in turn grow toward the chromosomes.

Metaphase

The next stage in mitosis is called *metaphase*. The chromosomes now begin to line up. Notice how nice and orderly they've become!

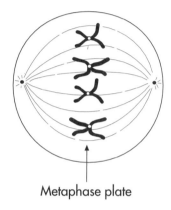

Metaphase plate

The spindle fibers are responsible for this neat arrangement: They line up the chromosomes at the middle of the cell along the **metaphase plate**.

Anaphase

During anaphase, the sister chromatids of each chromosome separate at the centromere and slowly move to opposite poles. A tug-of-war begins as the spindle fibers pull the chromosomes apart at the centromere.

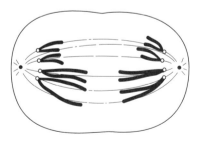

One member from each pair now zips off to opposing poles of the cell.

Telophase

The final phase of mitosis is telophase. A nuclear membrane forms around each set of chromosomes.

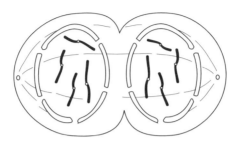

The nuclear membrane is ready to divide. Now it's time to split the cytoplasm in a process known as **cytokinesis**. Look at the figure below and you'll notice that the cell membrane has begun to split along a **cleavage furrow**:

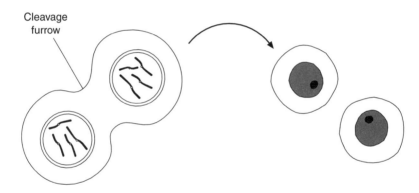

Cleavage furrow

A cell membrane forms around each cell and—pop!—they split into two daughter cells.

This is how cytokinesis occurs in animal cells. In plant cells, however, this final phase is slightly different. Plant cells do not form cleavage furrows. Instead, a partition called a **cell plate** forms down the middle region, separating the two daughter cells. Otherwise, mitosis for plant cells is the same as for animal cells.

MNEMONIC FOR MITOSIS

Here's a great way to remember the stages of mitosis. Use this mnemonic and you'll be sure to remember the major events.

PMAT

Prophase	*P* is for *p*repare (as the cell prepares for mitosis)
Metaphase	*M* is for *m*eet (when the chromosomes meet in the middle)
Anaphase	*A* is for *a*part (when the chromosomes draw apart)
Telophase	*T* is for *t*ear (as the cell tears in half, forming two daughter cells)

PURPOSE OF ASEXUAL REPRODUCTION

The purpose of asexual reproduction is to produce daughter cells that are identical copies of the parent cell. In animal cells, all cells except sex cells undergo mitosis. Just remember: Like begets like. Hair cells beget other hair cells, skin cells beget other skin cells, and so on.

DIFFERENT FORMS OF ASEXUAL REPRODUCTION

Binary Fission

Organisms have developed a number of ways to carry out asexual reproduction. Bacteria, for example, reproduce asexually by **binary fission**. Binary fission is just like mitosis. Bacteria replicate their chromosomes and divide into two identical daughter cells of equal size. This method of asexual reproduction is also common in *Paramecium* and *Amoeba*.

Budding

Other organisms, such as yeast and hydra, reproduce asexually by **budding**. Budding is a process in which a little bud sprouts from the parent and eventually separates into a fully formed offspring. In this case, the cell divides unequally.

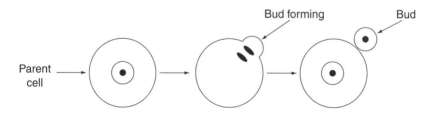

Sporulation

Another form of asexual reproduction is **sporulation**. Fungi, for example, produce spores (airborne cells) that are released from the parent organism.

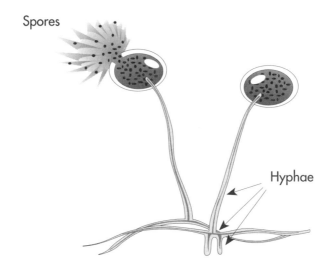

Spores

Hyphae

Once these tiny haploid cells land on fertile ground, they reproduce mitotically, generating other fungi. *Rhizopus*, a common bread mold, reproduces asexually by budding. As you know if you've ever opened a week-old bag of moldy bread, sporulation is a rather effective and swift way of reproducing.

Vegetative Propagation

Although most plants reproduce by fertilization, they can also reproduce asexually. This process is known as **vegetative propagation**. In vegetative propagation, some part of the parent plant—such as the root, stem, or leaf—produces another plant. Some examples of vegetative propagators include **tubers**, **runners**, **bulbs**, and **grafting**.

For example, if you wanted to make potato plants without fertilizing them, all you'd have to do is cut out the "eyes" of a potato and plant them. Each of the eyes would then develop into a complete potato plant. The eyes are actually rudimentary tubers.

Here's a list of the different types of vegetative propagation:

TYPES OF VEGETATIVE PROPAGATION		
Types	**Description**	**Examples**
Bulbs	Short stems underground	Onions
Runners	Horizontal stems above the ground	Strawberries
Tubers	Underground stems	Potatoes
Grafting	Cut a stem and attach it to a closely related plant	Seedless oranges

Regeneration

A last form of asexual reproduction is **regeneration**, which occurs when an organism grows back a missing body part. For example, starfish regenerate. If you were to cut up a starfish and leave the severed pieces in an aquarium, each of the five limbs would regenerate an entire starfish! Such extreme examples of regeneration are relatively rare in nature.

Now that we've looked at asexual reproduction, let's move on to sexual reproduction. We'll start by discussing meiosis.

MEIOSIS

Every organism has a specific number of chromosomes. For example, fruit flies have eight chromosomes, and humans have forty-six chromosomes. However, if you take a closer look at a human cell, you'll realize that there are actually only twenty-three *different* chromosomes. Where do the other twenty-three come from?

In normal eukaryotic cells, chromosomes exist in pairs called **homologues**. When a cell has a full complement of homologues or *homologous chromosomes*, as they're often called, it is said to be **diploid**. A normal, diploid human cell contains forty-six chromosomes altogether, two of each kind. We can therefore say that the **diploid number** for human beings is forty-six. Occasionally, cells possess only one set of chromosomes. For a human being, that would mean a total of twenty-three chromosomes. Such a cell is called a **haploid cell**.

The terms *diploid* and *haploid* are important when we talk about sexual reproduction. Although almost all the cells in the human body are diploid, there are special cells that are haploid. These haploid cells are called **sex cells**, or **gametes**. Why do we have haploid cells?

When a man and a woman decide to have a baby, both contribute chromosomes. The problem is that each of them has a full set. If they both threw in their full complement, the baby would have forty-six pairs of chromosomes instead of twenty-three. Within a few generations, kids would be born with 1,507,328 pairs of chromosomes. Imagine how complicated that would get! To preserve the diploid number of chromosomes in an organism, each parent must contribute only half of his or her chromosomes. Meiosis is the process by which sexually reproducing organisms accomplish this.

OVERVIEW OF MEIOSIS

Because sexually reproducing organisms need only haploid cells for reproduction, meiosis is limited to sex cells in special sex organs called

gonads. In males, the gonads are the **testes**; in females, they are the **ovaries**.

Meiosis actually involves two rounds of cell division: the **first meiotic division** and **second meiotic division**. As in mitosis, the chromosomes duplicate and double-stranded chromosomes are formed. At this point, we're already in the first phase of meiosis.

First Meiotic Division

Meiosis 1 consists of four stages: **prophase 1, metaphase 1, anaphase 1,** and **telophase 1**.

Prophase 1

Prophase 1 is a little more complicated than mitotic prophase. As in mitosis, the nuclear membrane disappears, the chromosomes become visible, and the centrioles move to opposite poles of the nucleus. That's where the similarity ends.

The major difference involves the movement of the chromosomes. In prophase 1, the chromosomes line up side by side with their counterparts. This event is known as **synapsis**.

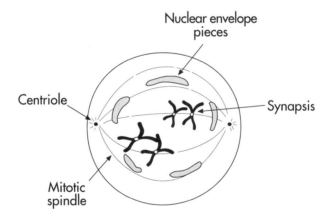

Synapsis involves two sets of chromosomes coming together to form a **tetrad**. A tetrad consists of four chromatids. Synapsis is followed by **crossing-over**, the exchange of segments of homologous chromosomes.

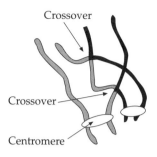

Crossover

Crossover

Centromere

What's unique in prophase 1 is that "pieces" of chromosomes are swapped between the homologous partners. This is one of the ways organisms produce genetic variation.

Metaphase 1

As in mitosis, the chromosome pairs—now called **tetrads**—line up at the metaphase plate.

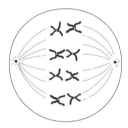

These pairs, or tetrads, are our famous homologous pairs.

Anaphase 1

During anaphase 1, each chromosome within a tetrad separates and moves to a pole of the cell. Notice that the chromosomes do not separate at the centromere. They separate with their centromeres intact.

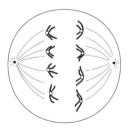

The chromosomes now go on to their respective poles.

Telophase 1

During telophase 1, a nuclear membrane forms around each set of chromosomes.

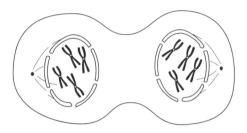

Finally, the cells undergo cytokinesis, leaving us with two daughter cells.

Second Meiotic Division

The second meiotic division is virtually identical to mitosis. After a brief period, the cell undergoes a second round of cell division. During prophase 2, the chromosomes once again condense. In metaphase 2, the chromosomes move toward the metaphase plate. During anaphase 2, the chromatids of each chromosome split at the centromere and move to opposite ends of the cell. During telophase 2, a new nuclear membrane envelope forms around each set of chromosomes and four new daughter cells are produced.

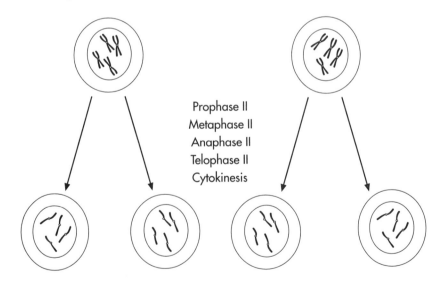

Prophase II
Metaphase II
Anaphase II
Telophase II
Cytokinesis

These resulting cells, each of which contains only half the total number of chromosomes, are known as **gametes**.

Gametogenesis

Because meiosis results in the formation of gametes, it is also known as **gametogenesis**. When meiosis takes place in the male, it results in the production of sperm cells. This is called **spermatogenesis**. During spermatogenesis, four sperm cells are produced for each root or parent cell.

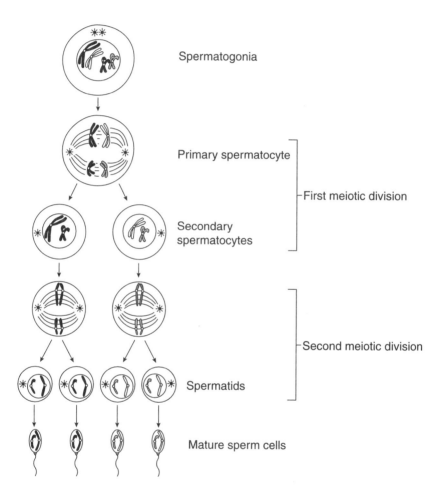

In a female, an egg cell or ovum is produced as the result of meiosis. This process is called **oogenesis**. Oogenesis differs slightly from spermatogenesis. During oogenesis, only one ovum is produced.

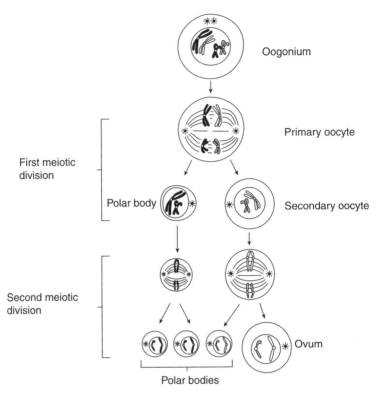

Oogonium

Primary oocyte

First meiotic division

Polar body

Secondary oocyte

Second meiotic division

Ovum

Polar bodies

The other three cells, called **polar bodies**, eventually degenerate. Why do we get only one ovum? Because the female wants to conserve as much cytoplasm as possible for the surviving gamete, the ovum. This means the ovum contains lots of stored nutrients.

COMPARISON OF MITOSIS AND MEIOSIS

Here's a summary of the major differences between mitosis and meiosis:

Mitosis:	Meiosis:
• Occurs in somatic (body) cells	• Occurs in germ (sex) cells
• Produces identical cells	• Produces gametes
• Diploid cell → diploid cells	• Diploid cell → haploid cells

HUMAN REPRODUCTIVE SYSTEM

Reproduction in humans, as in most higher organisms, involves the formation of new organisms from two gametes, a sperm, and an ovum. As we discuss the reproductive process, we'll also mention the hormones involved in the male and female reproductive systems.

FEMALE REPRODUCTIVE SYSTEM

Let's begin with the female reproductive system. In women, the ovaries are responsible for the production of **ova**, the female gametes. Yet, ovaries are also endocrine glands: They release hormones that play crucial roles in reproduction. These, then, are the ovaries' two main roles:

1. They manufacture **ova**.

2. They secrete **estrogen** and **progesterone**, sex hormones found principally in females.

Estrogen and progesterone are key components of the menstrual cycle. Here's a picture of the female reproductive system:

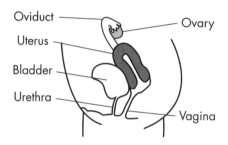

Menstrual Cycle

Phase 1: The Follicle Stage

In phase 1, the anterior pituitary secretes two hormones, **follicle-stimulating hormone (FSH)** and **luteinizing hormone (LH)**. FSH stimulates several follicles in the ovaries to grow. Eventually one of these follicles gains the lead and stops the growth of the others.

Because the follicles are undergoing growth in this phase, the phase itself is known as the **follicle phase**. Keep in mind that during all this time, the follicle is churning out **estrogen**. Estrogen eventually causes the pituitary to release a very large amount of LH. This dumping of LH is known as a **luteal surge**. LH triggers **ovulation**—the release of the follicle from the ovaries.

Here's a quick summary of the hormones associated with the follicle stage:

1. FSH

2. Estrogen (which originates in the follicle)

3. LH (which originates in the pituitary gland)

The luteal surge makes the follicle burst and release the ovum. The ovum then begins its journey into the **fallopian tube**, which is also known as the **oviduct**. This crucial event in the female menstrual cycle is known as **ovulation**. Once the ovum has been released, we've reached the end of the follicle stage. This entire stage lasts about 12 days.

Phase 2: The Corpus Luteum Stage

By the end of the follicle stage, the ovum has moved into the fallopian tube, and the follicle has been ruptured and left behind in the ovary. The ruptured follicle (now a fluid-filled sac) continues to function in the menstrual cycle. At this stage, it condenses into a little yellow blob, which we call the **corpus luteum**, which is Latin for "yellow body."

The corpus luteum continues to secrete estrogen. In addition, it now starts producing the other main hormone involved in female reproduction, **progesterone**. Progesterone is responsible for readying the body for pregnancy. It does this by preparing the uterine lining for implantation. Without progesterone, a fertilized ovum cannot latch onto the uterus and develop into an embryo. We can therefore think of progesterone as the pregnancy hormone.

After about 13–15 days, if fertilization and implantation have not occurred, the corpus luteum shuts down. Once the corpus luteum turns off, the uterus can no longer maintain its thickened walls and reabsorbs most of the tissue that progesterone encouraged it to grow. However, because there is too much to reabsorb, a certain amount is shed. This "sloughing off," or bleeding, is known as **menstruation**.

With the end of menstruation, the cycle starts all over again. Here's a graph of the concentration of the various female reproductive hormones during the menstrual cycle of humans:

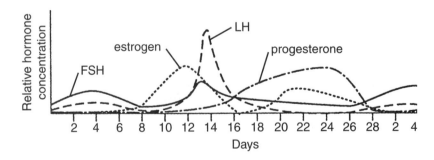

MALE REPRODUCTIVE SYSTEM

In human beings, sperm cells are produced in paired gonads called **testes**. The testes are contained within the **scrotum**, a skin-covered sac. The main sex hormone in males is **testosterone**. Testosterone is responsible for the development of the sex organs and secondary sex characteristics. In addition to the deepening of the voice, these characteristics include body hair, muscle growth, and facial hair, all of which indicate the onset of **puberty**.

Once sperm cells are produced, they are transported through conducting tubes and mix with secretions from accessory glands. The sperm and added fluids leave the body via the urethra. The structure that delivers the sperm into the female reproductive tract is the penis.

Here's a side view of the male reproductive system:

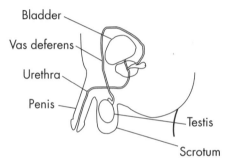

EMBRYONIC DEVELOPMENT

How does a tiny, single-celled egg eventually become a complex, multicellular organism? By growing, of course. As you already know, an entire organism arises from a single cell. The study of how this minuscule cell develops into the great variety of specialized tissues found within an organism is called **developmental biology**.

To understand some of the basic early steps of development, let's go right back to the beginning, when the female and male gametes, or ovum and sperm cell, first meet. This is called **fertilization** and results in a diploid cell called a **zygote**.

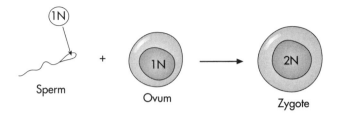

Fertilization can occur externally (outside the female organism) or internally (inside the female organism). External fertilization usually occurs among aquatic animals such as fish and amphibians. In more complex terrestrial organisms, fertilization occurs internally.

Here's one more thing you should remember: The sex of the organism is usually determined by the *sperm cell* involved in fertilization. Sperm cells carry either an X or a Y sex chromosome. As we'll see in the next chapter, it is the presence of this chromosome that determines the sex of the offspring. If the offspring receives an X chromosome from its father, it will be a female. If it receives a Y, it will be a male. The female gametes do not play a role in sex determination. As you'll see later, this is because females have two X chromosomes.

CLEAVAGE

Fertilization triggers the zygote to undergo a series of rapid cell divisions called **cleavage**. What's interesting at this stage is that the cells keep dividing until they form a solid, undifferentiated ball called a **morula**.

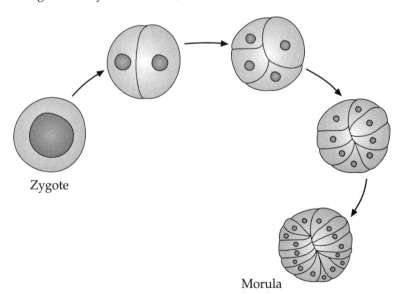

BLASTULA

In the next stage, the morula becomes a **blastula**. As the cells continue to divide they press against each other and produce a hollow ball:

Blastula (cross-section)

GASTRULA

As development continues, the blastula becomes a gastrula. During **gastrulation**, the zygote begins to change its shape. Cells now migrate into the blastocoele and form three layers of cells called **germ layers**. These three layers give rise to all the different tissues in the body. The three germ layers are the **ectoderm**, **mesoderm**, and **endoderm**.

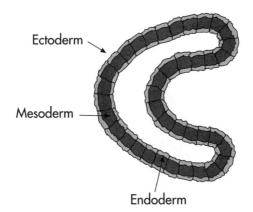

Gastrula (cross-section)

- The outer layer becomes the ectoderm.
- The middle layer becomes the mesoderm.
- The inner layer becomes the endoderm.

Here's a list of the organs that develop from each germ layer:

Cell layer	Tissues
Ectoderm	Skin, eyes, and nervous system
Endoderm	Lining of the digestive tract and respiratory tract, pancreas, gall bladder, and liver
Mesoderm	Bones; muscles; gonads; excretory, circulatory, and reproductive systems

DIFFERENTIATION

Over time, the cells in the various germ layers *specialize* and develop into the organs and tissues listed above. To summarize, the order of the stages within embryonic development run like this:

zygote → cleavage → blastula → gastrula → differentiation

WHAT ABOUT CHICK EMBRYOS?

In addition to the primary germ layers, some animals have extraembryonic membranes. Chickens, for example, possess these membranes. There are basically four extraembryonic membranes: the **yolk sac, amnion, chorion,** and **allantois.**

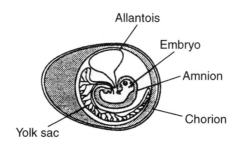

These extraembryonic membranes are common in terrestrial animals. Here's a list of the membranes and their functions:

Functions of Extraembryonic Membranes	
Extraembryonic membrane	Function
Yolk sac	Provides food for the embryo
Amnion	Forms a fluid-filled sac that protects the embryo
Allantois	Membrane involved in gas exchange
Chorion	Outermost membrane that surrounds all the other extraembryonic membranes

PLACENTAL AND NONPLACENTAL MAMMALS

One last thing you should remember: Some mammals have a **placenta**. A placenta is the structure that joins the embryo to the wall of the mother's uterus. This is how the embryos of mammals like ourselves get their nutrients and eliminate wastes.

Marsupial mammals, on the other hand, don't have a placenta. The developing embryo receives very little nourishment from the mother in the uterus. Marsupials nourish their young with milk provided through nipples inside a pouch in the abdominal region. Marsupial fetuses pop out about 8 days after fertilization and continue their maturation in their mother's pouch. Examples of marsupials are kangaroos, koalas, and opossums.

CHAPTER 7 QUIZ

1.   The diagrams below represent stages of a cellular process.

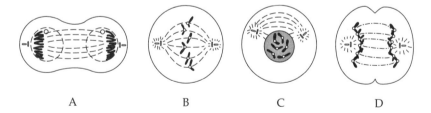

A	B	C	D

Which is the correct sequence of these stages?

(1) A → B → C → D

(2) B → D → C → A

(3) C → B → D → A

(4) D → B → A → C

2. Which statement best describes the division of the cytoplasm and the nucleus in budding?

   (1) Both the cytoplasm and the nucleus divide equally.

   (2) The cytoplasm divides unequally, but the nucleus divides equally.

   (3) The cytoplasm divides equally, but the nucleus divides unequally.

   (4) Both the cytoplasm and the nucleus divide unequally.

3. *Rhizopus*, a bread mold, usually reproduces asexually by

   (1) budding

   (2) sporulation

   (3) regeneration

   (4) fission

4. Which statement is true regarding plants produced by vegetative propagation?

   (1) They normally exhibit only dominant characteristics.

   (2) They normally have the monoploid number of chromosomes.

   (3) They normally obtain most of their nourishment from the seed.

   (4) They are normally genetically identical to the parent.

5. The chromatids of a double-stranded chromosome are held together at a region known as the

   (1) polar body

   (2) centromere

   (3) centriole

   (4) Golgi body

6. The yolk of a developing bird embryo functions as a

   (1) moist respiratory membrane

   (2) storage site for waste

   (3) food source

   (4) fluid environment

7. In humans, the fertilization of two eggs at the same time usually results in

    (1) chromosomal abnormalities

    (2) gene mutations

    (3) identical twins

    (4) fraternal twins

8. Which situation is a result of crossing-over during meiosis?

    (1) Genes are duplicated exactly, ensuring that offspring will be identical to the parents.

    (2) Chromatids thicken and align themselves, helping to ensure genetic continuity.

    (3) Genes are rearranged, increasing the variability of offspring.

    (4) Chromatids fail to sort independently, creating abnormal chromosome numbers.

9. The diagrams below represent the gametes and zygotes associated with two separate fertilizations in a particular species:

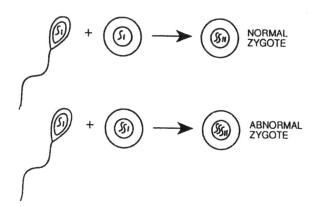

    The abnormal zygote is most likely the result of

    (1) polyploidy

    (2) nondisjunction

    (3) chromosome breakage

    (4) gene linkage

10. Which statement is true about the process of fertilization in both tracheophytes and mammals?

    (1) It normally results in the production of monoploid offspring.

    (2) It occurs externally in a watery environment.

    (3) It is followed by yolk production.

    (4) It occurs within female reproductive organs.

11. In sexually reproducing species, doubling of the chromosome number from generation to generation is prevented by events that take place during the process of

    (1) gametogenesis

    (2) cleavage

    (3) nondisjunction

    (4) fertilization

12. In a rabbit, the embryo normally develops within the

    (1) placenta

    (2) uterus

    (3) yolk sac

    (4) umbilical cord

13. The production of large number of eggs is necessary to ensure the survival of most

    (1) mammals

    (2) molds

    (3) fish

    (4) yeasts

8

Genetics

Genetics is the study of heredity. It explains how certain characteristics are passed on from parents to children. The basic principles of heredity were first discovered by Gregor Mendel, a nineteenth-century monk. Since then, the field of genetics has expanded greatly. Today, genetic engineering is science fact, not science fiction. Before we talk about the cutting edge of genetics, let's discuss Mendel's discoveries.

To discuss Mendel's work, you'll need some genetics vocabulary. The terms listed below are essential for the study of genetics, so make sure you're comfortable with them.

- **Genes**: Each trait—or expressed characteristic—is produced by a pair of hereditary factors known as genes. Within a chromosome, there are many genes, each controlling the inheritance of a particular trait. A gene is a segment of a chromosome that produces a particular trait. For example, in pea plants, there's a gene on the chromosome that codes for seed coat. The position of a gene on a chromosomes is called a *locus*.

- **Alleles**: A gene usually consists of a *pair* of hereditary factors. These factors are called **alleles**. Each organism carries two alleles for a particular trait. In other words, alleles make up a gene, which in turn produces a particular trait. Alleles are alternate forms of the same trait. For example, if we're talking about the height of a pea plant, there's an allele for tall and an allele for short. Both alleles are alternate forms of the gene for height.

- **Dominant and recessive alleles**: An allele can be **dominant** or **recessive**. In simple cases, an organism can express contrasting traits. For example, a plant can be tall or short. The convention is to assign a capital and a lowercase of the same letter for the two alleles. The dominant allele receives the capital letter, and the recessive allele receives the lowercase. For instance, we might give the dominant allele for height in pea plants a *T* for tall, and the recessive allele a *t* for short.

- **Phenotype** and **genotype**: When discussing the physical appearance of an organism, we refer to its **phenotype**. The phenotype tells us what the organism looks like. When talking about the genetic makeup of an organism, we refer to its **genotype**. The genotype tells us which alleles the organism possesses.

- **Homozygous** and **heterozygous**: When an organism has two identical alleles for a given trait, the organism is said to be **homozygous**. For instance, TT and tt would both represent the genotype of homozygous organisms, one homozygous dominant and the other homozygous recessive. If an organism has two different alleles for a given trait, the organism is **heterozygous**.

- **Parent** and **filial generations**: The first generation is always called the **parent**, or P1, generation. The offspring of the P1 generation are called the **filial**, or F1, generation.

MENDELIAN GENETICS

One of Mendel's primary pursuits was the study of the effects of cross-breeding on different strains of pea plants. Mendel worked exclusively with true-breeder pea plants. This means that the plants he used were genetically pure and consistently produced the same traits. Tall plants always produced tall plants, whereas short plants always produced short plants. Through his work he came up with three principles: the **law of dominance**, the **law of segregation**, and the **law of independent assortment**.

LAW OF DOMINANCE

Mendel crossed two true-breeding plants with contrasting traits: tall pea plants and short pea plants. This type of cross is called a *monohybrid cross*, which means that we're looking at only one trait. In this case, the trait is height.

To his surprise, when Mendel mated these plants, the characteristics didn't blend to produce plants of average height. Instead, all the offspring were tall.

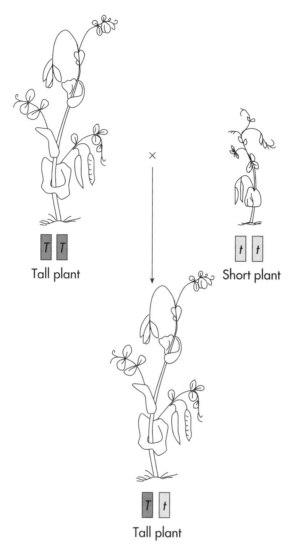

Tall plant   Short plant

Tall plant

He recognized that one trait must be masking the effect of the other trait. Mendel called this the *law of dominance*. The dominant tall allele, T, somehow masked the presence of the recessive short allele, t. Consequently a plant needed only one tall allele to make it tall.

PUNNETT SQUARES

A simple way to represent a cross is to set up a Punnett square. A Punnett square looks a bit like a small checkerboard. Punnett squares are used to predict the results of a cross. Let's construct a Punnett square to predict the results of a cross between a pure tall and pure short pea plant.

Because one parent was a pure tall pea plant, we'll give two dominant alleles (TT). The other parent was a pure short plant, so we'll give it two recessive alleles (tt). Let's put the alleles for one of the parents across the top of the box, and the alleles for the other parent along the side of the box:

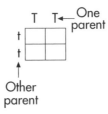

Now we can fill in the checkerboard by matching the letters. Here are the results of the F1 generation:

All of the offspring received one allele from each parent, one T and one t. They're all Tt! We would therefore say that these offspring are heterozygous: They all have one copy of each allele.

F2: THE NEXT GENERATION

Getting back to Brother Mendel . . . Mendel's next step was to take the offspring of the first cross and self-pollinate them. Let's use a Punnett square to spell out the results, using the plants from our original cross as our parents this time:

F2 Generation

One of the offspring was a short pea plant! The short-stemmed trait reappeared in the F2 generation. How did that happen? Once again, the alleles separated and recombined to produce a new combination. The cross resulted in one pair of recessive alleles, tt.

Although all of the F1 plants appeared to be tall, the alleles separated and recombined during the cross. This is an example of the **law of segregation**.

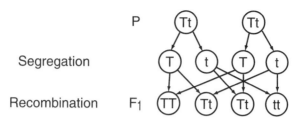

One important thing to keep in mind is that recombination is entirely random.

What are the genotype and phenotype for this cross? Remember, *genotype* refers to the genetic makeup of an organism, whereas *phenotype* refers to the physical characteristics. We have four offspring with two different phenotypes: Three of the offspring are tall, whereas one of them is short. On the other hand, we have three genotypes one TT, two Tt, and one tt.

We can summarize the results in a ratio form:

Phenotype is 3:1   Three tall: one short
Genotype is 1:2:1   One TT: two Tt: one tt

LAW OF INDEPENDENT ASSORTMENT

So far, we have looked at two alleles for one characteristic, height in pea plants. But what happens when we study two traits at the same time? The two traits still segregate randomly. This is known as *independent assortment*. For example, sticking with our pea plants, let's take a look at height and color at the same time.

As we've already seen, a pea plant can be either tall or short. When it comes to color, let's say that we've got green and yellow plants. Because green is dominant, we'll use G for the allele for green and g for the allele for yellow. If we combine these with our alleles for height, we wind up with four different possible combinations:

• TG, Tg, tG, and tg

Each trait is inherited independently of the other. For example, a plant that is tall can be either green or yellow. Similarly, a plant that is green can be either tall or short. If we were to figure out all the possible outcomes, our results would look something like this:

	TG	Tg	tG	tg
TG	TG TG	Tg TG	tG TG	tg TG
Tg	TG Tg	Tg Tg	tG Tg	tg Tg
tG	TG tG	Tg tG	tG tG	tg tG
tg	TG tg	Tg tg	tG tg	tg tg

For the sixteen offspring shown above there are:

- Nine tall and green
- Three tall and green
- Three short and yellow
- One short and yellow

If we combine these results, they yield a ratio of 9:3:3:1. Here's a summary of Mendel's three laws:

SUMMARY OF MENDEL'S LAW	
Laws	**Definition**
Law of Dominance	One trait masks the effects of another trait.
Law of Segregation	Alleles can segregate and recombine.
Law of Independent Assortment	Traits can segregate and recombine independently of other traits

GENE-CHROMOSOME THEORY

It wasn't until the mid-1900s that scientists became aware that Mendel's hereditary factors—now called *genes*—were carried on chromosomes. This theory connected Mendel's results to the movement of chromosomes during reproduction. It explained why genes occur in pairs, why each member of a gene pair comes from one parent, and why genes segregate during meiosis. This theory of inheritance is known as the **gene-chromosome theory**.

BEYOND MENDELIAN GENETICS

Not all patterns of inheritance obey the principles of Mendelian genetics. In fact, many traits occur due to a combined expression of alleles. Here are a couple of examples of non-Mendelian forms of inheritance:

- **Intermediate inheritance:** In some cases, the traits blend. For example, a white snapdragon plant (dominant) and a red snapdragon plant (recessive) produce a pink snapdragon plant.

- **Codominance**: Sometimes you'll see an equal expression of both alleles. One example is the roan coat in cattle. If one parent has a red coat, RR, and the other parent has a white coat, WW, the offspring will have a roan coat, RW (a mottled red and white coat). Both alleles are expressed.

- **Multiple alleles**: Sometimes the expression of a trait involves more than two alleles. For example, two genes are involved in the expression of AB blood group. The combination of genes determine the different blood types (A, B, AB, and O). In this case, both alleles are equally expressed.

SEX DETERMINATION

Humans have twenty-three pairs of chromosomes. Twenty-two of the pairs of chromosomes are called **autosomes** and code for many different traits. The other pair contains the **sex chromosomes**. As mentioned in chapter 7, this pair determines the sex of the individual. A female has two X chromosomes. A male has one X and one Y chromosome—the X from his mother and the Y from his father.

SEX LINKAGE

Some traits are carried on sex chromosomes. **Color blindness** and **hemophilia**, for example, are two disorders carried on the X chromosome. These are called **sex-linked traits**.

Because males have one X and one Y chromosome, what happens if a male has a defective X chromosome? Unfortunately, he'll express the sex-linked trait. Why? Because his one and only X chromosome is defective. However, if a female has only one defective X chromosome, she won't express the sex-linked trait. For her to express the trait, she has to inherit two defective X chromosomes. A female with one defective X is called a **carrier**. Although she appears normal, she can still pass the trait on to her children. If, however, she has two bad X chromosomes, she's out of luck. She will express the trait.

Punnett squares can be used to figure out the results of crosses involving sex-linked traits. This time, however, we will work with the sex chromosomes X and Y. Here's an example: A male who is normal for color vision marries a woman who is a carrier for color blindness. How many of the children will be color-blind? Let's check the possibilities with a Punnett square. We'll indicate the presence of the gene for color blindness by placing a bar above any X carrying the defective allele. Take a look:

$$
\begin{array}{c}
\quad\quad\quad\quad \text{X} \quad \bar{\text{X}} \;\leftarrow \text{Mother} \\
\text{Father} \rightarrow
\begin{array}{c|c|c|}
 & \text{X} & \bar{\text{X}} \\
\hline
\text{X} & \text{XX} & \text{X}\bar{\text{X}} \\
\hline
\text{Y} & \text{XY} & \bar{\text{X}}\text{Y} \\
\hline
\end{array}
\end{array}
$$

$\bar{\text{X}}$ = diseased X

According to our square, the couple could have one son who is color blind, a normal son, a daughter who is a carrier, or a normal daughter. Notice that in our cross, the affected child is a son. With the parents above, the only child who could possibly be color-blind is the son.

CHAPTER 8 QUIZ

1. Traits that are controlled by genes found on an X chromosome are said to be

    (1) dominant

    (2) recessive

    (3) codominant

    (4) sex-linked

2. In raccoons, a dark mask is dominant over a bleached face mask. Several crosses were made between raccoons that were heterozygous for dark face mask and raccoons that were homozygous for bleached face mask. What percentage of the offspring would be expected to have a dark face mask?

    (1) 0%

    (2) 50%

    (3) 75%

    (4) 100%

3. Mendel developed his basic principles of heredity by

    (1) microscopic study of chromosomes and genes
    (2) breeding experiments with *Drosophila*
    (3) mathematical analysis of the offspring of pea plants
    (4) ultracentrifugation studies of cell organelles

4. In screech owls, red feathers are dominant over gray feathers. If two heterozygous red-feathered owls are mated, what percentage of their offspring would be expected to have red feathers?

    (1) 25%
    (2) 50%
    (3) 75%
    (4) 100%

5. In humans, normal color vision (N) is dominant over color blindness (n). A man and woman with normal color vision produced two color blind sons and two daughters with normal color vision. The parental genotypes must be

    (1) $X^N Y$ and $X^N X^N$
    (2) $X^n Y$ and $X^N X^N$
    (3) $X^N Y$ and $X^N X^n$
    (4) $X^n Y$ and $X^n X^n$

Modern Genetics

DNA: THE BLUEPRINT OF LIFE

All living things exhibit an astonishing degree of organization. For the simplest single-celled organism and for the largest mammal, millions of reactions and events must be precisely coordinated for life to exist. This coordination is directed from the nucleus of the cell by **deoxyribonucleic acid (DNA)**. DNA is the hereditary blueprint of the cell.

The DNA of a cell is contained in structures called *chromosomes*. The chromosomes are basically enormous coils of DNA and proteins. Found in the nucleus, chromosomes direct and control all the activities necessary for life, including passing themselves and their information on to future generations.

STRUCTURE OF DNA

The DNA molecule consists of two strands that wrap around each other to form a long, twisted ladder called a **double helix.** The structure of DNA was first discovered in 1956 by two scientists named Watson and Crick.

DNA is made up of repeated subunits of **nucleotides**. Each nucleotide has a **sugar**, a **phosphate**, and a **nitrogenous base**. Take a look at the nucleotide below:

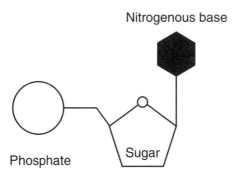

Nitrogenous base

Phosphate

Sugar

The name of the five-carbon sugar in DNA is **deoxyribose**, hence the name *deoxyribo*nucleic acid. Notice that the sugar is linked to two things: a phosphate and a base. A nucleotide can have four different bases:

- Adenine (A)
- Guanine (G)
- Cytosine (C)
- Thymine (T)

Any of these four bases can attach to the sugar. As we'll soon see, this is extremely important when it comes to the "sense" of the genetic code in DNA. Here's a picture of the four different kinds of nucleotides in DNA:

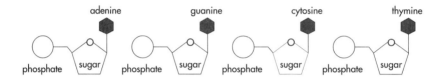

A Single Strand

The nucleotides link up in long chain to form a single strand of DNA. Here's a small section of a DNA strand:

The Double Strand

Now let's look at the way in which two DNA strands get together. You can think of DNA as a ladder. The sides of the ladder consist of alternating sugar and phosphate groups, and the rungs of the ladder consist of pairs of nitrogenous bases.

You'll notice from the diagram above that the nitrogenous bases pair up in a particular way. Adenine in one strand always binds to thymine in the other strand. Similarly, guanine always binds to cytosine. This matching of the bases is known as **base pairing**. Because of this predictable matching of bases, the two strands are said to be **complementary**. This means if you know the sequence of the bases in one strand, you'll know the sequence of the bases in the other strand. For example, if the base sequence in one strand is A-T-C, the base sequence in the complementary strand will be T-A-G.

One more thing to keep in mind: These DNA strands are joined together by weak hydrogen bonds.

DNA REPLICATION

Chromosomes are capable of replicating (duplicating) themselves. Because the DNA molecule is twisted over on itself, the first step of DNA replication is to unwind the double helix and break the hydrogen bonds between the two strands. Now each strand can serve as a **template**, a blueprint, for the synthesis of the other strand.

strand 1:
5' _____ 3'

strand 2:
3' _____ 5'

Free-floating DNA nucleotides in the cytoplasm are added one after the other to each strand. These bases match the appropriate bases contained in the template strand. For example, adenine nucleotides attach to thymine nucleotides, and guanine nucleotides attach to cytosine nucleotides. Because the new strands always form in this way under normal conditions, they are said to be **complementary** to the template strands.

These new stretches of nucleotides are eventually linked together to produce a continuous strand. In the last step of DNA replication, hydrogen bonds form between the new base pairs, leaving two identical copies of the original DNA molecule.

Now that we've seen how DNA is replicated, let's take a look at how the genetic code is expressed.

PROTEINS AND THE GENETIC CODE

DNA is crucial to the day-to-day operations of the cell. Without it, the cell would not be able to direct the manufacture of the proteins that regulate all the activities of the cell. However, DNA does not directly manufacture proteins. This job falls to intermediate molecules known as **ribonucleic acids (RNA)**.

RNA molecules carry out the instructions contained in the DNA, manufacturing the proteins that determine the course of life. The flow of genetic information is therefore:

$$DNA \rightarrow RNA \rightarrow proteins$$

Genetic information is passed from the DNA to the RNA, which then handles the production of polypeptides. (Don't forget that *polypeptide* is simply a fancy name for proteins. You'll see why in just a bit.) Before we discuss the way in which RNA makes proteins, let's talk about its structure. RNA differs from DNA in three principal ways:

1. RNA is single-stranded, not double-stranded.

2. The five-carbon sugar in RNA is ribose not deoxyribose.

3. The RNA nitrogenous bases are adenine, guanine, cytosine, and a new base called *uracil*. Uracil replaces thymine.

Here's a table to help you memorize the differences between DNA and RNA:

Differences between DNA and RNA		
	DNA	**RNA**
Sugar	deoxyribose	ribose
Bases:	adenine	adenine
	guanine	guanine
	cytosine	cytosine
	thymine	uracil

TYPES OF RNA

There are three types of RNA: **messenger RNA (mRNA), ribosomal RNA (rRNA),** and **transfer RNA (tRNA).** All three types of RNA are key players in the synthesis of proteins. mRNA carries the information from the DNA. rRNA makes up the ribosomes, the primary sites of protein synthesis. tRNA shuttles amino acids around the cell, bringing them into place on the ribosome. Now that we know about the different types of RNA, let's see how they direct the synthesis of proteins.

PROTEIN SYNTHESIS

Protein synthesis involves the production of polypeptides. The initial steps in protein synthesis are a lot like the initial steps in DNA replication. As in DNA replication, the first step is to unwind and unzip the DNA strands.

Because RNA is single-stranded, we only have to copy one of the DNA strands. This time, RNA nucleotides line up alongside a DNA strand to form an mRNA strand.

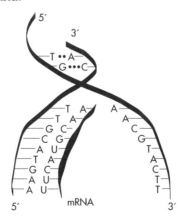

Free-floating RNA nucleotides are brought to the DNA strand. As we said earlier, guanine and cytosine pair up. However, this time adenine pairs up with uracil instead of thymine. Once a string of RNA nucleotides is attached, we've got a newly synthesized RNA strand. The new RNA has transcribed or "copied" the sequence of nucleotide bases directly from the exposed DNA strand. This process occurs in the nucleus.

Codons

Now the mRNA is ready to leave the nucleus and search for a ribosome. The mRNA molecule carries the message from DNA in the form of **codons**, a group of three bases or "letters" that corresponds to one of twenty amino acids. Codons are very specific. For example, the sequence A-U-G found on an mRNA molecule corresponds to the amino acid methionine.

The mRNA finds the ribosome, attaches itself and waits for the appropriate amino acid to pass by. This is where tRNA comes in. One end of the tRNA binds to an amino acid. The other end, called an **anticodon**, has three nitrogenous bases that pair up with the bases contained in the codon.

tRNA molecules are the "go-betweens" in protein synthesis. Each tRNA molecule picks up a free-floating amino acid in the cell's cytoplasm and "shuttles" it to the ribosome. For example, the tRNA with the anticodon U-A-C is methionine's personal shuttle: It carries no other amino acids. Every time mRNA hangs an A-U-G out there, it is certain to pick up methionine.

But Where's the Protein?

Remember that the mRNA contains many hundreds, even thousands, of codons or "triplets" of nucleotide bases. As each amino acid is brought to the mRNA, it is linked up by the formation of a peptide bond. When many amino acids link up, that's a **polypeptide**.

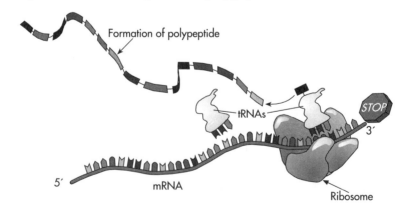

Formation of polypeptide, tRNAs, mRNA labeled 5' and 3', Ribosome, STOP

THE ONE GENE–ONE POLYPEPTIDE HYPOTHESIS

We've already talked about genes. Originally, we said that a gene is a region of the chromosome that codes for a particular trait. Now that we've discussed protein synthesis and the role of proteins in the cell, we can slightly revise our definition of a gene. We just saw that proteins direct the processes of the cell. We can therefore say that

- a gene is a region of DNA that codes for a single polypeptide

This is known as the one gene-one polypeptide hypothesis and comes a little nearer a "true" definition of a gene. As we saw earlier, to define genes simply in terms of traits leads to some confusion. Many traits are the consequence of the interaction of several genes. However, when we define a gene as a region of the genetic code that codes for a specific polypeptide, it's much easier for us to pinpoint where one gene begins and where the other ends.

Because polypeptides express themselves as traits, we can describe the expression of genes in this way:

$$DNA \rightarrow gene \rightarrow polypeptide \rightarrow trait$$

MUTATIONS

A cell uses some twenty amino acids to construct its proteins. However, these amino acids are not always attached in the right order. Errors occasionally occur during DNA replication. For example, suppose a short segment of a template DNA strand has the base sequence T-A-C. The complementary DNA segment should be A-T-G. If, for some reason, another thymine is inserted in the last position instead of guanine, the new strand of DNA would read A-T-T and would lead, in turn, to the insertion of the wrong amino acid in a given protein. One error of this sort is enough to inactivate the entire protein!

A change in one or more of the nucleotide bases is called a **mutation**. Mutations can occur when DNA is exposed to radiation (x-rays and UV light) or chemical agents.

There are many types of gene mutations. If an error results from a change in a single base, it can produce a **base substitution** (the exchange of one base for another), an **addition** (the addition of a base), or **deletion** (the removal of a base). For example, albinism—the lack of skin pigmentation—is a condition resulting from a change in a single gene.

CHROMOSOME MUTATIONS

Mutations can also occur on a grander scale in chromosomes. Sometimes a set of chromosomes has an extra or missing member. This can occur because of **nondisjunction**, the failure of the chromosomes to separate properly during meiosis. Such an error produces the wrong number of chromosomes in a cell, resulting in severe genetic defects. For example, Down syndrome, a form of mental retardation with characteristic physical deformities, results from the presence of an extra twenty-first chromosome. An individual afflicted with Down syndrome has *three*, rather than two, copies of this single chromosome.

Chromosomal abnormalities also occur when a segment of a chromosome breaks. The most common examples are **translocation** (when a segment of a chromosome moves to another chromosome), **inversion** (when a segment of a chromosome is inserted in the reverse orientation), and **deletion** (when a segment of a chromosome is lost).

MANIPULATING THE CODE

So far, we've seen how organisms can be affected by mutations in their genes and chromosomes. Modern technology has also helped scientists manipulate genetic information either indirectly by **artificial selection** or directly by **genetic engineering**.

A number of techniques can indirectly manipulate the inheritance of genes in plants and animals. In artificial selection, desirable characteristics are "bred into" populations. This is done quite simply by allowing only those organisms with the desired characteristics to interbreed. For example, by pollinating flowers by hand, rose-breeders have produced thousands of special roses. Other breeding techniques include **hybridization** (in which animals are crossbred to maximize the favorable traits of both varieties of a given species) and **inbreeding** (to produce pure breeds). Examples of these breeding patterns are found in corn, flowers, fruits, cattle, and dogs, among other familiar organisms.

GENETIC ENGINEERING

Scientists have found new ways of changing organisms through the *transfer* of individual genes from one organism to another. This is known as *genetic engineering*.

Genetic engineering is a technology that produces new organisms by transferring genes between cells. DNA is cut from one cell and transferred to another. The host DNA is now called **recombinant DNA**. When the cell undergoes protein synthesis, it will read the inserted portion of

DNA as if it were its own. As we've already seen, this leads to the production of specific proteins.

This technique has resulted in the successful production of such proteins as insulin and growth hormone. For example, the DNA that instructs a human cell to make insulin can be transferred to a bacterium. As this bacterium divides, it passes the gene for insulin to its offspring. Pretty soon you've got millions upon millions of bacteria churning out insulin. Once it is isolated from the solution in which the bacteria are raised, the insulin can be used by diabetics to help regulate their blood sugar.

LOOKING FOR DEFECTS

Many genetic defects are detectable even before an organism is born. Researchers and doctors use several techniques to identify such defects:

- Genetic screening: a technique used to identify abnormal conditions by detecting the presence or absence of certain chemicals in the blood or urine.

- Amniocentesis: a technique in which a sample of amniotic fluid is taken from the mother's womb. In the amniotic fluid is an abundance of fetal cells. By examining the fetal cells, doctors can detect severe disorders that may pose a risk to the fetus, the mother, or both.

- Karyotyping: a technique in which paired chromosomes are arranged based on shape and size. This procedure helps to identify such chromosomal abnormalities as extra or missing chromosomes. The chromosomes are organized into a karyotype:

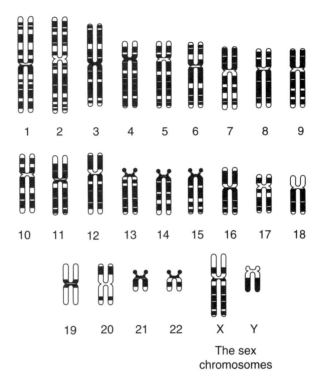

1 2 3 4 5 6 7 8 9

10 11 12 13 14 15 16 17 18

19 20 21 22 X Y

The sex
chromosomes

GENETIC DISORDERS

Here's a list of some genetic disorders you should be aware of:

- Phenylketonuria (PKU): a genetic disorder in which the body is unable to metabolize the amino acid phenylalanine. This condition can lead to mental retardation.

- Sickle cell anemia: a genetic disorder in which red blood cells are abnormally shaped.

- Tay-Sachs: a genetic disorder in which the nervous system malfunctions due to the accumulation of fat in the brain.

CHAPTER 9 QUIZ

1.   Which event is not part of the process of DNA replication?

(1) Nitrogenous base pairs are formed.

(2) Hydrogen bonds are broken.

(3) A double-stranded molecule unwinds.

(4) Ribosomes are synthesized.

2. DNA molecules serve as a template for the synthesis of molecules of

    (1) amino acids

    (2) carbohydrates

    (3) mRNA

    (4) lipids

3. What is the role of DNA in controlling cellular activity?

    (1) DNA provides energy for all cell activities.

    (2) DNA determines which enzymes are produced by a cell.

    (3) DNA is used by cells for the excretion of nitrogenous wastes.

    (4) DNA provides nucleotides for the construction of plasma membrane.

4. In addition to a phosphate group, a DNA nucleotide could contain

    (1) thymine and deoxyribose

    (2) uracil and deoxyribose

    (3) thymine and ribose

    (4) uracil and ribose

5. Which of the following molecules is found in RNA molecules but not in DNA molecules?

    (1) phosphorus

    (2) adenine

    (3) uracil

    (4) thymine

6. The correct sequence between genes and their expression is

    (1) RNA → DNA → protein → trait

    (2) DNA → RNA → protein → trait

    (3) trait → DNA → protein → RNA

    (4) protein → trait → protein → DNA

7. Although genetic mutations can occur spontaneously in organisms, the incidence of such mutation can be increased by

(1) radioactive substances in the environment

(2) lack of vitamins in the diet

(3) long exposure to humid climates

(4) a short exposure to freezing temperatures

10

Evolution

All of the organisms we see today arose from earlier organisms. This process, known as **evolution**, can be described as a change in the gene pool of a population over time. Much of what we now know about evolution is based on the work of **Charles Darwin**. Darwin was a nineteenth-century British naturalist who sailed the world in a ship called the HMS *Beagle*. Darwin developed his theory of evolution after studying animals in the Galapagos Islands off the western coast of South America. Purely from observation, Darwin deduced that different populations of animals must have once belonged to the same species.

Darwin came to this conclusion on the basis of two very simple facts: (1) Different groups of animals had similar traits, and (2) they had dissimilar traits. There's nothing necessarily surprising in animals having similar and dissimilar traits. But what Darwin found most striking was that the differences among these animals seemed ideally suited to their environments. For example, tortoises living on islands where low vegetation was scarce had very long necks. This worked out well for them, because most of their food grew above ground. Without their long necks, these tortoises would have starved to death. Tortoises on other islands where low vegetation was abundant did not have such long necks.

Darwin believed that these differences were evidence of **natural selection**, the driving force of evolution. By natural selection, Darwin meant the process by which nature "chooses" which organisms survive. Which ones are they? The ones most fit to survive. To take the example of our tortoises, on an island without low-growing vegetation, tortoises with longer necks are simply more fit to survive. As a consequence, they outlive those tortoises with shorter necks and produce more offspring. Over time, this pattern of competition and extinction (as the short-necked tortoises die off) results in the formation of new species.

To summarize, Darwin's key observations were as follows:

- Each species produces more offspring than can survive.
- These offspring compete with one another for the limited resources available to them.
- In every population, different organisms have different traits.
- The offspring with the most favorable traits are the ones most likely to survive and produce offspring.

Taken together, these observations led him to conclude that natural selection leads to the process of evolution.

LAMARCK'S INFAMOUS GIRAFFES

Darwin was not the first to propose a theory explaining the variety of life on earth. One of the most widely accepted theories of evolution in Darwin's day was that proposed by Jean-Baptiste de Lamarck.

In the eighteenth century, Lamarck proposed that acquired traits were inherited and passed on to offspring. For example, he thought that giraffes had long necks because they were constantly reaching for higher leaves while feeding. Giraffes with longer necks survived and had more offspring. In time, all giraffes had long necks. This theory is referred to as the "law of use and disuse," or, as we might say now, "use it or lose it."

We know now that Lamarck's theory was wrong: Acquired changes—that is, changes in body cells—cannot be passed on to germ cells. For example, if you were to lose one of our fingers, your children would not inherit this trait.

EVIDENCE FOR EVOLUTION

Today we find support for the theory of evolution in several areas:

- **Geological** or **fossil records**. The study of fossils has revealed to us both the variety of organisms and the major lines of evolution. Scientists study the fossilized remains and traces of extinct organisms to gain some sense of the path of evolution. Such famous examples as *Archaeopteryx*, a winged, feathered reptile from the age of the dinosaurs, have helped scientists trace the development of life on earth. *Archaeopteryx* has led biologists to conclude that birds are in fact distant descendants of the great dinosaurs.

- **Comparative embryology**, or the study of the development of various organisms. If you look at the early stages in vertebrate development, all the embryos look alike! All vertebrates, including fish, amphibians, birds, and even us, possess similar paths of development. At a very early stage, the embryos of all vertebrates even have gill slits! Naturally, terrestrial animals lose them long before birth.

- **Comparative anatomy**, or the study of the anatomy of various animals. Scientists have discovered that some animals have similar structures that serve different functions. For example, a bat's wing, a whale's fin, and a human's arm are all appendages that have evolved to serve different purposes. These structures, called **homologous structures**, point to common ancestors.

- **Comparative biochemistry**, or the study of the polypeptides of various organisms. Scientists look at the DNA sequences and the polypeptides from different organisms to identify similarities at the biochemical level. They've found that organisms that are closely related have a greater proportion of polypeptides in common than do distantly related species.

SPECIES

A house cat and a butterfly obviously cannot reproduce together. We would therefore say that they are different **species**. However, a tabby and an angora (those big, furry house cats) *could* reproduce. We would not say that they are different species; they are merely different breeds. **Speciation**, or the production of different species, occurs when organisms that were once members of the same species can no longer interbreed. It is this emergence of a new species that marks an "evolutionary stage," or a step forward in evolution.

Two factors lead to the process of speciation: **geographic isolation** and **reproductive isolation**. In geographic isolation, a geographic barrier separates two groups of organisms. For example, if an earthquake thrust a mountain between two different groups of birds, we would say that they were geographically isolated. At this point, they are still the same species: They are just cut off from one another.

Over time, however, environmental pressures can lead to drastic changes in these two groups. For example, let's say that the mountain catches all the moisture on its western slope, turning its eastern slope into a desert. The only birds that would survive on its eastern slope would be those least susceptible to desiccation. Over eons, this group of birds may become so different from the original group that the two would no longer be able to interbreed. At this point, we would say that a new species of bird had evolved.

However, a new species might also arise due to reproductive isolation. Imagine that erosion wipes away our mountain, leaving our two groups of birds to interact once again. Even if the birds haven't evolved into two totally separate species, they may still not be able to interbreed. One group may breed in the summer, when it's warm and moist; whereas the other group, the desert birds, may breed only in the winter, when it's cool enough to seek out a mate. Such a factor could be considered reproductive isolation. Over time, these two would eventually become totally separate species, incapable of interbreeding even if they could synchronize their mating seasons.

EVOLUTION: FAST OR SLOW?

Scientists have long debated whether evolution occurs gradually or suddenly. Some believe that evolution is a gradual process. This view is known as **gradualism**. Proponents of this theory believe that such large changes as speciation happen only because of many small changes over long stretches of time.

Other scientists believe in **punctuated equilibrium**. According to the theory of punctuated equilibrium, there are long stretches of time where essentially nothing happens. A status quo is reached. Although organisms are constantly reproducing, competing for resources and dying, we would not say that they are *evolving*. Evolution only occurs, according to this view, under extreme environmental stress. For example, if a massive comet had not struck the earth, wiping out the dinosaurs (as many contend), mammals would never have taken over. Mammals already existed during the age of the dinosaurs. They were mostly small, scurrying creatures, much like today's rodents. However, it took a massive shake-up—the extinction a large proportion of the world's species—for this moment in evolution to occur. This is an example of punctuated equilibrium: The equilibrium of the Cretaceous era (the final age of the dinosaurs) was shattered or "punctuated" by some major catastrophe. Was it a comet? We'll never know for sure, but one thing is certain: Without the sudden extinction of the dinosaurs, we might not be around to ask the question in the first place.

Here are two graphs illustrating the difference between the two theories:

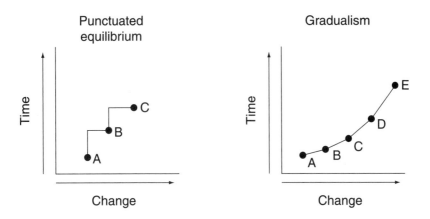

THE HETEROTROPH HYPOTHESIS

One question that is still hotly debated among scientists is the origin of life. Most scientists believe that the earliest precursors of life were non-living matter—basically gases—in the primitive oceans of the earth. But this theory didn't take shape until the 1920s. Two scientists, Oparin and Haldane, proposed that the primitive atmosphere contained the following gases: methane (CH_4), ammonia (NH_3), hydrogen (H_2), and water (H_2O). Interestingly enough, there was almost no free oxygen (O_2) in this early atmosphere. This mixture formed a sort of "primordial soup" in which these gases collided, producing chemical reactions that eventually led to the organic molecules we know today.

Oparin and Haldane's theory didn't receive any substantial support until 1953. In that year, Stanley Miller and Harold Urey simulated the conditions of primitive earth in a laboratory. They put the gases together in a flask, struck them with electrical charges to mimic lightning, and *voilà* . . . organic compounds similar to amino acids appeared!

It's been a long journey from these basic amino acids to the unbeliev-able complexity of modern-day organisms. However, scientists speculate that the earliest forms of life were heterotrophs. This is known as the **heterotroph hypothesis**.

By "consuming" organic molecules in the primordial soup, these earliest organisms acquired the energy necessary for life. Because no one was around to observe them, we'll never know for sure what they were like or how they lived. However, biologists generally accept that the first "living things" survived by consuming organic molecules. It was only much, much later that autotrophs, organisms capable of making their own food, appeared on Earth, filling the atmosphere with oxygen gas and paving the way for evolution.

CHAPTER 10 QUIZ

1. According to the heterotroph hypothesis, which event immediately preceded the evolution of aerobes?

   (1) the production of oxygen by autotrophs

   (2) the production of ammonia by heterotrophs

   (3) the production of carbon dioxide by autotrophs

   (4) the production of carbon dioxide by heterotrophs

2. One theory about the extinction of dinosaurs is that the collision of an asteroid with the Earth caused environmental changes that killed off the dinosaurs in a relatively short time, changing the course of evolution. This theory is an example of which evolutionary concept?

   (1) gradualism

   (2) competition

   (3) the heterotroph hypothesis

   (4) punctuated equilibrium

3. Since the time of Darwin, increased knowledge of heredity has resulted in

   (1) the addition of use and disuse to Lamarck's theory

   (2) the elimination of all previous evolutionary theories

   (3) increased support for the theory of natural selection

   (4) disagreement with Mendel's discoveries

4. Which phrase best defines evolution?

   (1) an adaptation of an organism to its environment

   (2) a sudden replacement of one community by another

   (3) a geographic or reproductive isolation of organisms

   (4) a process of change in organisms over a period of time

5. Which statement would most likely be in agreement with Lamarck's theory of evolution?

(1) Black moths have evolved in an area because they were better adapted to the environment and had high rates of survival and reproduction.

(2) Geographic barriers can lead to reproductive isolation and the production of new species.

(3) Giraffes have long necks because their ancestors stretched their necks reaching for food.

(4) Most variations in animals and plants are due to random chromosomal and gene mutation.

6. Organisms with favorable variations reproduce more successfully than organisms with less favorable variations. This statement best describes the concept of

(1) overproduction

(2) use and disuse

(3) inheritance of acquired characteristics

(4) survival of the fittest

7. How does natural selection operate to cause change in a population?

(1) The members of a population are equally able to survive any environmental change.

(2) The members of the population differ so that only some survive when the environment changes.

(3) The members of the population do not adapt to environmental changes.

(4) All the members of the population adapt to environmental changes.

8. The concept that evolution is the result of long period of stability interrupted by geologically brief periods of significant change is known as

(1) gradualism

(2) natural selection

(3) geographic isolation

(4) punctuated equilibrium

11

Diversity of Living Things

TAXONOMY

People have long been aware of the diversity of life. But figuring out exactly how organisms are related to one another has taken some work. From the very beginning, naturalists could spot similarities among many organisms. For example, they knew that dogs and wolves were closely related. After all, they resemble one another and behave in similar ways. But what about birds and bats? Or sharks and dolphins? Sharks and dolphins also look nearly identical, with their fins and tails, and they both live in the sea. Wouldn't it seem perfectly reasonable to lump them together as well?

As you can imagine, determining the best way to classify all the creatures on the planet was no easy task. Interestingly, just like those earliest scientists, we now place organisms into different groups on the basis of shared characteristics or traits. Although these first biologists classified organisms solely on the basis of appearance and habitat, we now classify living things on the basis of evolutionary relatedness.

From this perspective, sharks and a dolphins are not that closely related. As you probably know, sharks breathe with gills, whereas dolphins have lungs. These two very different traits, acquired over the long process of evolution, lead us to conclude that sharks and dolphins split off somewhere way back on the evolutionary tree. Consequently, although they both live in the sea, they are no more than very distant relations. As we now know, sharks are fish, and dolphins are mammals. To a student of biology, this comes as no surprise. But as little as 200 years ago, if you had proposed that dolphins were more closely related to human beings than to sharks, you would have been laughed out of the classroom!

Let's take a look, then, at the ways in which we currently classify living things. The science of classifying organisms according to their traits is known as **taxonomy**.

HOW CLASSIFICATION WORKS

The simplest way to think about taxonomy is to remember that organisms are classified on the basis of shared characteristics. The order of classification is: **kingdom**, **phylum**, **class**, **order**, **family**, **genus**, and **species**. As we move from kingdom to species, we find that organisms have more traits in common. The kingdom is the largest grouping and contains organisms that share very few traits. The species is the smallest grouping, and its members have the most traits in common.

THE NITTY GRITTY OF CLASSIFICATION

Let's take a closer look at how organisms are actually ordered into various levels. We'll start with the highest level, the kingdom. All organisms belong to one of five kingdoms: **Monera**, **Protista**, **Fungi**, **Plantae**, and **Animalia**. There's a quick summary of the five kingdoms on the next two pages. You'll notice that the kingdoms are further broken down into major phyla and classes, along with some of the main characteristics particular to each. Although you don't have to know all of the classes, you should be familiar with at least the major phyla:

CLASSIFICATION OF FUNGI

Phylum	Characteristics	Examples	
Fungi	Lack chlorophyll; produce spores	Molds, yeast, mushrooms	

CLASSIFICATION OF ANIMALS

Phylum	Characteristics	Examples	
1. Porifera	Two layers of cells with pores	Sponge	
2. Coelenterata	Two layers of cells; hollow digestive cavity with tentacles	Hydra, jellyfish	
3. Platyhelminthes (Flatworms)	Three layers of cells; flat; bilateral symmetry	Tapeworm, planaria, fluke	
4. Nematoda (Roundworms)	Digestive system with a mouth and anus; round	Hookworm	
5. Rotifera	Digestive system	Rotifer	
6. Annelida (Segmented worms)	Long, segmented body; digestive system; open circulatory system	Earthworm	
7. Mollusca	Soft bodies; hard shell	Clam, snail	
8. Arthropoda	Segmented body; jointed legs; exoskeleton		
Class Crustacea	Gills for breathing; jointed legs	Crab, lobster	
Insecta	Three body parts; one pair of antennae; six legs; tracheal breathing system	Bee, grasshopper	
Arachnida	Two body parts; eight legs	Spider	
Chilopoda	One pair of legs per segment	Centipede	
Diplopoda	Two pairs of legs per segment	Millipede	
9. Echinodermata (Spiny-skinned)	Spiny exoskeleton; complete digestive system	Starfish, sea urchin, sea cucumber	

CLASSIFICATION OF ANIMALS (Continued)

Phylum	Characteristics	Examples	
10. Chordata	Notochord; dorsal nerve cord; gill slits		
Subphylum Vertebrate	Backbone		
Class Pisces (fish)	Gills; scales; two-chambered heart	Salmon	
Amphibia	Breathe through gills, lungs and thin, moist skin; three-chambered heart	Frog	
Reptilia	Eggs with a chitinous covering; cold-blooded; scales; three-chambered heart	Snake	
Aves	Warm-blooded; four-chambered heart; eggs with shell; wings	Owl	
Mammalia	Warm-blooded; hair; produce milk to feed young	Human, kangaroo	

Notice that organisms in particular kingdoms possess specific characteristics. For example, **Monera** includes bacteria, the smallest and most primitive of all living organisms. As we saw in chapter 2, monerans lack a nuclear membrane, mitochondria, and several other organelles. Organisms in this kingdom are also known as **prokaryotes**. All other organisms, which have a nuclear membrane, are called **eukaryotes**.

All organisms are given scientific names consisting of a species name and genus name. This classification scheme, called the *binomial classification system*, was developed by Carolus Linnaeus. For example, humans are called *Homo sapiens*. *Homo* is our genus name, and *sapiens* is our species names. *Homo* means man, and *sapiens* means wise. Obviously we fancy ourselves the wisest of the bunch!

CHAPTER 11 QUIZ

1. A fungus is classified as a heterotroph rather than an autotroph because it

    (1) grows by mitosis

    (2) absorbs food from the environment

    (3) manufactures its own food

    (4) transforms light energy into chemical energy

2. Which is the most specific term used to classify humans?

    (1) *sapiens*

    (2) animals

    (3) *Homo*

    (4) fungi

3. In which group do all the organisms belong to the same kingdom?

    (1) yeast, mushroom, maple tree

    (2) paramecium, amoeba, euglena

    (3) bacteria, amoeba, euglena

    (4) bacteria, moss, geranium

4. In modern classification, blue-green algae, plants, and algae are known as

    (1) heterotrophs

    (2) autotrophs

    (3) animals

    (4) plants

5. Which of the following terms includes the other three?

    (1) genus

    (2) species

    (3) kingdom

    (4) phylum

6. In attempting to classify a newly discovered organism, the following characteristics were observed under a microscope: It is unicellular, heterotrophic, and contains a nucleus. Which kingdom is the organism most likely to be classified under?

(1) Protista

(2) Monera

(3) Plant

(4) Fungi

12

Ecology

We've spent most of our time discussing individual organisms. However, in the real world, organisms are in constant interaction with other organisms and the environment. The study of the interactions between living things and their physical environment is known as **ecology**.

The best way to understand the various levels of ecology is to start with the big picture, the biosphere, and work our way down to the smallest ecological unit, the population. We can rank the various levels of ecological organization in a clear hierarchy, each of which represents a different degree of interaction:

- **Biosphere**: the entire part of the earth where living things exist. This includes abiotic factors (nonliving) such as soil, water, light, and air. In comparison to the overall mass of the earth, the biosphere is relatively small. If you think of the earth as a basketball, the biosphere is equivalent to a coat of paint over its surface.

- **Ecosystem**: the interaction of living (**biotic**) and nonliving (**abiotic**) things.

- **Community**: a group of populations interacting in the same area.

- **Population**: a group of individuals that belong to the same species.

BIOSPHERE

The biosphere can be divided into large regions called *biomes*. Biomes are massive areas that are classified mostly on the basis of their climate and plant life. Because of the different climates and terrains on the earth, the distribution of living organisms varies. It's important to know both the names of the different biomes and their characteristic **flora** (plant life) and **fauna** (animal life).

Here's a summary of the major **terrestrial** (land) **biomes**:

Major Biomes

Tundra

Regions—northernmost regions

Plant life—few, if any, trees; primarily grasses and wildflowers

Characteristics—contains permafrost (a layer of permanently frozen soil); has a short growing season.

Animal life—includes lemmings, arctic foxes, snowy owls, caribou, and reindeer

Taiga

Region—northernmost regions

Plant life—wind-blown conifers (evergreens), stunted in growth, possess modified spikes for leaves

Characteristics—very cold, long winters

Animal life—includes caribou, wolves, moose, bear, rabbits, and lynx

Temperate Deciduous Forest

Regions—northeast and middle eastern United States, western Europe

Plant life—deciduous trees which drop their leaves in winter

Characteristics—moderate precipitation; warm summers, cold winters

Animal life—includes deer, wolves, bear, small mammals, birds

Grasslands

Regions—American Midwest, Eurasia, Africa, South America

Plant life—grasses

Characteristics—hot summers, cold winters; unpredictable rainfall

Animal life—includes prairie dogs, bison, foxes, ferrets, grouse, snakes, and lizards

Deserts

Regions—western North America, Arctic

Plant life—sparse, includes cacti, drought-resistant plants

Characteristics—arid, low rainfall; extreme diurnal temperature shifts

Animal life—includes jackrabbits (in North America), owls, kangaroo rats, lizards, snakes, tortoises

Tropical Rain Forests

Regions—South America, Colombia

Plant life—high biomass; diverse types

Characteristics—high rainfall and temperature; impoverished soil

Animal life—includes sloths, snakes, monkeys, birds, leopards, and insects

Remember that the biomes tend to be arranged along particular latitudes. For instance, if you hiked from Alaska to Kansas, you'd pass through the following biomes: tundra, taiga, temperate deciduous forests, and grasslands.

The biomes can also be arranged along particular altitudes. For instance, if you hiked up a snow-capped mountain in South America, you'd pass through the following biomes: tropical rain forest, temperate deciduous forests, taiga, and tundra.

ECOSYSTEM

Now let's look at an even smaller group, the ecosystem. Ecosystems are self-contained regions that include both living and nonliving components. For example, a lake, its surrounding forest, the atmosphere above it, and all the organisms that live in or feed off the lake would be considered an ecosystem. As you probably know, there is an exchange of materials between the components of an ecosystem. Take a look at the flow through a typical ecosystem:

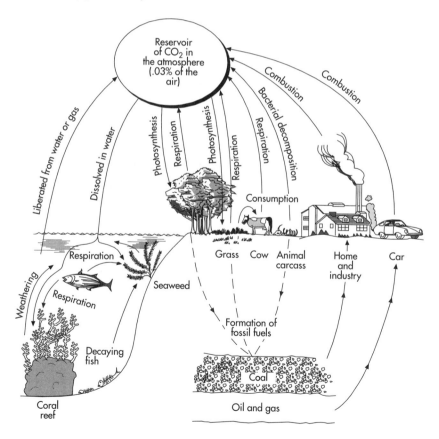

You'll notice that carbon, hydrogen, and oxygen are recycled throughout the ecosystem. In other words, energy flows through ecosystems. In photosynthesis, plants use carbon dioxide (CO_2) and water (H_2O) to make glucose, releasing oxygen gas (O_2) in the process. Consumers then use this oxygen to access the energy stored in glucose, releasing carbon dioxide and water back into the environment. Other examples of continuous cycles are the **nitrogen cycle** and the **water cycle**.

NITROGEN CYCLE

Plants need nitrogen to survive. They need nitrogen to make plant proteins. However, in most places, the soil is relatively poor in nitrogen. Although the atmosphere is rich in nitrogen, the nitrogen in the air is not in a usable form. Fortunately for plants living in nitrogen-poor soil, there are bacteria that are able to use or "fix" this atmospheric nitrogen. **Nitrogen-fixing bacteria** live in the roots of plants and convert atmospheric nitrogen to a useable form called **nitrates**. Nitrates are then used to make plant proteins.

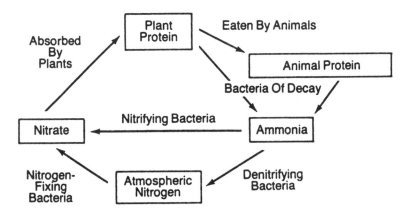

WATER CYCLE

Water is vital to life as we know it. Most living things require water to survive. In the water cycle, such processes as precipitation, evaporation, and condensation distribute water throughout the ecosystem.

COMMUNITY

A **community** refers to groups of plants and animals that interact and show some degree of interdependence. For instance, you, your dog, and the fleas on your dog are all members of the same community. All organisms within a community perform one of the following roles: They're either **producers, consumers,** or **decomposers**.

PRODUCERS

Producers have the ability to make their own food. Think about your average houseplant. Sure, it needs its square foot of soil, from which it extracts some base nutrients, but for the most part, it does just fine with air, sunlight, and a little water. Your houseplant is a typical producer. From water and the gases that abound in the atmosphere and with the aid of the sun's energy, autotrophs manage to convert light energy to chemical energy. As we saw in chapter 4, they accomplish this through photosynthesis.

CONSUMERS

Consumers, or heterotrophs, are forced to find their energy sources in the outside world. Basically, heterotrophs are the eaters, and autotrophs are the eaten (though plenty of consumers also get munched on). Heterotrophs digest the carbohydrates of their prey into carbon, hydrogen, and oxygen and then use these molecules to make organic substances. Examples of heterotrophs are **herbivores** (organisms that eat plants), **carnivores** (organisms that eat animals), **omnivores** (organisms that eat plants and animals), and **saprophytes** (organisms that eat decaying organic matter).

The bottom line is that heterotrophs or "consumers" get their energy from the things they consume.

DECOMPOSERS

All organisms at some point must finally yield to **decomposers.** Decomposers are the organisms that break down organic matter into simple products. Generally, fungi and bacteria are the decomposers.

THE FOOD CHAIN

Each organism has its own **niche**—its position or function in a community. Because every species occupies a niche, it's going to have an effect on all the other organisms. These connections are shown in the **food chain**. A food chain describes the ways in which different organisms depend on one another for food. There are basically four levels to the food chain: **producers, primary consumers, secondary consumers**, and **tertiary consumers.**

Autotrophs produce all of the available food. They make up the first **trophic** (feeding) level. They possess the highest biomass (the total mass of all the organisms in an area) and exist in the greatest numbers. Did you know that plants make up about 99% of the Earth's total biomass?

Primary consumers or **herbivores** are organisms that feed directly on producers. A good example are cows. They make up the second trophic level. The energy flow, biomass, and numbers for members within an ecosystem can be represented in an **pyramid**. Organisms that are "higher up" on the pyramid are less numerous and have less biomass and energy:

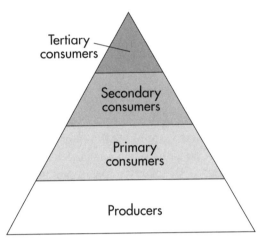

This simply means that primary consumers have less **biomass** (amount of living material) and are therefore less numerous than producers. The next level consists of organisms that feed on primary consumers. They are the **secondary consumers** and they make up the third trophic level. Finally, there are the **tertiary consumers** (like ourselves) who eat just about everything. So now we've got our four complete levels of the food chain:

1. Producers, which make their own food

2. Primary consumers (herbivores), which eat producers

3. Secondary consumers (heterotrophs and carnivores), which eat primary consumers

4. Tertiary consumers (heterotrophs and omnivores), which eat all of the above

But what about decomposers? Where do they fit in on the food chain? They don't. They are not considered part of the food chain. Decomposers are usually placed just below the food chain to show that they can decompose any organism.

SYMBIOTIC RELATIONSHIPS

We've already mentioned that organisms interact with one another. Many organisms coexist in what we call **symbiotic relationships**. Examples of

such organisms include remoras, or "sucker fish," which attach themselves to the backs of sharks, and lichen, the fuzzy, mold-like stuff that
grows on rocks. Lichen appears to be one organism: In fact, it is two
organisms—a fungus and an alga or photosynthetic bacterium—living in
a complex symbiotic relationship.

Overall, there are three basic types of symbiotic relationships:

1. **Mutualism**, in which both organisms win (e.g., the
   lichen)

2. **Commensalism**, in which one organism lives off another
   with no harm to the "host" organism (e.g., the remora)

3. **Parasitism**, in which the organism actually harms its host

Regardless of which one we refer to, all three are examples of "symbiotic"
relationships. Make sure you're clear on the difference between the three.
Here's a simple (if slightly goofy) summary of the benefits or harm
derived by different organisms in symbiotic relationships:

Relationship	Organism I	Organism II
Commensalism	😐	🙂
Parasitism	🙁	🙂
Mutualism	🙂	🙂

ECOLOGICAL SUCCESSION

Communities of organisms don't just spring up on their own; they develop
gradually over time. **Ecological succession** describes this process, a predictable procession of plant communities over a relatively short period of
time (decades or centuries). Centuries may not seem like a short time to us,
but if you consider that evolution occurs over millions of years, you'll see
that it is pretty short. Ecological succession begins with pioneer organisms.

PIONEERS

How does an abandoned area full of rocks and overgrown weeds eventually turn into a gorgeous field? The job usually falls to a community of
lichens. Lichens are hardy organisms. They can invade an area, land on

bare rocks, and erode the rocks' surfaces, turning them to soil. Lichens are considered **pioneer organisms**.

Once lichens have made an area more habitable, the stage is set for other organisms to settle. Communities establish themselves in an orderly fashion. Lichens are replaced by mosses and ferns, which in turn are replaced by tough grasses, then low shrubs, then deciduous trees and evergreen trees. Why are lichens replaced? Because they can't compete with the new plants for sunlight and minerals.

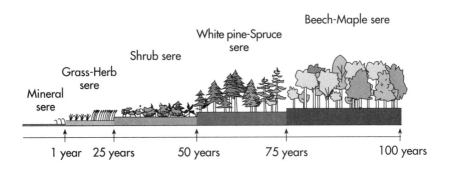

Each succession occurs until we reach a final community, called the **climax community**. The climax community is the most stable. In our example, the beech-maple trees are part of the climax community.

HUMANS AND THE ENVIRONMENT

Before the 1850s, the human population was low because it was kept in check by **limiting factors** such as disease and food shortages. Since the mid-nineteenth century, the human population growth has increased at a rapid rate and is now increasing by about 200,000 individuals per day!

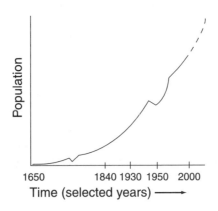

This population growth has put a lot of stress on the environment. As if overpopulation weren't bad enough, we've also managed to harm our environment in many other ways. Take a look:

The Problems:

- **Overhunting**: Many species have been hunted into extinction, some for food, others merely for sport.

- **Exploitation of organisms**: Many exotic plants and animals are killed for commercial trade. For example, the white rhino is routinely slaughtered simply for its horn.

- **Poor land-use management**: Land has been abused through overfarming and unchecked development.

- **Technological oversight**: New technologies have been used without consideration of the effect on the environment. These technologies have often polluted our air and water supply. For example, **biocide use**—the use of chemicals such as pesticides and herbicides to control pests—often damages the soil and increases water and land pollution.

However bad the situation may be, it isn't all bad. In recent years, we've begun to make an effort to remedy some of these problems. Here is a list of some of the ways we are working to improve our environment:

The Solutions:

- **Population control**: People are now encouraged to practice family planning.

- **Conservation of resources**: People are now practicing reforestation and water conservation to help protect the soil.

- **Species preservation**: Wildlife refuges and international bans on hunting have been enacted to protect endangered species.

- **Biological controls**: Natural enemies are often used to control pests instead of dangerous chemicals.

- **Environmental laws**: Various laws are passed to preserve and protect the environment.

CHAPTER 12 QUIZ

1. Which is an example of an ecosystem?

    (1) a population of monarch butterflies

    (2) the interdependent biotic and abiotic components of a pond

    (3) all the abiotic factors found in a field

    (4) all the mammals that live in the Atlantic Ocean

2. In the nitrogen cycle, plants use nitrogen compounds to produce

    (1) glucose

    (2) starch

    (3) lipids

    (4) proteins

3. A flea in the fur of a mouse benefits at the mouse's expense. This type of relationship is known as

    (1) commensalism

    (2) parasitism

    (3) saprophytism

    (4) mutualism

Directions for 4–5: Base your answer to questions 4 and 5 on the diagram below and on your knowledge of biology.

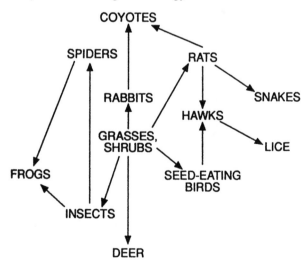

4. Which organisms would contain the greatest amount of available energy?

   (1) rabbits and deer

   (2) grasses and shrubs

   (3) lice

   (4) hawks

5. The primary consumers include

   (1) rabbits and snakes

   (2) insects and seed-eating birds

   (3) rats and frogs

   (4) spiders and coyotes

6. Which statement best describes an energy pyramid?

   (1) There is more energy at the consumer level than at the producer level.

   (2) There is more energy at the producer level than at the consumer level.

   (3) There is more energy at the secondary-consumer level than at the primary-consumer level.

   (4) There is more energy at the decomposer level than at the consumer level.

13

Laboratory Skills

All biology courses include a laboratory component that gives students hands-on experience regarding some of the biology topics covered in class. Through these laboratory exercises, you can learn the scientific method, laboratory techniques, and problem-solving skills.

These labs usually test two things: (1) how well you understand the key concepts in biology and (2) how well you think analytically. For instance, can you design experiments, manipulate data, and draw conclusions from experiments?

SCIENTIFIC METHOD

Let's begin by discussing the **scientific method**. Have you ever heard of the scientific method? It's just a fancy name for the steps an investigator takes in conducting an experiment. One of the key steps in conducting an experiment is to state the **problem** to be studied. The problem is the dilemma or mystery the experiment intends to explain. For example, an experiment may be designed to study the effect of pH on enzyme activity. The problem here can be phrased as a simple question: How does pH affect the activity of a given enzyme?

The expected results in a study are then presented in the form of a **hypothesis**. A hypothesis is a possible explanation for the observable facts. For example, a hypothesis for the effect pH has on enzyme activity may be that enzymes are designed to work at specific pH levels.

VARIABLES

Next, a student should be able to identify the **variables** in the study. The variables are the parts of the experiment that are altered to obtain results. Let's take the problem mentioned before. If we were to conduct an experiment to test our hypothesis, we would have to test the rate of an enzyme-assisted reaction as a function of one or more variables. In this case, our principal variable would be the pH of the solution in which we place our enzyme.

By altering the pH and keeping careful track of the effect this variation has on the enzyme, we come up with a bunch of data. This data is called the **results**.

RESULTS

Once we've compiled our results, we can organize them into a chart or graph. Let's look at a typical coordinate graph. The coordinate graph has a horizontal axis (x axis) and a vertical axis (y axis):

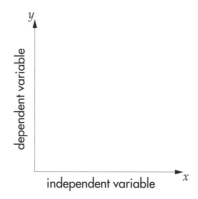

The x axis usually contains the independent variable, the component being manipulated. The y axis contains the dependent variable, the component affected when the independent variable is changed.

Now let's look at what happens when we place our data on the graph. Every point on the graph represents both an independent variable and a dependent variable.

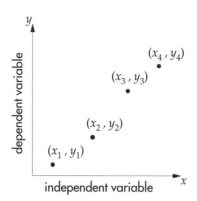

To make a graph, draw both axes and label the axes with the independent and dependent variable. Then you can begin to plot the points on the graph. The graph below shows how the rate of our reaction changed as pH increased:

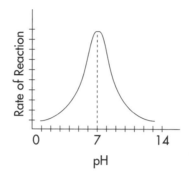

Notice how the dots were connected to form a curved line. The graph shows that the rate of the reaction is greatest at a pH of 7.

Once the data has been collected and presented in a readable form, we can make **conclusions** and draw **inferences** (conclusions based on the facts). The conclusion is the final statement based on the findings in the study. For our particular study, our conclusion may be that pH does exert an effect on enzyme activity. In the case of the enzyme we examined, a pH of 7 turned out to be optimal.

GENERALIZATION

Based on the results, you should now be able to make a generalization or broad conclusion based on the study. In our example, the generalization would be that pH has a definite effect on enzyme activity. The best way to confirm these results is to repeat the study several times.

CONTROLS IN YOUR EXPERIMENTS

Almost every experiment has at least one variable that remains constant throughout the study. This variable is called the **control**. A control is simply a standard of comparison. It enables the investigator to be certain that the outcome of the study is due to the changes in the independent variable and nothing else.

Let's look at an example. Let's say the principal of your school thinks that students who eat breakfast do better on standardized tests than those who don't eat breakfast. He takes a group of ten students from your class and gives them free breakfast every day for a year. When the school year is over, he administers a standardized test, and they all score brilliantly!

Did they do well because they ate breakfast every day? We don't know for sure. Maybe the principal picked only the smartest kids in the class to participate in the study.

The best way to be sure that eating breakfast made a difference in this case is to pick students in the class who *never* eat breakfast and follow them for a year. At the end of the year, have them take the same standardized test and see how they score. It they do just as well as the group that ate breakfast, then we'll know that eating breakfast didn't make a difference. The group of students that didn't eat breakfast is called the *control group*. They were not "exposed" to the variable of interest, in this case, breakfast.

COMPOUND LIGHT MICROSCOPE

One of the most common tools used to study tiny structures is the **compound light microscope**. A compound microscope magnifies the size of a specimen. The main components of the microscope are the **eyepiece lens**, **objective lens**, **stage**, **diaphragm**, **coarse-adjustment knob**, and **fine-adjustment knob**. Let's review the parts of a light microscope and how they work.

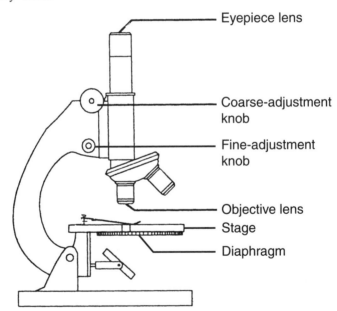

- **Eyepiece (ocular) lens**: the lens through which the image is observed directly.
- **Objective lens**: the lens closest to the specimen.

- **Stage**: the platform on which the specimen is placed to be viewed.

- **Coarse-adjustment knob**: brings the image into rough focus.

- **Fine-adjustment knob**: brings the image into sharp focus.

- **Light source**: the object that provides the light used to illuminate the specimen.

- **Diaphragm**: controls the amount of light trained on the specimen.

- **Magnification**: the apparent enlargement of the specimen.

- **Resolution**: the degree to which the microscope distinguishes detail.

To find the total magnification, multiply the power of the eyepiece by the power of the objective lens. For example, if the eyepiece power is 10×, and the objective lens is 40×, then the total magnification is 10×40, which equals 400. This means the specimen studied under high power is magnified 400×.

Here's one more thing you should remember: The object is not only magnified but also reversed and inverted.

STAINING

To view structures under a light microscope, you need to provide contrast between cells and cell structures. This is accomplished through staining techniques. The two most common stains are **iodine** and **methylene blue**.

OTHER INSTRUMENTS

We can obtain additional information about cells using the other instruments listed below:

- **Electron microscope**: uses a beam of electrons to increase the magnification in excess of 100,000×. Only nonliving things can be observed.

- **Dissecting microscope**: a low-power microscope that gives us a three-dimensional image of the specimen.

- **Ultracentrifuge**: spins cells in a machine and separates them according to their mass.

- **Microdissection instrument**: a tool used to dissect or transfer tiny structures.

OTHER LAB TECHNIQUES

MEASURING THE LENGTH OF CELLS

Cells, which are extremely small, are usually measured in micrometers (μm). For example, most cells are approximately 10 μm in size. One millimeter (mm) is equal to 1,000 micrometers (μm).

INDICATORS

An indicator is a substance that is used to determine the chemical characteristics of a sample or solution. The most common indicators are **pH paper, bromthymol blue, Benedict's (Fehling's) solution,** and **iodine (Lugol's) solution**.

- **pH paper**: measures the acidity of a solution. pH paper turns red in an acidic solution and blue in a basic solution.

- **Bromthymol blue**: used to test for the presence of carbon dioxide in a solution.

- **Benedict's (Fehling's) solution**: used to test for the presence of simple sugars in a solution. When a solution containing sugar and Benedict's solution is heated, the sample turns colors ranging from yellow to red, depending on the concentration of the sugar.

- **Iodine (Lugol's) solution**: used to test for the presence of starch in a solution. It turns blue-black when added to a sample that contains starch.

CHAPTER 13 QUIZ

1. Which indicators could be used to test for the presence of simple sugar and starch in a fluid solution?

   (1) Benedict's solution and Lugol's iodine

   (2) bromthymol blue solution and pH paper

   (3) Fehling's solution and bromthymol blue

   (4) pH paper and Lugol's iodine

2. Which procedure is usually used to help determine whether a child will be born with Down syndrome?

(1) amniocentesis

(2) cloning

(3) microdissection of sperm cells and egg cells

(4) analysis of urine samples from the mother

3. The diagram below represents a sample of crushed ion cells that was centrifuged. Cell and cell components were dispersed in layers as illustrated.

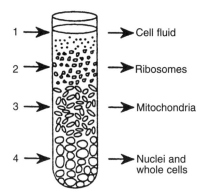

The organelles that act as the sites of protein synthesis are found in the greatest concentration in layer

(1) 1   (3) 3
(2) 2   (4) 4

4. When viewed with a compound light microscope, which letter would best illustrate that the microscope inverts and reverses an image?

(1) A   (3) F
(2) W   (4) D

5. Which technique enabled scientists in the 1800s to identify cell organelles?

    (1) electron microscopy

    (2) ultracentrifugation

    (3) staining

    (4) dissection

14

Answers and Explanations

CHAPTER 1 QUIZ

1. Choice 4 is the correct answer. Notice the compound attached to the enzyme. This compound (which has rings) is a disaccharide. The addition of water breaks the disaccharide into two monosaccharides. This process is called *hydrolysis.*

    (1) The synthesis of a polypeptide requires amino acids. The compound shown doesn't contain any amino acids.

    (2) The emulsification of a fat is the breakdown of a fat molecule into smaller fat molecules.

    (3) Synthesis refers to the formation of complex molecules from simpler ones. During synthesis, water is removed, not added.

2. Choice 3 is the correct answer. Maltose is a disaccharide that is formed from two monosaccharides via dehydration synthesis. This means water is *removed* to form a bond.

    (1) *Dipeptide synthesis* refers to the removal of water to form a dipeptide. In dipeptide synthesis, amino acids are joined, not molecules of glucose.

    (2) *Intracellular digestion* refers to chemical digestion within the cell.

    (4) *Biological oxidation* refers to the production of energy (ATP) in the presence of oxygen.

3. Choice 1 is the correct answer. The structural formula of urea is given in this question. Fortunately, you don't need to know anything about urea except that it contains carbon, hydrogen, and nitrogen. It is therefore an organic compound.

(2) Urea is not an inorganic compound: It contains carbon.

(3) Urea is not a carbohydrate. Carbohydrates contain carbon, hydrogen, and oxygen in a ratio of 1:2:1 and do not contain nitrogen.

(4) Urea is not a nucleic acid because it doesn't contain a sugar, phosphate, and a nitrogenous base.

4. Choice 1 is the correct answer. Inorganic compounds do not contain carbon atoms. Water (H_2O) and salts (like NaCl) are both inorganic compounds.

(2) Proteins and carbohydrates are organic compounds.

(3) Fats and oils are lipids; they're organic compounds.

(4) Enzymes and nucleic acids are organic compounds.

5. Choice 2 is the correct answer. Use the process of elimination. To identify a carbohydrate, the ratio of carbon to hydrogen to oxygen must be 1:2:1. The only chemical formula with the correct ratio is answer choice 2.

6. Choice 2 is the correct answer. A lipid is composed of a glycerol molecule and three fatty acids.

(1) Water molecules are released when a lipid is formed.

(3) and (4) Lipids do not contain amino groups.

7. Choice 4 is the correct answer. The activity of an enzyme is influenced by the pH of the reaction. That's because enzymes function best at a particular pH.

(1) and (3) Most enzymes operate at a neutral pH—a pH of 7. Some enzymes, however, operate at a low pH (a pH lower than 4).

(2) Adding more acid influences the reaction rate of an enzyme. As you add more acid to a solution, the pH goes down.

CHAPTER 2 QUIZ

1. Choice 4 is the correct answer. An animal cell does not contain chloroplasts; a plant cell does. Chloroplasts are the primary sites of photosynthesis. All of the other organelles are found in animal cells.

2. Choice 3 is the correct answer. The rough endoplasmic reticulum is a continuous channel that is involved in protein synthesis. It is found in the cytoplasm.

    (1) Ribosomes also participate in protein synthesis. However, they are round, discrete structures, not continuous channels.

    (2) Golgi bodies, which look like flattened sacs, package and distribute materials destined to be sent out of the cell.

    (4) The mitochondria, oblong-shaped organelles, are the powerhouses of the cell.

3. Choice 3 is the correct answer. Plant cells have a cell wall, whereas animal cells do not. The cell wall is a protective outer covering made of cellulose. Both plant and animal cells contain a plasma membrane, mitochondria, a nucleus, and vacuoles.

4. Choice 4 is the correct answer. Prokaryotes are primitive cells that do not have membrane-bound nuclei. Their DNA floats around within the plasma membrane.

    (1) Although prokaryotes lack a nuclear membrane, they do have a plasma membrane.

    (2) Prokaryotes are primitive cells that *lack* organelles.

    (3) Although prokaryotes lack a nuclear membrane, they do have DNA.

5. Choice 4 is the correct answer. Vacuoles are sacs that store water, food, or pigments.

6. Choice 3 is the correct answer. Centrioles are paired organelles that are active during cell division. They migrate to opposite poles of the cell and aid in the separation of homologous chromosomes.

7. Choice 2 is the correct answer. Lysosomes are structures that carry digestive or "hydrolytic" enzymes.

CHAPTER 3 QUIZ

1. Choice 2 is the correct answer. The key phrase in this question is *complete oxidation*. The complete oxidation of glucose refers to aerobic respiration. It produces a net gain of 36 ATP. If you forgot that aerobic respiration produces 36 ATP, you could figure out the number of ATP produced in each step based on the equations given. Keep in mind that the first step (equation A) is known as *glycolysis* and requires the input of 2 molecules of ATP. Consequently the net gain is not 38, as it would appear to be if you simply added the end products of the two equations. This is the gross gain. The net gain is 36: 2 ATP from glycolysis and 34 ATP from aerobic respiration.

2. Choice 1 is the correct answer. *Respiratory end products* refer to the final products of cellular respiration. Because species A always produces ATP, CO_2, and H_2O, it undergoes aerobic respiration. Species B, on the other hand, produces ethyl alcohol. It therefore undergoes anaerobic respiration. Choice 1 is the only one that describes this situation.

3. Choice 1 is the correct answer. During aerobic respiration the energy-rich bonds within a glucose molecule are used to make ATP.

    (2) The enzymes for aerobic respiration are not produced by lysosomes. Lysosomes contain digestive enzymes that destroy worn-out organelles.

    (3) Lactic acid is produced within muscle cells during anaerobic respiration.

    (4) Alcohol is produced by yeast and bacteria during anaerobic respiration.

4. Choice 1 is the correct answer. During glycolysis, glucose is converted to pyruvic acid.

5. Choice 3 is the correct answer. Alcoholic fermentation, a form of anaerobic respiration, produces ethanol.

6. Choice 4 is the correct answer. Water is produced in the final stage of aerobic respiration.

7. Choice 2 is the correct answer. Lactic acid builds up in muscle cells when they carry out fermentation.

CHAPTER 4 QUIZ

1. Choice 4 is the correct answer. When photosynthetic protists are exposed to sunlight, the pigments absorb red and blue light. Light in the red and blue range activates chlorophyll in the light reactions of photosynthesis. The reason protists look green is that they reflect green light.

2. Choice 1 is the correct answer. Guard cells control the opening and closing of the stomates, allowing for gas exchange.

   (2) Thylakoids are flattened sacs that contain chlorophyll.

   (3) A grana is a stack of thylakoids.

   (4) The stroma is the area in a chloroplast in which the dark reactions of photosynthesis take place.

3. Choice 3 is the correct answer. Use the process of elimination. Because photosynthesis requires sunlight, we can eliminate answer choices 1 and 2. The starting materials for photosynthesis are CO_2 (for carbon fixation) and water (for photolysis), not O_2 (oxygen) and water.

4. Choice 1 is the correct answer. Photolysis—the splitting of water—occurs during the light reaction. This step is part of photochemical reactions.

5. Choice 2 is the correct answer. If we're going to trace the radioactive carbon in carbon dioxide, it would show up in the glucose molecule produced during carbon fixation. Carbon dioxide is the starting material used to make glucose.

6. Choice 1 is the correct answer. Electrons are passed down to electron carriers to produce ATP and NADPH. This occurs only during the photochemical reactions.

CHAPTER 5 QUIZ

1. Choice 4 is the correct answer. The chart in question provides a lot of information about the two plants. Notice that Plant B contains roots, stems, and leaves. This means it is a tracheophyte, not a bryophyte. You can therefore eliminate answer choices 1 and 3.

Plant A does not contain xylem and phloem (transport vessels). So eliminate answer choice 2.

2. Choice 3 is the correct answer. When a plant is placed in a horizontal position, the cells in the stem grow unequally because the distribution of auxin influences plant growth. Auxin is a plant hormone that serves many functions.

    (1) Auxin does not cause stomates to close.

    (2) The distribution of auxin doesn't cause leaves to develop.

    (4) Auxin stimulates cell growth.

3. Choice 4 is the correct answer. The cotyledon provides food for the germinating plant.

    (1) The epicotyl forms the upper portion of the plant.

    (2) The hypocotyl forms the lower portion of the plant.

    (3) The fruit protects the ovary from drying out.

4. Choice 2 is the correct answer. The stamen, the male part of the flower, consists of the anther (structure B) and filament (structure H).

    (1) Structure A is the stigma, and structure F is the stem of the flower.

    (3) Structure C is the petal, and structure D is the sepal.

    (4) Structure E is the ovary, and structure G is the ovule. They are both part of the female part of the flower—the pistil.

5. Choice 1 is the correct answer. During pollination, pollen is transferred from the anther (structure B) to the stigma (structure A).

    (2) Structure C is the petal. It serves to attract insects. Structure D is the sepal. It protects the pistil and stamen.

    (3) Structure G is the ovule, the site of egg production.

    (4) Structure F is the stem that supports the flower, and H is the filament.

6. Choice 1 is the correct answer. Lenticels are small pores on woody stems that facilitate gas exchange.

    (2) Cambium, also known as *lateral meristem*, is the region of actively dividing cells that gives girth to the plant.

(3) Xylem is the vascular tissue that carries water.

(4) Phloem is the vascular tissue that carries food and minerals.

7. Choice 1 is the correct answer. Plant growth occurs in regions known as *meristems*—the plant tissues containing actively dividing cells. This tissue is found in the tips of roots, stems, and leaves.

(2) Lenticels are small pores in woody stems that allow for gas exchange.

(3) The palisade layer is the part of the leaf that contains lots of chloroplasts.

(4) Vascular tissues include xylems and phloems: They conduct materials throughout the plant.

CHAPTER 6 QUIZ

1. Choice 4 is the correct answer. This question tests your ability to identify the correct pathway of carbon dioxide as it passes *out* of the respiratory system. Use the process of elimination. Carbon dioxide must first pass from the alveoli (in the lungs) to the bronchioles. You can therefore eliminate answer choices 1, 2, and 3.

2. Choice 4 is the correct answer. Cerebral palsy is a motor disorder that results in a loss of muscle control or "motor functions."

3. Choice 2 is the correct answer. A stroke occurs when the blood vessels fail to deliver oxygen-rich blood to the brain due to a blockage.

4. Choice 3 is the correct answer. Meningitis is a disease in which the tissues covering the brain and spinal cord (the meninges) are infected and inflamed.

5. Choice 1 is the correct answer. Both short-tailed shrews and ruby-throated hummingbirds have high metabolic rates. Animals with high metabolic rates burn energy much more rapidly than do those with lower metabolic rates.

(2) Animals with high metabolic rates need lots of food.

(3) The number of predators has nothing to do with metabolic rates.

(4) Metabolic rates have no relation to patterns of hibernation.

6. Choice 3 is the correct answer. To maintain a stable internal environment, animals must do several things: remove waste products, transport compounds throughout their bodies, and regulate bodily activities. Reproduction does not help maintain a stable internal environment.

7. Choice 3 is the correct answer. A protist belongs to the kingdom Protista. More specifically, this organism is a *Paramecium*. Structure X is the oral groove that is involved in the process of ingestion—the taking in of food.

   (1) *Extracellular digestion* refers to the breaking down of food *outside* the cell.

   (2) *Enzymatic hydrolysis* refers to the addition of water to break up a polymer.

   (4) *Transpiration* refers to the evaporation of water from leaves.

8. Choice 2 is the correct answer. An amoeba is a one-celled organism. It gets rid of wastes such as ammonia and carbon dioxide via diffusion across its cell membrane.

   (1) Ammonia and carbon dioxide are not absorbed, they are excreted.

   (3) *Respiratory gas exchange* refers to the intake of oxygen and the excretion of carbon dioxide.

   (4) *Egestion* refers to the elimination of undigested food material.

9. Choice 4 is the correct answer. Tendons are connective tissues that connect muscles to bone.

   (1) Cartilage is a flexible connective tissue found between bones. It helps protect the bones from damage.

   (2) Ligaments connect bones to bones.

   (3) Voluntary (skeletal) muscles are tissues that provide a wide range of motion.

10. Choice 1 is the correct answer. Let's review structures A through D. Structure A is a group of blood cells; structure B is a neuron; structure C is a portion of tissue; and structure D is a portion of a muscle. A neuron (B) can cause a muscle cell (D) to contract.

    (2) Blood cells (A) are not produced by muscle cells (D).

(3) Tissue (C) does not transport oxygen to blood cells (A).

(4) Neurons (B) are not used to repair tissue (C).

11. Choice 3 is the correct answer. These processes are examples of synthesis. *Synthesis* refers to the making of complex compounds from simpler ones.

   (1) *Regulation* refers to how organisms respond to the environment.

   (2) *Respiration* refers to how organisms take in oxygen and get rid of wastes such as carbon dioxide.

   (4) *Excretion* refers to how organisms get rid of wastes.

12. Choice 4 is the correct answer. A hydra, which is a simple animal, takes in oxygen from the surrounding medium through its external surfaces via diffusion. An earthworm takes in oxygen across its moist skin by diffusion.

   (1) They do not absorb oxygen through a system of tubes.

   (2) Neither the hydra nor the earthworm has cilia.

   (3) Only earthworms use capillaries to transport oxygen throughout the body. A hydra absorbs oxygen directly across its cell membranes.

13. Choice 2 is the correct answer. Keep in mind that all insects, including grasshoppers, have *open* circulatory systems and tracheal tubes.

   (1) Grasshoppers do not have alveoli. Alveoli are structures found in vertebrate circulatory systems.

   (3) Earthworms, not grasshoppers, absorb oxygen via their moist skin.

   (4) The life function of transport in grasshoppers involves a dry external body surface, but doesn't involve hemoglobin.

14. Choice 3 is the correct answer. The key phrase in this question is *waste product*. During dehydration synthesis, water is removed.

   (1) The waste product in respiration is carbon dioxide, not oxygen.

   (2) During protein synthesis, amino acids are linked together, not given off as a waste product.

   (4) During hydrolysis water is used to break up a complex organic compound.

15. Choice 3 is the correct answer. The diagram shows a plant bending toward sunlight. This occurs because of plant hormones known as *auxins*.

    (1) Acetylcholine is a neurotransmitter found in the terminal branches of neurons.

    (2) Minerals are substances absorbed by the roots of plants.

    (4) Vascular tissues have no effect on the growth response of plants.

16. Choice 1 is the correct answer. The human heart consists of four chambers. The two top chambers are called *atria* and the two bottom chambers are called *ventricles*. The structure labeled X is therefore a ventricle.

    (2) The top chambers in the heart are called *atria*.

    (3) Valves separate the atria from the ventricles.

    (4) The aorta is the artery that carries blood away from the heart toward the body.

17. Choice 2 is the correct answer. A hawk uses its eyes to find food. The eyes therefore serve as receptors: They pick up information from the environment.

    (1) Effectors (such as muscles) respond to a nerve impulse.

    (3) Stimuli are agents that produce responses.

    (4) Neurotransmitters are chemical substances released by a neuron.

18. Choice 4 is the correct answer. According to the question, methyl cellulose slows down the movement of paramecia. This chemical must somehow have an effect on the cilia that paramecia use for locomotion.

    (1) Pseudopodia are structures used by amoeba for locomotion.

    (2) The flagella is the structure used by euglena for locomotion.

    (3) Setae are the short bristles used by the earthworm for locomotion.

19. Choice 4 is the correct answer. Don't be intimidated by the phrase *ciliated mucous membranes. Ciliated* simply refers to our old friends cilia. As you already know, there are cilia in the respiratory tract that help keep foreign particles out of the body (i.e., "filter" the air).

(1) Gas exchange occurs at the alveoli.

(2) Rings of cartilage within the trachea help keep the respiratory tract open.

(3) Involuntary smooth muscles are found throughout the respiratory tract. They control the volume of air that enters the body.

20. Choice 2 is the correct answer. The epiglottis is a flap of skin that keeps food from entering the trachea.

(1) The diaphragm is a muscle that facilitates breathing.

(3) Villi are finger-like projections found in the small intestine.

(4) Ribs are bones that are part of the chest cavity.

21. Choice 1 is the correct answer. In humans, the function of the nephrons (excretory organs) and alveoli (respiratory organs) are similar to nephridia (excretory organs) and the skin (respiratory organ) of the earthworm.

(2) The Malpighian tubules are excretory organs found in grasshoppers, while muscles are used for locomotion.

(3) In hydras, the nerve nets are made up of neurons, and the gastrovascular cavities serve both as digestive and circulatory systems.

(4) Cilia and pseudopodia are structures used for locomotion in protozoans.

22. Choice 3 is the correct answer. The cerebrum, the largest part of the brain, controls memory and reasoning.

(1) The spinal cord serves as the center of reflex.

(2) The cerebellum maintains muscle coordination.

(4) The medulla controls involuntary actions such as the heart rate.

CHAPTER 7 QUIZ

1. Choice 3 is the correct answer. The correct sequence of mitosis is prophase, metaphase, anaphase, and telophase. During prophase (C), the centrioles move to opposite ends of the cell. During metaphase (B), the chromosomes line up in the middle of the cell. During anaphase (D), the chromosomes separate. During telophase (A), two daughter cells are finally formed.

2. Choice 2 is the correct answer. In budding, the nucleus divides evenly, but the cytoplasm divides unequally. You can therefore eliminate answer choices 3 and 4.

   (1) In both mitosis and binary fission, the nucleus and cytoplasm divide equally.

3. Choice 2 is the correct answer. *Rhizopus*, a bread mold, reproduces asexually by sporulation. Spores are tiny airborne cells released from the parent organism.

   (1) Budding is a type of asexual reproduction in which a bud sprouts from the parent cell and eventually separates as a complete organism.

   (3) Regeneration is the growing back of missing body parts.

   (4) Fission (also known as *binary fission*) is a form of asexual reproduction that is common in bacteria.

4. Choice 4 is the correct answer. Vegetative propagation is a method used by some plants to reproduce *asexually*. The offspring are therefore identical to the parent.

   (1) Vegetation propagation has nothing to do with dominant or recessive characteristics.

   (2) These plants have the diploid number of chromosomes, just like their parents.

   (3) After double fertilization, the embryo obtains nourishment from the seed.

5. Choice 2 is the correct answer. The centromere is the round structure that holds the chromatids together.

   (1) A polar body is a tiny, nonfunctioning cell that forms during oogenesis. It contains almost no cytoplasm.

   (3) Centrioles are paired structures that are involved in cell division.

   (4) A Golgi body is a organelle that packages and distributes materials destined to be sent outside of the cell.

6. Choice 3 is the correct answer. The yolk of a bird is an extraembryonic sac that provides food for the animal.

   (1) The chorion functions as a moist respiratory membrane.

   (2) The allantois functions as the storage site for wastes.

(4) The amnion provides a fluid environment that protects the embryo.

7. Choice 4 is the correct answer. When two eggs are fertilized at the same time by two separate sperm cells, fraternal twins are produced.

  (1) and (2) Fertilization of two eggs at the same time doesn't normally produce chromosome abnormalities or gene mutations.

  (3) When one egg is fertilized and splits into two viable halves, identical twins are produced.

8. Choice 3 is the correct answer. Crossing-over is the exchange of segments of the chromosomes during meiosis. This process leads to the rearrangement of chromosomal segments and genetic variability.

  (1) Crossing-over does not produce offspring that are identical to the parents.

  (2) Chromosomes thicken during prophase and align themselves during metaphase in both mitosis and meiosis.

  (4) During meiosis, chromatids do not fail to sort independently.

9. Choice 2 is the correct answer. In the top figure, the haploid sperm and the haploid egg unite to form a normal diploid zygote. In the bottom figure, the haploid sperm unites with a *diploid* egg, which produces an abnormal zygote. This occurred because the chromosomes in the egg did not separate properly.

  (1) *Polyploidy* refers to an extra set of chromosomes in an organism.

  (3) *Chromosome breakage* refers to a mutation in the chromosomes.

  (4) Gene linkage is the tendency of two or more genes to segregate together during meiosis.

10. Choice 4 is the correct answer. Fertilization occurs within female reproductive organs: the ovary in tracheophytes and the fallopian tube in mammals.

  (1) The offspring in both tracheophytes and mammals are diploid, not monoploid.

  (2) Fertilization does not occur in a watery environment for these organisms. Fertilization occurs *internally* in both tracheophytes and mammals.

  (3) Yolk production does not occur in tracheophytes or mammals.

11. Choice 1 is the correct answer. *Gametogenesis* refers to the formation of gametes. During this process, the diploid number of chromosomes is reduced to the haploid or monoploid number. This prevents the chromosome number from increasing over time.

   (2) *Cleavage* is the rapid division of a zygote after fertilization.

   (3) *Nondisjunction* is the unequal separation of the chromosomes during meiosis.

   (4) *Fertilization* is the union of an egg and sperm to form a zygote.

12. Choice 2 is the correct answer. The rabbit embryo develops in the uterus of the mother.

   (1) In many vertebrates, the placenta provides nourishment for the embryo.

   (3) In chick embryos, the yolk sac is an extraembryonic membrane that provides food for the embryo.

   (4) In mammals, the umbilical cord connects the fetus to the placenta.

13. Choice 3 is the correct answer. Aquatic animals, such as fish, must produce large numbers of eggs to ensure fertilization.

   (1) Mammals produces fewer eggs, because fertilization occurs internally, not externally.

   (2) and (4) Molds and yeasts don't produce eggs.

CHAPTER 8 QUIZ

1. Choice 4 is the correct answer. Sex-linked traits, such as hemophilia and color blindness, are controlled by genes on the X chromosome.

   (1) and (2) A trait controlled by genes found on an X chromosome is not necessarily dominant or recessive.

   (3) *Codominance* refers to the ability of two alleles to express themselves equally in an organism.

2. Choice 2 is the correct answer. When a heterozygous raccoon crosses with a homozygous recessive raccoon, the percentage of offspring with the dark face mask will be 50%. When in doubt, do a test cross using a Punnett square. Such a cross (Dd × dd) will give us offspring that are 50% Dd and 50% dd.

3. Choice 3 is the correct answer. Mendel, the father of genetics, developed his basic principles of heredity by studying pea plants.

   (1) Mendel didn't know about chromosomes and genes.

   (2) Mendel did not work with *Drosophila* (fruit flies).

   (4) An ultracentrifuge is an instrument used to spin organelles and separate them according to their mass.

4. Choice 3 is the correct answer. Let's take a look at a test cross with two heterozygous red-feathered owls. $Rr \times Rr = RR, Rr, Rr,$ and rr. Three of four of the offspring are red.

5. Choice 3 is the correct answer. If the couple produced two color-blind sons, the mother must be a carrier. The father is therefore normal, and the mother is a carrier of this gene on one of her X chromosomes. Make a Punnett square to verify your results:

	X^N	X^n
X^N	$X^N X^N$	$X^N X^n$
Y	$X^N Y$	$X^n Y$

Given the information contained in the question, the parental genotypes must be $X^N Y$ and $X^N X^n$.

CHAPTER 9 QUIZ

1. Choice 4 is the correct answer. This question tests your knowledge of DNA replication. We know that during DNA replication the double-stranded molecule unwinds (3), the hydrogen bonds are then broken (2), and the nitrogenous base pairs are linked together (1). Ribosomes are not synthesized during DNA replication.

2. Choice 3 is the correct answer. During the first stage of protein synthesis, DNA serves as a template for messenger RNA.

   (1) Amino acids are the building blocks of proteins.

   (2) and (4) Carbohydrates are organic molecules that serve as fuel for the cell. Lipids are complex organic molecules that are composed of glycerol and three fatty acids. Neither of these classes of molecules uses DNA as a template.

3. Choice 2 is the correct answer. DNA contains the "directions" for protein synthesis. Because enzymes are proteins, their manufacture is directed by the DNA as well. Therefore, we could say that DNA determines which enzymes are produced by the cell.

   (1) ATP provides energy for the cell's activities.

   (3) DNA does not participate in the excretion of wastes.

   (4) DNA does not provide nucleotides for the making of the cell membrane. The cell membrane is composed of lipids and proteins.

4. Choice 1 is the correct answer. DNA contains a *deoxy*ribose and not a ribose sugar. You can therefore eliminate answer choices (3) and (4). DNA does not contain the nitrogenous base uracil. Uracil is found only in RNA. This eliminates answer choice 2. The correct answer is therefore (1).

5. Choice 3 is the correct answer. Uracil is found in RNA but not in DNA.

   (1), (2), and (4) Phosphorus, adenine, and thymine are found in both DNA and RNA.

6. Choice 2 is the correct answer. The sequence always begins with DNA and ends with the expression of the trait. The only answer choice that begins with DNA is answer choice 2.

7. Choice 1 is the correct answer. Radioactive substances can damage the DNA, which can lead to mutations.

   (2), (3), and (4) A lack of vitamins, long exposure to humid climates, or a short exposure to freezing temperatures do not increase the incidence of mutation.

CHAPTER 10 QUIZ

1. Choice 1 is the correct answer. According to the heterotroph hypothesis, aerobes did not appear until oxygen was present in the atmosphere. Oxygen gas was produced by autotrophs.

    (2) Ammonia was present in the atmosphere during primitive earth.

    (3) and (4) Carbon dioxide was not part of the primitive atmosphere.

2. Choice 4 is the correct answer. If such an abrupt change did in fact cause the extinction of the dinosaurs, it would provide proof for the theory of punctuated equilibrium.

    (1) The theory of gradualism assumes that evolutionary change is gradual and continuous.

    (2) Competition occurs when different species in an area must compete for limited resources.

    (3) The heterotroph hypothesis explains the origin of life and the evolution of the earth's atmosphere.

3. Choice 3 is the correct answer. Increased knowledge of heredity has supported Darwin's theory of evolution by natural selection.

    (1) Lamarck's theory of evolution was dismissed long before the increase in our knowledge of heredity.

    (2) Our knowledge of heredity did not dismiss all previous evolutionary theories: Darwin's elegant theory did.

    (4) Our knowledge of heredity does not disagree with Mendel's discoveries: It merely complements and clarifies them.

4. Choice 4 is the correct answer. The phrase that best defines evolution is *a process of change in organisms over time.*

    (1) Evolution does not refer to the adaptation of a single organism to its environment. It refers to changes in a population over time.

    (2) Evolution is not the sudden replacement of one community by another.

    (3) New species can develop from geographic and reproductive isolation. However, this doesn't necessarily *define* evolution. Rather, such an occurrence *leads* to evolution.

5. Choice 3 is the correct answer. Lamarck believed that traits are *acquired*. The classic example is that giraffes had long necks because they used them to reach for acacia leaves. The other answer choices do not describe Lamarck's theory of evolution.

6. Choice 4 is the correct answer. This statement best describes the concept of the survival of the fittest. Organisms with favorable characteristics are able to successfully reproduce and pass on these traits to their offspring.

    (1) The concept of overproduction is the first part of Darwin's theory of natural selection. Each species produces more offspring than can survive.

    (2) The concept of use and disuse is part of Lamarck's theory of evolution.

    (3) Lamarck believed that certain characteristics were acquired.

7. Choice 2 is the correct answer. One prerequisite for natural selection is variation in the population. That is, organisms possess different traits. Some of these traits enable organisms to survive better than others.

    (1) Members of a population are not equally able to survive environmental changes.

    (3) This is not how natural selection operates.

    (4) Members cannot adapt to environmental changes: They already possess the traits that either allow them to survive or do not.

8. Choice 4 is the correct answer. Punctuated equilibrium says that evolution occurs due to stresses imposed by abrupt changes in the environment. These periods of relatively rapid change are preceded by long periods of little or no evolutionary change.

    (1) Other scientists believe that new species arise because of gradual change. This is known as *gradualism*.

    (2) Natural selection is the engine of Darwin's theory of evolution.

    (3) Geographic isolation is a physical factor that decreases interbreeding between different populations or species.

CHAPTER 11 QUIZ

1. Choice 2 is the correct answer. A fungus belongs to the kingdom Fungi. Fungi are classified as heterotrophs, because they don't make their own food. They absorb nutrients directly through their cell walls and membranes.

    (1) Fungi are organisms that grow either by budding or sporulation.

    (3) Fungi are heterotrophs; they can't make their own food. Only autotrophs are capable of manufacturing their own food.

    (4) Fungi do not convert light energy to chemical energy. Only autotrophs convert energy from the sun into chemical energy in the form of glucose.

2. Choice 1 is the correct answer. Use the process of elimination. The binomial name for humans is *Homo sapiens*. *Homo* (3) is the genus, and *sapiens* is the species. The most specific term for humans is therefore *sapiens*.

    (2) Although humans belong to the animal kingdom, it is not the most specific term listed.

    (4) Humans are not fungi; they're animals.

3. Choice 2 is the correct answer. The paramecium, amoeba, and euglena belong to the kingdom Protista. They are all unicellular organisms.

    (1) Yeast and mushrooms are fungi, whereas maple trees are plants.

    (3) Bacteria are monerans, whereas amoeba and euglena are protists.

    (4) Bacteria are monerans, whereas mosses and geraniums are plants.

4. Choice 2 is the correct answer. Blue-green algae, plants, and algae are autotrophs: They make their own food.

    (1) These organisms are not heterotrophs.

    (3) None of these organisms belongs to the animal kingdom.

    (4) Blue-green algae belong to the kingdom Monera. Plants belong to the kingdom Plantae. Algae belong to the kingdom Protista.

5. Choice 3 is the correct answer. The term that includes all of the other terms is *kingdom*. It is the biggest and most numerous group. The order of classification from fewest to most characteristics in common is kingdom, phylum, class, order, family, genus, and species.

6. Choice 1 is the correct answer. The characteristics listed are found among organisms that belong to the kingdom Protista. Protists are one-celled organisms that are eukaryotic and heterotrophic.

   (2) The unknown organism can't be a moneran because it contains a nucleus.

   (3) The unknown organism can't be a plant because it is heterotrophic, not autotrophic.

   (4) The unknown organism can't be an animal because it is unicellular.

CHAPTER 12 QUIZ

1. Choice 2 is the correct answer. An ecosystem consists of both abiotic (nonliving) factors and biotic (living) factors.

   (1) and (4) These answer choices include only biotic factors.

   (3) This answer choice includes only abiotic factors.

2. Choice 4 is the correct answer. Plants are unable to use nitrogen from the atmosphere. Plants have a mutualistic relationship with nitrogen-fixing bacteria to convert nitrogen to nitrates to make plant proteins. This relationship is part of the nitrogen cycle.

   (1), (2), and (3) Glucose, starch, and lipids do not contain nitrogen.

3. Choice 2 is the correct answer. This example describes the relationship between a flea and a mouse. The flea benefits by living in the fur of a mouse. The mouse, on the other hand, is harmed by the flea. This type of relationship is called *parasitism*.

   (1) Commensalism occurs when one organism benefits, while the other is unaffected.

   (3) Saprophytism refers to an organism that lives off dead organisms.

   (4) Mutualism occurs when both organisms benefit from the relationship.

4. Choice 2 is the correct answer. In a food web, the organisms that contain the greatest amount of available energy are producers—organisms that make their own food. Grasses and shrubs are the only producers in the food web.

(1) Rabbits and deer are primary consumers: They eat grasses and shrubs.

(3) Lice are tertiary consumers, because they eat hawks (secondary consumers).

(4) Hawks are secondary consumers, because they eat seed-eating birds (primary consumers).

5. Choice 2 is the correct answer. Organisms that eat producers are primary consumers. They include rabbits, insects, seed-eating birds, rats, and deer. Frogs, snakes, spiders, and coyotes are secondary and tertiary consumers.

6. Choice 2 is the correct answer. The distribution of energy in a community can be pictured as a pyramid, with the first level (producers) at the base and the last level (consumers) at the top. Energy decreases as you move up the pyramid. Consequently, there is more energy at the producer level than at the consumer level.

(1) There is *less* energy at the consumer level than at the producer level.

(3) There is *less* energy at the secondary consumer level than at the primary consumer level.

(4) Decomposers are not part of the energy pyramid. They are usually pictured below the pyramid because they consume dead organic matter.

CHAPTER 13 QUIZ

1. Choice 1 is the correct answer. Benedict's (Fehling's) solution is an indicator that tests for simple sugar. Lugol's iodine is an indicator that tests for the presence of starch.

(2), (3), and (4) Bromthymol blue solution tests for the presence of carbon dioxide, and pH paper measures the acidity of a substance.

2. Choice 1 is the correct answer. The method used to determine whether a child has Down syndrome is amniocentesis. Amniocente-

sis is a technique in which cells cast off by the growing fetus are gathered by inserting a needle into the amniotic cavity of the mother.

(2) Cloning is the production of genetically identical cells or organisms.

(3) Microdissection is a tool used to dissect such tiny structures as sperm and egg cells.

(4) Urinalysis is a procedure used to detect abnormal substances in the urine.

3. Choice 2 is the correct answer. The diagram shows a sample of crushed onion cells that was centrifuged (i.e., spun so that the cell components separated by mass). This question tests your ability to recognize that protein synthesis occurs in the ribosomes. Ribosomes are found in level 2.

(1) Cell fluids are found in the cytoplasm.

(3) Mitochondria are the sites of ATP production.

(4) The nucleus controls the activities of the cell.

4. Choice 3 is the correct answer. You need to pick a letter that shows a difference when inverted and reversed. *F* is the only letter that shows a difference for both.

5. Choice 3 is the correct answer. Staining enables scientists to identify organelles by providing a contrast between the cell and its structures.

(1), (2), and (4) These technologies were either nonexistent or not sufficiently developed in the 1800s to be of any use for the examination of a cell.

15

Practice Exams

EXAM ONE

PART I: Answer all 59 questions in this part. [65]

Directions (1–59): For *each* statement or question, select the word or expression that, of those given, best completes the statement or answers the question. Record your answer on the separate answer sheet provided.

---

1   In plants, glucose is converted to cellulose, and in human muscle cells, glucose is converted to glycogen. These processes are examples of which life activity?
   1   regulation   3   synthesis
   2   respiration   4   excretion

2   Which organelles outside the cell nucleus contain genetic material?
   1   lysosomes and cell walls
   2   chloroplasts and mitochondria
   3   endoplasmic reticula and cell membranes
   4   vacuoles and Golgi complex

3   The diagrams below represent unicellular organisms. In the past, they were difficult to classify as either plants or animals.

 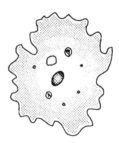

Currently, these organisms are classified as
   1   coelenterates   3   tracheophytes
   2   annelids   4   protists

4   Which technique enabled scientists in the 1800's to identify cell organelles?
   1   electron microscopy   3   staining
   2   ultracentrifugation   4   dissection

5   Which substance is an organic compound?
   1   water   3   maltase
   2   glucose   4   insulin

6 Which chemical formula represents a carbohydrate?
 (1) CH_4 (3) $C_{12}H_{22}O_{11}$
 (2) $C_3H_7O_2N$ (4) CO_2

7 The equation below summarizes the process that produces the flashing light of a firefly. The molecule luciferin is broken down, and energy is released in the form of heat and light.

$$\text{luciferen} \xrightarrow[\text{luciferase}]{\text{ATP}} \text{heat} + \text{light}$$

 In this process, luciferase functions as
 1 a reactant
 2 a substrate
 3 an inorganic catalyst
 4 an enzyme

8 Which statement best describes the process of digestion in fungi and bacteria?
 1 It occurs as a result of the dehydration synthesis of foods within these organisms.
 2 It results in the production of starch and protein molecules.
 3 It occurs as a result of the enzymatic hydrolysis of foods outside these organisms.
 4 It occurs within a highly specialized digestive system.

9 If a grasshopper's gastric caeca stopped functioning, which activity would be affected first?
 1 chemical breakdown of food in the digestive tube
 2 transmission of impulses by the nerve cord
 3 taking in of air by the spiracles
 4 release of hormones into the transport system

10 An iodine test of a tomato plant leaf revealed that starch was present at 5:00 p.m. on a sunny afternoon in July. When a similar leaf from the same tomato plant was tested with iodine at 6:00 a.m. the next morning, the test indicated that less starch was present in this leaf than in the leaf tested the day before. This reduction in starch content occurred because starch was
 1 changed into cellulose
 2 transported out of the leaves through the stomates
 3 conducted downward toward the roots through the vessels
 4 digested into simple sugars

11 The diagram below illustrates the transport of oxygen and carbon dioxide.

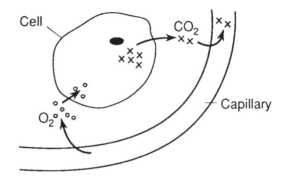

In which organisms does this type of transport occur?
1   hydra and ameba
2   human and frog
3   grasshopper and chicken
4   paramecium and earthworm

12 Which process requires cellular energy?
    1   diffusion   3   active transport
    2   passive transport   4   osmosis

13 The diagram below represents a cross section of a leaf.

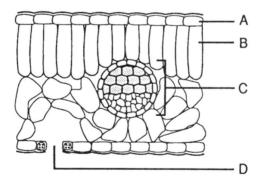

Food manufactured in the leaf is conducted to the rest of the plant by structure
(1) A   (3) C
(2) B   (4) D

14 What is a direct result of aerobic respiration?
1 The potential energy of glucose is transferred to ATP molecules.
2 The enzymes for anaerobic respiration are produced and stored in lysosomes.
3 Lactic acid is produced in muscle tissue.
4 Alcohol is produced by yeast and bacteria.

15 Hemoglobin is found in the blood of humans and earthworms, but not in the blood of grasshoppers. Which conclusion is best supported by this statement?
1 The human and the earthworm have lungs, but the grasshopper does not have lungs.
2 The human and the earthworm transport far more oxygen with their blood than the grasshopper transports with its blood.
3 The human and the earthworm have open circulatory systems, but the grasshopper has a closed circulatory system.
4 The human and the earthworm are adapted for anaerobic respiration, but the grasshopper is adapted for aerobic respiration.

16 In a branch of a cherry tree, gases are exchanged between the environment and the cells through
1 lenticels   3 xylem
2 cambium   4 phloem

17 Some metabolic wastes produced by plant cells are
1 used by cells for the synthesis of chitin
2 used by centrioles to produce spindle fibers
3 stored by nuclei for DNA replication
4 stored in vacuoles, where they do not harm the cell

18 Nitrogenous wastes such as ammonia, urea, and uric acid all result from
1 dehydration synthesis
2 protein metabolism
3 aerobic respiration
4 carbohydrate metabolism

19 The growth of roots on plant cuttings may be stimulated by
1 a decrease in enzymes
2 the use of auxins
3 the use of endocrine secretions
4 a decrease in soil minerals

20 In humans, certain glands produce the chemicals that are distributed by the circulatory system and influence the various target organs. These glands are classified as
1 intestinal glands   3 gastric glands
2 salivary glands   4 endocrine glands

21 A change in environment that initiates the transmission of an electrochemical charge along a neuron is known as
1 a reflex   3 an impulse
2 a response   4 a stimulus

22 Which specialized structures for locomotion are correctly paired with the organism that possesses those structures?
1 setae—earthworm
2 chitinous appendages—paramecium
3 flagella—grasshopper
4 pseudopods—human

23 Which process is illustrated in the diagrams below?

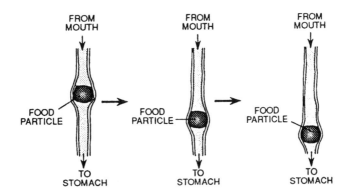

1 circulation   3 peristalsis
2 absorption   4 ingestion

24 Which statement best describes arteries?
1 They have thick walls and transport blood away from the heart.
2 They have thick walls and transport blood to the heart.
3 They have thin walls and transport blood away from the heart.
4 They have thin walls and transport blood toward the heart.

25 To receive necessary nutrients and eliminate wastes, all
    human body cells must be
    1   surrounded by cilia
    2   endocrine in nature
    3   able to carry on phagocytosis
    4   surrounded by a transport medium

26 The nephron is the structural unit of the human
    1   lung   3   kidney
    2   liver   4   intestine

27 In the human respiratory system, bronchioles directly connect
    the
    1   trachea and pharynx
    2   bronchi and alveoli
    3   nasal cavity and trachea
    4   epiglottis and larynx

28 The connective tissue that cushions the vertebrae and pro-
    vides flexibility to joints is known as
    1   tendon   3   cartilage
    2   muscle   4   bone

29 The diagrams below represent a cell process.

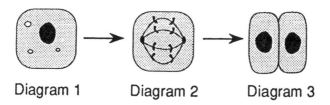

Diagram 1   Diagram 2   Diagram 3

    If the cell in diagram 1 contains 4 chromosomes, what is the
    total number of chromosomes in each cell in diagram 3?
    (1) 8   (3) 16
    (2) 2   (4) 4

30 The chromatids of a double-stranded chromosome are held
    together at a region known as the
    1   polar body   3   centriole
    2   centromere   4   Golgi complex

31 Which statement is true regarding plants produced by vegetative propagation?
1 They normally exhibit only dominant characteristics.
2 They normally have the monoploid number of chromosomes.
3 They normally obtain most of their nourishment from the seed.
4 They are normally genetically identical to the parent.

32 After gametogenesis takes place, which process restores the diploid chromosome number of the species for the next generation?
1 oogenesis   3 fertilization
2 mitosis   4 meiosis

33 In the diagram below, which number indicates a structure that transmits impulses from a receptor to an interneuron?

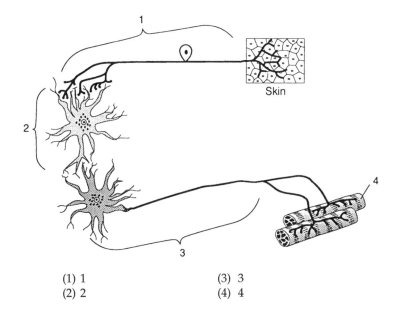

Skin

(1) 1   (3) 3
(2) 2   (4) 4

34 In many aquatic vertebrates, reproduction involves external fertilization. What is a characteristic of this type of fertilization?
1 Gametes fuse outside the body of the female.
2 Gametes fuse in the moist reproductive tract of the female.
3 Offspring produced have twice as many chromosomes as each of the parents.
4 Offspring produced have only half the number of chromosomes as each of the parents.

35 In a rabbit, the embryo normally develops within the
    1 placenta   3 yolk sac
    2 uterus   4 umbilical cord

36 The pistil of the flower includes the
    1 stigma, anther, and filament
    2 stamen, stigma, and anther
    3 stigma, style, and ovary
    4 petals, sepals, and pollen grains

37 In a plant, which structure enables sperm nuclei to reach the
    ovule?
    1 stigma   3 stamen
    2 pollen tube   4 seed coat

38 In screech owls, red feathers are dominant over gray feathers.
    If two heterozygous red-feathered owls mated, what percent-
    age of their offspring would be expected to have red feathers?
    (1) 25%   (3) 75%
    (2) 50%   (4) 100%

39 Two genes for two different traits located on the same chro-
    mosome are said to be
    1 homozygous
    2 independently assorted
    3 mutagenic agents
    4 linked

40 Diagram *A* below illustrates the chromosomes of a normal
    female insect. Diagram *B* illustrates the chromosomes found
    in an abnormal female insect of the same species.

Diagram A   ## Diagram B

The chromosomal alteration in diagram *B* most likely
resulted from
    1 codominance   3 sex linkage
    2 crossing-over   4 nondisjunction

41 Identical twins were separated at birth and raised by different families. The best explanation for any differences between the twins in height, weight, and IQ scores is that the genes regulating these traits were
1 independently assorted
2 codominant
3 linked
4 environmentally influenced

42 In humans, normal color vision (N) is dominant over color blindness (n). A man and a woman with normal color vision produced two colorblind sons and two daughters with normal color vision. The parental genotypes must be
(1) $X^N Y$ and $X^N X^N$ (3) $X^N Y$ and $X^N X^n$
(2) $X^n Y$ and $X^N X^N$ (4) $X^n Y$ and $X^n X^n$

43 If the pattern of inheritance for a trait is complete dominance, then an organism heterozygous for the trait would normally express
1 the recessive trait, only
2 the dominant trait, only
3 a blend of the recessive and dominant traits
4 a phenotype unlike that of either parent

44 Although genetic mutations may occur spontaneously in organisms, the incidence of such mutations may be increased by
1 radioactive substances in the environment
2 lack of vitamins in the diet
3 a long exposure to humid climates
4 a short exposure to freezing climates

45 In addition to a phosphate group, a DNA nucleotide could contain
1 thymine and deoxyribose
2 uracil and deoxyribose
3 thymine and ribose
4 uracil and ribose

46 Which phrase best defines evolution?
1 an adaptation of an organism to its environment
2 a sudden replacement of one community by another
3 a geographic or reproductive isolation of organisms
4 a process of change in organisms over a period of time

47 Which statement would most likely be in agreement with
    Lamarck's theory of evolution?
    1 Black moths have evolved in an area because they were
       better adapted to the environment and have high rates of
       survival and reproduction.
    2 Geographic barriers may lead to reproductive isolation
       and the production of new species.
    3 Giraffes have long necks because their ancestors stretched
       their necks reaching for food, and this trait was passed on
       to their offspring.
    4 Most variations in animals and plants are due to random
       chromosomal and gene mutation.

48 Organisms with favorable variations reproduce more success-
    fully than organisms with less favorable variations. This state-
    ment best describes the concept of
    1 overproduction
    2 use and disuse
    3 inheritance of acquired characteristics
    4 survival of the fittest

49 How does natural selection operate to cause change in a
    population?
    1 The members of the population are equally able to survive
       any environmental change.
    2 The members of the population differ so that only some
       survive when the environment changes.
    3 The members of the population do not adapt to environ-
       mental changes.
    4 All the members of the population adapt to environmental
       changes.

50 Evolution is often represented as a tree similar to the one shown in the diagram below.

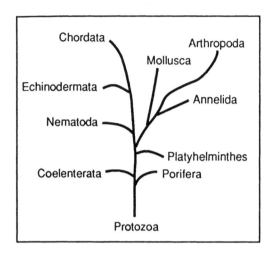

This diagram suggests that
1 different groups of organisms may have similar characteristics because of common ancestry
2 because of biochemical differences, no two groups of organisms could have a common ancestor
3 evolution is a predictable event that happens every few years, adding new groups of organisms to the tree
4 only the best adapted organisms will survive from generation to generation

51 The concept that evolution is the result of long periods of stability interrupted by geologically brief periods of significant change is known as
1 gradualism
2 natural selection
3 geographic isolation
4 punctuated equilibrium

52 According to the heterotroph hypothesis, which gas given off by autotrophic activity made the evolution of aerobes possible?
1 oxygen   3 carbon dioxide
2 hydrogen   4 nitrogen

53 All the red foxes inhabiting a given forest constitute a
1 population   3 biome
2 community   4 biosphere

54 The diagram below shows living and nonliving factors and
the interaction between them.

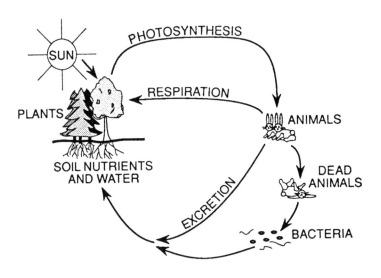

1 a species   3 a community
2 a population   4 an ecosystem

55 Which statement best describes an energy period?
1 There is more energy at the consumer level than at the
producer level.
2 There is more energy at the producer level than at the consumer level.
3 There is more energy at the secondary-consumer level
than at the primary-consumer level.
4 There is more energy at the decomposer level than at the
consumer level.

56 The exchange of useful chemicals between organisms and
their abiotic environment is an example of
1 a material cycle   3 a limiting factor
2 competition   4 succession

57 In an ecosystem, the more living requirements that two different species have in common, the more intense will be their
1 ecological succession
2 competition
3 energy requirements
4 evolution

58   The diagrams below represent four members of a food chain.

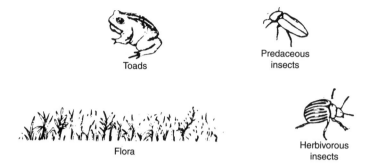

Toads

Predaceous insects

Flora

Herbivorous insects

Which sequence best represents the transfer of energy between these organisms?

1   toads → predaceous insects → herbivorous insects → plants
2   predaceous insects → herbivorous insects → plants → toads
3   plants → herbivorous insects → predaceous insects → toads
4   plants → herbivorous insects → toads → predaceous insects

59   Based on the graph below, which conditions most likely existed during the period from 1860 to 1865?

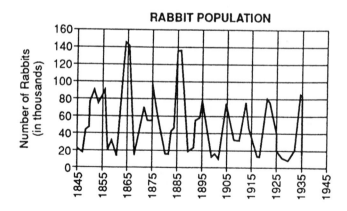

RABBIT POPULATION

1   Plenty of food was available and there were few predators.
2   Food was scarce and there were few predators.
3   Plenty of food was available and there were many predators.
4   No conclusion can be drawn from the information given.

PART II: This part consists of five groups, each containing ten questions. Choose two of these five groups. Be sure that you answer all ten questions in each group chosen. Record the answers to these questions on the separate answer sheet provided.

GROUP 1 — BIOCHEMISTRY

If you choose this group, be sure to answer questions 60–69.

Base your answers to questions 60 through 63 on the chemical equation below which represents a metabolic activity and on your knowledge of biology.

60 Which chemical substance is labeled C?
   1 a lipid   3 a disaccharide
   2 a dipeptide   4 a nucleotide

61 Which substance is represented by letter D?
   1 water   3 ammonia
   2 salt   4 carbon dioxide

62 Molecule C belongs in the general class of substances known as
   1 vitamins   3 inorganic acids
   2 minerals   4 organic compounds

63 Which structural group is represented at A and B?

Base your answers to questions 64 through 66 on the information below and on your knowledge of biology.

> *A solution of enzyme normally found in the human body was added to a flask containing proteins in distilled water, and then the flask was stoppered. This mixture was then maintained at a temperature of 27°C and a pH of 7 for 48 hours. When the mixture was analyzed, the presence of amino acids was noted.*

64 Which substances would most likely be present in the solution in the flask after 48 hours?
1 amino acids, only
2 amino acids and polypeptides, only
3 polypeptides, amino acids, and enzyme molecules
4 polysaccharides, amino acids, and enzyme molecules

65 One way to speed up the production of amino acids in the flask would be to
1 increase the temperature from 27°C to 37°C
2 increase the pH from 7 to 12
3 place the flask in bright light
4 decrease the amount of enzyme added

66 The enzymatic solution most likely contained
1 carbohydrates
2 maltases
3 lipases
4 proteases

Directions (67–68): **For each phrase in questions 67 and 68 select the photosynthetic reactions, *chosen from the list below*, that are best described by that phrase. Then record the *number* of the reactions on the separate answer sheet.**

Photosynthetic Reactions
(1) Photochemical reactions, only
(2) Carbon-fixation reactions, only
(3) Both photochemical and carbon-fixation reactions

67 The reactions in which the radioactive isotope carbon-14 can be used to trace the chemical pathway of the carbon in carbon dioxide

68 The reactions in which photolysis occurs

69 Which intermediate substance in produced in both alcohol
and lactic acid fermentation?
1 oxygen   3 nitrogen
2 pyruvic acid   4 starch

Group 2 — Human Physiology

If you choose this group, be sure to answer questions 70–79.

Base your answers to questions 70 through 73 on the diagram below and on your knowledge of biology.

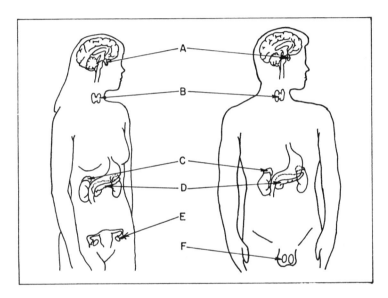

70 Which two glands produce gametes?
(1) *A* and *B*   (3) *C* and *F*
(2) *B* and *E*   (4) *E* and *F*

71 Which gland is associated with the malfunction known as
goiter?
(1) *E*   (3) *C*
(2) *B*   (4) *D*

72 Which gland produces adrenalin?
(1) *A*   (3) *C*
(2) *B*   (4) *D*

73 Removing part of gland *D* would most likely result in
1 a decrease in the secretions of other glands
2 a decrease in the blood calcium level
3 an increase in the growth rate of the individual
4 an increase in the blood sugar level

Directions (74–76): For each statement in questions 74 through 76 select the part of the human transport system, *chosen from the list below,* that is best described by that statement. Then record its *number* on the separate answer sheet.

Parts of the Human Transport System
(1) Pulmonary circulation
(2) Systemic circulation
(3) Coronary circulation
(4) Lymphatic circulation

74 Cardiac muscle tissue is supplied with nutrients and oxygen.

75 The concentration of carbon dioxide in the blood decreases, and the concentration of oxygen increases.

76 Oxygen is delivered to the liver from the heart.

77 Which of the blood types in the ABO system may be safely given to a person with AB blood?
(1) O or AB, only   (3) B or AB, only
(2) A or B, only   (4) A, B, AB, or O

78 The movement of blood from the legs toward the heart is hindered by gravity. The effect of gravity is counteracted by
1 smooth muscle in the capillaries
2 cilia lining the blood vessels
3 valves in the veins
4 lymph nodes near major vessels

79 Which disease is linked to smoking and results in a reduction in the number and elasticity of alveoli?
1 emphysema   3 bronchitis
2 asthma   4 meningitis

If you choose this group, be sure to answer questions 80–89.

Base your answers to questions 80 through 84 on the diagram below of some events in the human female reproductive cycle and on your knowledge of biology.

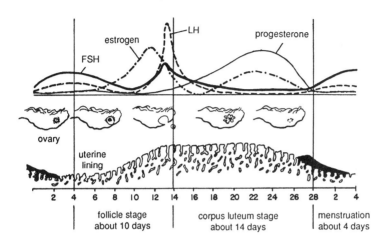

80 During which part of this cycle does the shedding of the thickened uterine lining occur?
1 ovulation
2 corpus luteum stage
3 menstruation
4 follicle stage

81 On or about which day does ovulation occur?
(1) 8th day   (3) 20th day
(2) 14th day   (4) 28th day

82 Which hormones are secreted by the ovaries?
(1) progesterone and estrogen
(2) FSH and estrogen
(3) FSH and LH
(4) LH and estrogen

83 What is the average length of this reproductive cycle?
(1) 32 days   (3) 14 days
(2) 28 days   (4) 4 days

84   The permanent cessation of this cycle is known as

1   puberty   3   fertilization
2   pregnancy   4   menopause

Base your answers to questions 85 through 87 on the diagram below of some stages in the development of an embryo and on your knowledge of biology.

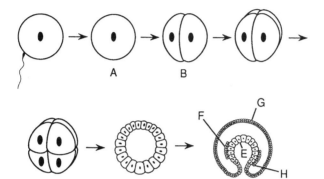

85   Which stage represents a zygote?

(1) *A*   (3) *C*
(2) *B*   (4) *D*

86   Which cell layer develops into the linings of the digestive and respiratory tracts?

(1) *E*   (3) *G*
(2) *F*   (4) *H*

87   Diagram *D* illustrates a

1   late blastula stage   3   fetus
2   gastrula   4   stage of meiosis

88   Which event would most probably result in the production of fraternal twins?

1   One egg is fertilized by two sperm cells.
2   Two egg cells are fertilized by one sperm cell.
3   Two egg cells are each fertilized by separate sperm cells.
4   Two eggs develop without fertilization.

89　In the human female reproductive system, the union of sperm and ovum normally takes place within the

1　ovary　　　　　　　3　uterus
2　vagina　　　　　　4　oviduct

GROUP 4 — MODERN GENETICS

If you choose this group, be sure to answer questions 90–99.

Base your answers to questions 90 through 92 on the diagram below and on your knowledge of biology.

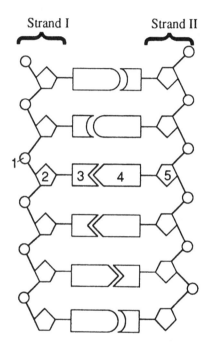

90　Structures 1, 2, and 3 make up a

1　nucleic acid　　　　3　nucleolus
2　ribosome　　　　　4　nucleotide

91　If strand I represents a segment of a replicating DNA molecule with bases A-T-C-C-G-A, the complementary DNA strand would contain the bases

(1) T-A-G-G-C-T　　　　(3) U-A-G-G-C-U
(2) T-U-G-G-C-T　　　　(4) A-T-G-G-C-T

92 Structures 3 and 4 are held together by
  1 weak peptide bonds
  2 strong hydrogen bonds
  3 weak hydrogen bonds
  4 strong peptide bonds

Directions (93–94): For *each* statement in questions 93 and 94 select the genetic disorder, *chosen from the list below,* that is best described by that statement. Then record its *number* on the separate answer paper.

Genetic Disorders
(1) Phenylketonuria (PKU)
(2) Sickle-cell anemia
(3) Down's syndrome
(4) Tay-Sachs disease

93 The formation of abnormal hemoglobin results in severe pain due to obstructed blood vessels.

94 Fatty material accumulates because a specific enzyme cannot be synthesized, causing a deterioration of the nervous system.

95 Amino acid molecules are bonded together in a specific sequence on cell structures known as
  1 ribosomes   3 mitochondria
  2 vacuoles   4 centromeres

96 The core of a virus may contain either DNA or RNA. To identify which nucleic acid is present, a biochemist could chemically analyze the virus for the presence of
  1 guanine   3 cytosine
  2 ribose   4 phosphate

97 The sum of all the genes for all the heritable traits in a population is called the gene
  1 frequency   3 pool
  2 combination   4 system

98 A change in the base sequence of DNA is known as
  1 a gene mutation   3 nondisjunction
  2 a karyotype   4 polyploidy

99 In a large, randomly mating population of deer mice, the gene frequencies have stayed constant for several generations. Over this time interval, the rate of evolution in this mouse population most likely has
1 decreased, only
2 increased, only
3 increased, then decreased
4 remained the same

GROUP 5 — ECOLOGY

If you choose this group, be sure to answer questions 100–109.

Base your answers to questions 100 and 101 on the chart below and on your knowledge of biology.

Characteristics	Climax Flora	Dominant Fauna
long, severe winters; summers with thawing subsoil	conifers	moose and black bears

100 Which biome is most accurately described by the data in the chart?
1 taiga
2 tropical rain forest
3 tundra
4 temperate deciduous forest

101 The climax flora in this biome are characterized by
1 leaves that are shed in the fall
2 needle-like leaves
3 no leaves at all
4 no stomates or lenticels

Base your answers to questions 102 and 103 on the passage below and on your knowledge of biology.

Algae live inside the body cells of a species of hydra. The hydra uses the products of the alga's photosynthesis. Ammonia resulting from the hydra's metabolism is thought to contribute to the alga's nutrition.

102 The relationship between the hydra and the alga is best described as
1 commensalism   3 saprophytism
2 mutualism   4 parasitism

103　The ammonia is a part of which important ecological cycle?
　　　1　oxygen cycle　　　　　3　carbon cycle
　　　2　water cycle　　　　　4　nitrogen cycle

104　Releasing sterilized male insects of a certain species into the
　　　environment can lead to a reduction in population size of that
　　　species. This process is an example of
　　　1　the use of biological control
　　　2　the use of a biocide
　　　3　the effect of pesticides on reproduction rate
　　　4　a technique used for species preservation

105　Which abiotic factor limits the distribution of life in the
　　　oceans, but does not usually limit the distribution of life on
　　　land?
　　　1　minerals　　　　　　3　nitrogen
　　　2　water　　　　　　　4　oxygen

**Base your answers to questions 106 through 109 on the diagrams
below and on your knowledge of biology. The diagrams show various
stages of plant development on a volcanic island over a 300-year
period after it was formed.**

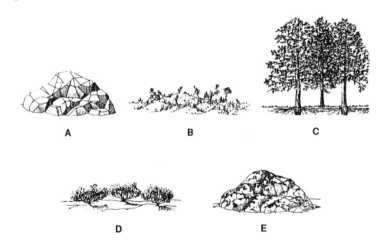

106　Pioneer organisms are the dominant flora in
　　　(1) E　　　　　　　　(3) C
　　　(2) B　　　　　　　　(4) D

107 If stage C illustrates the climax flora of the region, the dominant fauna would most likely include
   1 kangaroo rats and lizards
   2 snakes and monkeys
   3 squirrels and deer
   4 caribou and snowy owls

108 What is most likely the sequence of the stages of development that occurred on the island over the 300-year period?
   (1) $A \rightarrow B \rightarrow C \rightarrow D \rightarrow E$
   (2) $E \rightarrow B \rightarrow D \rightarrow C \rightarrow A$
   (3) $A \rightarrow E \rightarrow B \rightarrow D \rightarrow C$
   (4) $B \rightarrow D \rightarrow C \rightarrow E \rightarrow A$

109 Which type of organisms could most successfully colonize stage A of the volcanic island?
   1 ferns   3 woody shrubs
   2 lichens   4 flowering plants

PART III: This part consists of five groups. Choose three of these five groups. For those questions that are followed by four choices, record the answers on the separate answer sheet. For all other questions in this part, record your answers in accordance with the directions given in the question. [15]

GROUP 1

If you choose this group, be sure to answer questions 110–114.
Base your answers to questions 110 through 114 on the reading passage below an on your knowledge of biology.

Lyme Disease

Thousands of people have been bitten by deer ticks and infected with the bacterial spirochete Borrelia burgdorferi, the cause of Lyme disease. About half of these people will not realize that they have been infected. After the initial infection, their immune systems will begin to control the bacterium, but not to eliminate it altogether. Up to several years after the tick bite, the victims may develop complications such as crippling arthritis, neurological damage, and cardiac malfunctions. Now, researchers think they have determined one way B. burgdorferi manages to elude an activated immune system.

Five white-footed mice were infected with B. burgdorferi. The blood of the mice was sampled shortly thereafter, and it was confirmed that the mice were producing large quantities of antibodies that attacked the invading bacteria.

Four months later, B. burgdorferi *were extracted from the infected mice and mixed with the same type of mouse antibodies. This time the bacteria initiated only a weak response, indicating that the antibodies were less able to recognize the bacteria. Since antibodies recognize a bacterium by binding to specific protein molecules on the bacterial surface, these surface molecules may somehow have changed over time. In this way, the bacteria are better able to escape early recognition by antibodies produced by the human immune system.*

110 Shortly after the initial infection, the mice apparently
    1 got rid of the bacteria
    2 had no reaction to the infection
    3 produced antibodies against the disease
    4 suffered permanent neurological damage

111 The organisms that cause Lyme disease are able to
    1 cause problems in plants as well as several species of animals
    2 change their proteins, thus making recognition by the mouse's immune system more difficult
    3 destroy mouse antibodies by chemically breaking them down into harmless end products
    4 be transmitted directly from one mouse to another

112 According to the passage, which symptom of Lyme disease in humans might appear several years after the initial tick bite?
    1 a severe rash   3 kidney failure
    2 a high fever   4 joint inflammation

113 Which kingdom includes the organism that causes Lyme disease?
    1 Monera   3 Fungi
    2 Protista   4 Animal

114 The genus name of the organism that causes Lyme disease is
    1 *spirochete*   3 *burgdorferi*
    2 *Bacterium*   4 *Borrelia*

GROUP 2

If you choose this group, be sure to answer questions 115–119.

115 A student sees the image at the right when observing the letter "f" with the low-power objective lens of a microscope. Which diagram below most closely resembles the image the student will see after switching to high power?

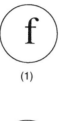

(1)

(3)

(2)

(4)

116 A student views some cheek cells under low power. Before switching to high power, the student should
1 adjust the eyepiece
2 center the image being viewed
3 remove the slide from the stage
4 remove the coverslip

117 A student changes the objective of a microscope from 10× to 50×. If this is the only change made, what will happen to the field of view?
1 Its diameter will decrease.
2 Its diameter will increase.
3 Its brightness will increase.
4 Its brightness will remain the same.

118 When an onion cell is stained with iodine, which organelle becomes more visible under the compound light microscope?
1 mitochondrion   3 ribosome
2 lysosome   4 nucleus

119 The diagram below represents the field of view of a compound light microscope. Three unicellular organisms are located across the diameter of the field.

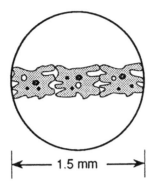

← 1.5 mm →

What is the approximate length of each unicellular organism?
(1) 250 µm   (3) 1,000 µm
(2) 500 µm   (4) 1,500 µm

GROUP 3

If you choose this group, be sure to answer questions 120–124.
Base your answers to questions 120 through 122 on the information below and on your knowledge of biology.

> *In a laboratory experiment, a student prepared a wet mount of the common aquarium plant elodea. After he used the low-power objective of a compound microscope to focus on the leaf cells, he switched to high power. In this field of view, he observed small green bodies moving along the boundary of each cell.*

Directions (120–122): Your answers to questions 120 through 122 must be written in ink. Write your answers in the spaces provided on the separate answer paper.

120 Identify the small green bodies that the student observed within the elodea cells.

121 Identify one cell structure other than the small green bodies that the student should be able to observe in each cell under high power.

122   By which process do the small green bodies move within a cell?

123   A block of wood is measured, as shown in the diagram
      below.

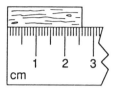

      What is the length of the wooden block in millimeters?
      (1) 2.60 mm   (3) 260 mm
      (2) 26.0 mm   (4) 2,600 mm

124   Iodine and Benedict's solution were both used to test for cer-
      tain nutrients in a sample of food. If both tests were positive
      for the nutrients, the sample must contain
      1   polysaccharide and simple sugar
      2   protein and fat
      3   carbohydrate and lipid
      4   polysaccharide and protein

GROUP 4

If you choose this group, be sure to answer questions 125–129.
Base your answers to questions 125 through 127 on the graph below
and on your knowledge of biology. The graph illustrates the growth
curve for two types of bacteria (*A* and *B*) under differing pH values.

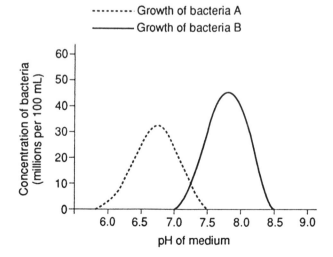

125 Bacteria *A* grows best in a medium that is

    1 slightly acid   3 slightly basic

    2 neutral   4 very basic

126 Which conclusion concerning bacteria *A* and bacteria *B* can correctly be drawn from the data provided in the graph?

    1 They could not coexist in the same medium.

    2 Their optimum pH values are different.

    3 Bacteria *A* grows at a faster rate that bacteria *B*.

    4 Bacteria *A* is larger than bacteria *B*.

127 A growth medium at pH 6.5 supports approximately what concentration of bacteria *A*?

    (1) 15 million/100 mL   (3) 35 million/100 mL

    (2) 25 million/100 mL   (4) 45 million/100 mL

Directions (128–129): Your answers must be written in complete sentences and must be written in ink. Write your answers in the spaces provided on the separate answer paper.

128 A student observed that on sunny days, green single-celled organisms in a lake were located several feet below the surface of the water. On cloudy days, she observed that these same organisms were only a few inches below the surface. Give a possible explanation for these observations.

129 The diagrams below show the setups for a particular experiment. Describe the relationship being studied in the experiment.

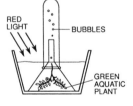 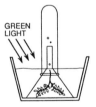 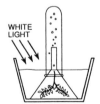

GROUP 5

If you choose this group, be sure to answer questions 130–134.

Base your answers to questions 130 through 133 on the information and data table below and on your knowledge of biology.

An experiment was set up to determine the effect of light intensity on the rate of photosynthesis in two cultures of the alga *Chlorella*, each grown in a different concentration of CO_2. The results are shown in the data table below.

Light Intensity (foot-candles)	Rate of Photosynthesis (bubbles of O_2 per minute)	
	Low CO_2 Concentration	High CO_2 Concentration
250	14	20
500	22	41
750	29	63
1,000	30	80
1,250	30	88
1,500	31	90
1,750	30	91
2,000	30	90

Directions (130–132): Using the information in the data table, construct a line graph on the grid provided on your answer paper, following the directions below. Pen or pencil may be used for your final answer.

The grid on the next page is provided for practice purposes only. Be sure your final answer appears *on your answer paper*.

130   Mark an appropriate scale on each axis.

131   Plot the data for the low CO_2 concentration on the graph. Surround each point with a small triangle and connect the points.

Example:

132 Plot the data for the high CO_2 concentration on the graph.
     Surround each point with a small circle and connect the
     points.

Example: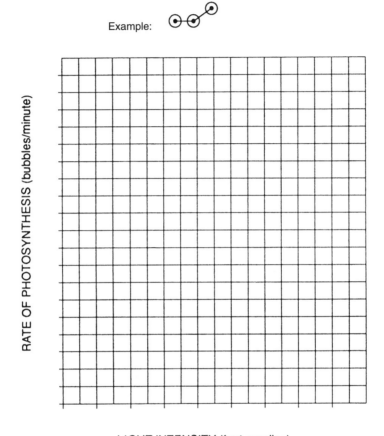

RATE OF PHOTOSYNTHESIS (bubbles/minute)

LIGHT INTENSITY (foot-candles)

KEY

⚠ LOW CO_2 CONCENTRATION

⊙ HIGH CO_2 CONCENTRATION

Directions (133): Your answer to question 133 must be written in ink. Write your
answer in the space provided on the separate answer paper.

133 Using one or more complete sentences, state one factor in the
     experiment that affects the rate of photosynthesis from 250 to
     1,000 foot-candles of light intensity and state this factor's
     effect on that rate.

134 An investigation was conducted using three groups of laboratory rats, X, Y, and Z, to determine the relative effects of glucose and adrenaline on the rate of heartbeat. The experimental conditions for each group of rats were kept the same except for the type of solution injected, as shown in the data table below.

Data Table

Group	Solution Injected
X	1 mL adrenaline in distilled water
Y	1 mL glucose in distilled water
Z	1 mL distilled water, only

According to the data table, which group of rats functioned as the control?

(1) X, only
(2) Y, only
(3) Z, only
(4) both X and Y

ANSWER KEY
EXAM ONE

PART I

1. 3
2. 2
3. 4
4. 3
5. 1
6. 3
7. 4
8. 3
9. 1
10. 4
11. 2
12. 3
13. 3
14. 1
15. 2
16. 1
17. 4
18. 2
19. 2
20. 4
21. 4
22. 1
23. 3
24. 1
25. 4
26. 3
27. 2
28. 3
29. 4
30. 2
31. 4
32. 3
33. 1
34. 1
35. 2
36. 3
37. 2
38. 3
39. 4
40. 4
41. 4

42. 3
43. 2
44. 1
45. 1
46. 4
47. 3
48. 4
49. 2
50. 1
51. 4
52. 1
53. 1
54. 4
55. 2
56. 1
57. 2
58. 3
59. 1

PART II

60. 3
61. 1
62. 4
63. 2
64. 3
65. 1
66. 4
67. 2
68. 1
69. 2
70. 4
71. 2
72. 3
73. 4
74. 3
75. 1
76. 2
77. 4
78. 3
79. 1
80. 3
81. 2

82.	1
83.	2
84.	4
85.	1
86.	1
87.	2
88.	3
89.	4
90.	4
91.	1
92.	3
93.	2
94.	4
95.	1
96.	2
97.	3
98.	1
99.	4
100.	1
101.	2
102.	2
103.	4
104.	1
105.	4
106.	1
107.	3
108.	3
109.	2

PART III

110.	3
111.	2
112.	4
113.	1
114.	4
115.	1
116.	2
117.	1
118.	4
119.	2
120.	chloroplasts
121.	nucleus or vacuole or cell wall

122.	cyclosis or cytoplasmic streaming
123.	2
124.	1
125.	1
126.	2
127.	2

The answers below represent sample responses. Other complete-sentence responses are acceptable.

128. These organisms require a certain amount of sunlight for photosynthesis. On cloudy days, this amount of sunlight does not penetrate as far into the lake as it does on sunny days. Therefore the organisms exist at shallower depths on cloudy days.

129. The experiment is being conducted to study the relationship between color of light and the rate of photosynthesis in a green aquatic plant.

130–132.

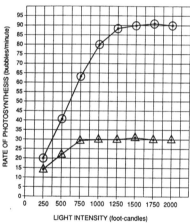

133. One factor that affects the rate of photosynthesis is the amount of CO_2 in the water. The greater the amount of CO_2, the greater the rate of photosynthesis as the light intensity increases from 250 to 1,000 foot-candles.

134. 3

EXAM TWO

PART I: Answer all 59 questions in this part. [65]

Directions (1–59): For each statement or question, select the word or expression that, of those given, best completes the statement or answers the question. Record your answer on the separate answer sheet provided.

---

1 Short-tailed shrews and ruby-throated hummingbirds have high metabolic rates. As a result, these animals
   1 utilize energy rapidly
   2 need very little food
   3 have very few predators
   4 hibernate in hot weather

2 Which activity would *not* be carried out by an organism in order to maintain a stable internal environment?
   1 removal of metabolic waste products
   2 transport of organic and inorganic compounds
   3 production of offspring by the organism
   4 regulation of physiological processes

3 Which statement about viruses is true?
   1 They carry on aerobic respiration.
   2 They reproduce both sexually and asexually.
   3 They are photosynthetic organisms.
   4 They are an exception to the cell theory.

4 The structural formula below represents urea.

This structural formula indicates that urea is
   1 an organic compound
   2 an inorganic compound
   3 a carbohydrate
   4 a nucleic acid

5 Which activity is an example of cyclosis?
   1   the movement of water from the soil into a root hair
   2   the movement of food vacuoles through the cytoplasm of
       a paramecium
   3   blood cells moving through the capillaries in a goldfish
       tail
   4   the pumping action of a contractile vacuole in an ameba

6 The diagram below represents a sample of crushed onion
   cells that was centrifuged. Cells and cell components were
   dispersed in layers as illustrated.

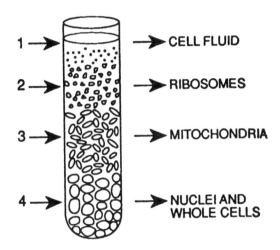

The organelles that act as the sites of protein synthesis are
found in the greatest concentration within layer
(1) 1   (3) 3
(2) 2   (4) 4

7 Maltose molecules are formed from glucose by the process of
   1   dipeptide synthesis
   2   intracellular digestion
   3   dehydration synthesis
   4   biological oxidation

8 Two species of bacteria produce different respiratory end products. Species A always produces ATP, CO_2, and H_2O; species B
   always produces ATP, ethyl alcohol, and CO_2. Which conclusion can correctly be drawn from this information?
   1   Only species A is aerobic.
   2   Only species B is aerobic.
   3   Species A and species B are both anaerobic.
   4   Species A and species B are both aerobic.

9 Two plants were observed to have the characteristics indicated in the chart below. An X indicates that the characteristic was present.

Specimen	Multicellular	Photosynthetic	Vascular Tissue	Roots	Stems	Leaves
Plant A	X	X				
Plant B	X	X	X	X	X	X

According to the chart, which statement about these plants is correct?
1 Plant A is a tracheophyte, and plant B is a bryophyte.
2 Plant A has xylem and phloem, but plant B does not.
3 Plant A could be a pine tree, and plant B could be a moss.
4 Plant A is a bryophyte, and plant B is a tracheophyte.

10 The diagram below represents a protist.

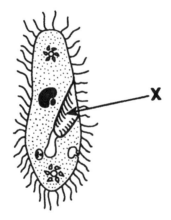

Structure X is most directly involved in the process of
1 extracellular digestion
2 enzymatic hydrolysis
3 ingestion
4 transpiration

11 A fungus is classified as a heterotroph rather than an autotroph because it

    1 grows by mitosis
    2 absorbs food from the environment
    3 manufactures its own food
    4 transforms light energy into chemical energy

12 The concentration of nitrates is often higher in plant roots than in the soil around them. Plants maintain this difference in concentration through

    1 active transport   3 diffusion
    2 osmosis   4 waste egestion

13 A wet-mount slide of photosynthetic protists was prepared and then exposed to light that had been broken up into a spectrum. When viewing this preparation through the microscope, a student would most likely observe that most of the protists had clustered in the regions of

    1 yellow and blue light
    2 orange and green light
    3 green and yellow light
    4 red and blue light

14 In an ameba, which process is best represented by the arrows shown in the diagram below?

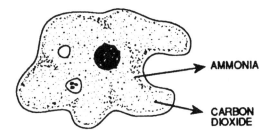

    1 absorption by active transport
    2 excretion by diffusion
    3 respiratory gas exchange
    4 egestion of digestive end products

15 Which statement describes a relationship between the human cells illustrated in the diagrams below?

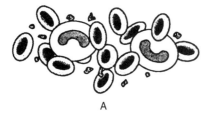

A

C

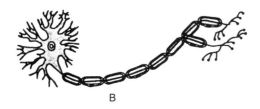

B

D

(1) *B* may cause *D* to contract.
(2) *A* is produced by *D*.
(3) *C* transports oxygen to *A*.
(4) *B* is used to repair *C*.

16 One way in which the intake of oxygen is similar in the hydra and the earthworm is that both organisms
   1 absorb oxygen through a system of tubes
   2 utilize cilia to absorb oxygen
   3 use capillaries to transport oxygen
   4 absorb oxygen through their external surfaces

17 The life function of transport in the grasshopper involves
   1 an internal gas exchange surface and alveoli
   2 an open circulatory system and tracheal tubes
   3 moist outer skin and hemoglobin
   4 a dry external body surface and hemoglobin

18 Which process is correctly paired with its major waste product?
   1 respiration — oxygen
   2 protein synthesis — amino acids
   3 dehydration synthesis — water
   4 hydrolysis — carbon dioxide

19   The diagram below represents a growth response in a plant.

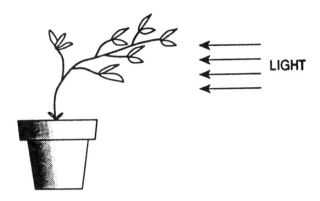

This growth response was most likely due to the effect of light on

1   acetylcholine   3   auxin distribution
2   minerals   4   vascular tissue

20   The diagram below represents three steps of a chemical reaction.

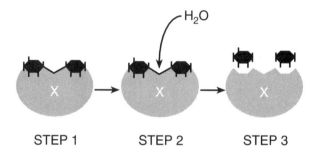

STEP 1   STEP 2   STEP 3

This diagram best illustrates the

1   deamination of amino acids
2   emulsification of a fat
3   synthesis of a polysaccharide
4   hydrolysis of a carbohydrate

21   Which statement best describes protein metabolism in the hydra?

1   It produces excess carbon dioxide, which is recycled for photosynthesis.
2   It produces urea, which is eliminated by nephridia.
3   It produces ammonia, which is transported out of the animal into the environment.
4   It produces mineral salts, all of which are retained for other metabolic processes.

22 The diagram below shows a longitudinal section of the human heart.

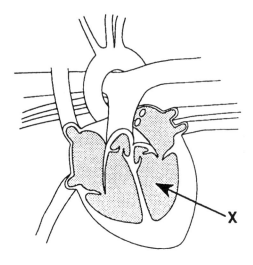

The structure labeled X is known as

1   a ventricle   3   a valve
2   an atrium   4   the aorta

23 A hawk sees a field mouse, which it then captures for food. In this activity, the eyes of the hawk function as

1   effectors   3   stimuli
2   receptors   4   neurotransmitters

24 Methyl cellulose is a chemical that slows the movement of paramecia on a slide. This chemical most likely interferes with the movement of

1   pseudopods   3   setae
2   flagella   4   cilia

25 Which adaptation found within the human respiratory system filters, warms, and moistens the air before it enters the lungs?

1   clusters of alveoli
2   rings of cartilage
3   involuntary smooth muscle
4   ciliated mucous membranes

26 Food is usually kept from entering the trachea by the

1   diaphragm   3   villi
2   epiglottis   4   ribs

27 The nephrons and alveoli of humans are most similar in function to the
    1 nephridia and skin of earthworms
    2 Malpighian tubules and gastric caecae of grasshoppers
    3 nerve nets and gastrovascular cavities of hydras
    4 cilia and pseudopods of protozoa

28 The diagrams below represent stages of a cellular process.

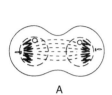   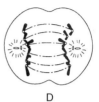

A   B   C   D

    Which is the correct sequence of these stages?
    (1) $A \rightarrow B \rightarrow C \rightarrow D$
    (2) $B \rightarrow D \rightarrow C \rightarrow A$
    (3) $C \rightarrow B \rightarrow D \rightarrow A$
    (4) $D \rightarrow B \rightarrow A \rightarrow C$

29 Which part of the human central nervous system is correctly paired with its function?
    1 spinal cord — coordinates learning activities
    2 cerebellum — serves as the center for reflex actions
    3 cerebrum — serves as the center for memory and reasoning
    4 medulla — maintains muscular coordination

30 Tendons are best described as
    1 tissue that is found between bones and that protects them from damage
    2 cords that connect bone to bone and that stretch at the point of attachment
    3 striated tissue that provides a wide range of motion
    4 fibrous cords that connect muscles to bones

31 Which statement best describes the division of the cytoplasm and the nucleus in budding?
    1 Both the cytoplasm and the nucleus divide equally.
    2 The cytoplasm divides unequally, but the nucleus divides equally.
    3 The cytoplasm divides equally, but the nucleus divides unequally.
    4 Both the cytoplasm and the nucleus divide unequally.

32 *Rhizopus*, a bread mold, usually reproduces asexually by
    1 budding   3 regeneration
    2 sporulation   4 fission

33 In sexually reproducing species, doubling of the chromosome
    number from generation to generation is prevented by events
    that take place during the process of
    1 gametogenesis   3 nondisjunction
    2 cleavage   4 fertilization

34 Which statement is true about the process of fertilization in
    both tracheophytes and mammals?
    1 It normally results in the production of monoploid off-
       spring.
    2 It occurs externally in a watery environment.
    3 It is followed by yolk production.
    4 It occurs within female reproductive organs.

35 The production of large numbers of eggs is necessary to
    insure the survival of most
    1 mammals   3 fish
    2 molds   4 yeasts

36 Mendel developed his basic principles of heredity by
    1 microscopic study of chromosomes and genes
    2 breeding experiments with drosophila
    3 mathematical analysis of the offspring of pea plants
    4 ultracentrifugation studies of cell organelles

37   The diagrams below represent the gametes and zygotes asso-
     ciated with two separate fertilizations in a particular species.

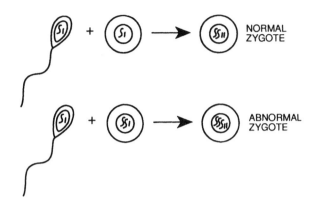

The abnormal zygote is most likely the result of
1   polyploidy
2   nondisjunction
3   chromosome breakage
4   gene linkage

**Base your answers to questions 38 and 39 on the diagram below of a
flower and on your knowledge of biology.**

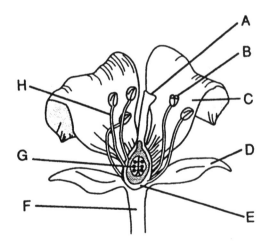

38   Which structures form the stamen?
     (1) A and F   (3) C and D
     (2) B and H   (4) E and G

39 During pollination, pollen is transferred from
   (1) *B* to *A*   (3) *B* to *G*
   (2) *C* to *D*   (4) *F* to *H*

40 Pea plants heterozygous for both height and color of seed
    coat (*TtYy*) were crossed with pea plants that were homozy-
    gous recessive for both traits (*ttyy*). The offspring from this
    cross included tall plants with green seeds, tall plants with
    yellow seeds, short plants with green seeds, and short plants
    with yellow seeds. This cross best illustrates
    1   gene mutation
    2   environmental influence on heredity
    3   independent assortment of chromosomes
    4   intermediate inheritance

41 In raccoons, a dark face mask is dominant over a bleached
    face mask. Several crosses were made between raccoons that
    were heterozygous for dark face mask and raccoons that were
    homozygous for bleached face mask. What percentage of the
    offspring would be expected to have a dark face mask?
    (1) 0%   (3) 75%
    (2) 50%   (4) 100%

42 Traits that are controlled by genes found on an X-chromo-
    some are said to be
    1   autosomal dominant
    2   autosomal recessive
    3   codominant
    4   sex-linked

43 The diagram below represents possible lines of evolution of primates.

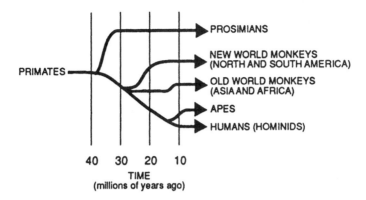

Which inference can best be made based on the diagram?
1 Acquired adaptations for living in trees are inherited.
2 Humans and apes have a common ancestor.
3 The embryos of monkeys and apes are identical.
4 The period of maturation is similar in most primates.

44 Which situation is a result of crossing-over during meiosis?
1 Genes are duplicated exactly, ensuring that offspring will be identical to the parents.
2 Chromatids thicken and align themselves, helping to ensure genetic continuity.
3 Genes are rearranged, increasing the variability of offspring.
4 Chromatids fail to sort independently, creating abnormal chromosome numbers.

45 What is the role of DNA in controlling cellular activity?
(1) DNA provides energy for all cell activities.
(2) DNA determines which enzymes are produced by a cell.
(3) DNA is used by cells for the excretion of nitrogenous wastes.
(4) DNA provides nucleotides for the construction of plasma membranes.

46 The best scientific explanation for differences in structure, function, and behavior found between life forms is provided by the
1 heterotroph hypothesis
2 lock-and-key model
3 theory of use and disuse
4 theory of organic evolution

47 Substances that increase the chance of gene alterations are known as
  1 mutagenic agents
  2 genetic agents
  3 chromosomal agents
  4 adaptive agents

48 Fossils of two different organisms, A and B, are found in different undisturbed layers of rock. The layer containing fossil A is located above the layer containing fossil B. Which statement about these fossils is most likely true?
  1 Fossil B is older than fossil A.
  2 Fossils A and B represent organisms that are closely related and evolved from a common ancestor.
  3 Fossil A represents an organism that evolved from fossil B.
  4 Fossil B represents an organism that evolved from fossil A.

49 Since the time of Darwin, increased knowledge of heredity has resulted in
  1 the addition of use and disuse to Lamarck's theory
  2 the elimination of all previous evolutionary theories
  3 increased support for the theory of natural selection
  4 disagreement with Mendel's discoveries

50 The diagrams below represent homologous structures.

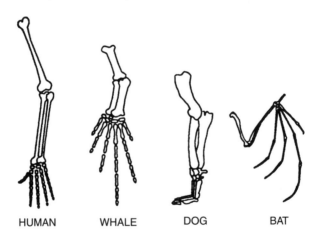

HUMAN   WHALE   DOG   BAT

The study of the evolutionary relationships between these structures is known as comparative
  1 cytology   3 anatomy
  2 biochemistry   4 embryology

51 Which processes are directly involved in the carbon-hydrogen-oxygen cycle?
1   respiration and photosynthesis
2   transpiration and evaporation
3   nutrition and ecological succession
4   diffusion and alcoholic fermentation

52 Which title would be most appropriate for a textbook on general ecology?
1   *The Interactions Between Organisms and Their Environment*
2   *The Cell and Its Organelles*
3   *The Physical and Chemical Properties of Water*
4   *The Hereditary Mechanisms of Drosophila*

53 Which is an example of an ecosystem?
1   a population of monarch butterflies
2   the interdependent biotic and abiotic components of a pond
3   all the abiotic factors found in a field
4   all the mammals that live in the Atlantic Ocean

54 According to the heterotroph hypothesis, which event immediately preceded the evolution of aerobes?
1   the production of oxygen by autotrophs
2   the production of ammonia by heterotrophs
3   the production of carbon dioxide by autotrophs
4   the production of carbon dioxide by heterotrophs

55 In a self-sustaining ecosystem, which component *cannot* be recycled because it is lost from food chains and becomes unavailable?
1   carbon   3   water
2   nitrogen   4   energy

56 Termites can be found living in dead trees partially buried under soil and stones. Within the tree trunks, the termites feed on the wood fiber, creating passageways having a high humidity. The wood fiber is digested by protozoans living within the digestive tract of the termite.
What are the biotic factors in this habitat?
1   tree trunk, stones, and protozoans
2   soil and humidity
3   termites and protozoans
4   humidity, soil, and stones

57 One theory about the extinction of dinosaurs is that the collision of an asteroid with the Earth caused environmental changes that killed off the dinosaurs in a relatively short time, changing the course of evolution. This theory is an example of which evolutionary concept?

1 gradualism
2 competition
3 the heterotroph hypothesis
4 punctuated equilibrium

58 The cartoon below illustrates a type of nutrition.

"Just think . . . Here we are, the afternoon sun beating down on us, a dead, bloated rhino underfoot, and good friends flying in from all over. . . . I tell you, Frank, this is the best of times."

Frank and the other birds in this cartoon are classified as

1 saprophytes   3 scavengers
2 herbivores   4 producers

59 Which types of organism is *not* represented in the diagram below?

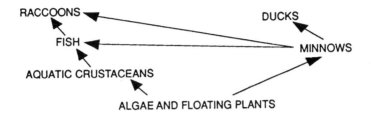

1 secondary consumers   3 carnivores
2 producers   4 decomposers

PART II: This part consists of five groups, each containing ten questions. Choose two of these five groups. Be sure that you answer all ten questions in each group chosen. Write the answers to these questions in the space provided on the separate answer sheet. [20]

GROUP 1 — BIOCHEMISTRY

If you choose this group, be sure to answer questions 60–69.

Base your answers to questions 60 through 62 on the structural formulas below and on your knowledge of biology.

60 By which formula can molecule *D* be represented?
  (1) $C_6H_{12}O_6$ (3) $C_3H_5(OH)_3$
  (2) $C_5H_{12}O_5$ (4) C_3H_5COOH

61 Which structural formulas present the building blocks of a lipid?
    (1) *A* and *C*   (3) *C* and *E*
    (2) *B* and *E*   (4) *F* and *G*

62 A single carboxyl group is represented by
    (1) *F*   (3) *C*
    (2) *B*   (4) *G*

63 According to the summary equations below, what is the net gain of ATP molecules from the complete oxidation of one glucose molecule?

    (*A*) 1 glucose + 2 ATP $\xrightarrow{\text{enzymes}}$
                  2 pyruvic acid + 4 ATP

    (*B*) 2 pyruvic acid + oxygen $\xrightarrow{\text{enzymes}}$
                  carbon dioxide + water + 34 ATP

    (1) 34   (3) 38
    (2) 36   (4) 40

64 If an enzyme works best at a neutral pH, in which pH range is that enzyme expected to function?
    (1) 1–3   (3) 6–8
    (2) 3–5   (4) 10–12

65 Bread dough that contains yeast and sugar expands during alcoholic fermentation as a result of an increase in the
    1 production of molecular oxygen
    2 absorption of minerals
    3 secretion of ATP
    4 production of carbon dioxide

Base your answers to questions 66 and 67 on the diagrams below of some stages of an enzyme-controlled reaction and on your knowledge of biology.

A   B   C   D

66 An enzyme-substrate complex is represented by diagram

(1) *A*   (3) *C*
(2) *B*   (4) *D*

67 A nonprotein vitamin required for this reaction would function as a

1   product   3   polypeptide
2   substrate   4   coenzyme

Base your answers to questions 68 and 69 on the diagram below which represents some of the events that take place in a plant cell.

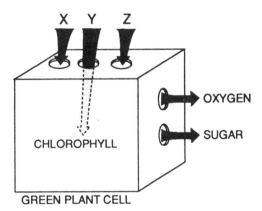

68 The oxygen and sugar leaving the cell were most likely produced by the processes of

1   hydrolysis and anaerobic respiration
2   dehydration synthesis and aerobic respiration
3   photolysis and carbon fixation
4   deamination and fermentation

69　The letters X, Y, and Z most likely represent
  (1) N_2, O_2, and H_2O
  (2) CO_2, light, and H_2O
  (3) light, ammonia, and H_2O
  (4) light, O_2, and methane

GROUP 2 — HUMAN PHYSIOLOGY

If you choose this group, be sure to answer questions 70–79.

Base your answers to questions 70 through 72 on the diagram below and on your knowledge of biology.

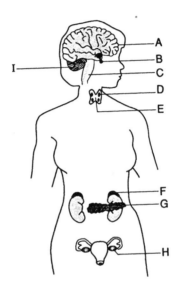

70　Which structure produces secretions that regulate E and H?
  (1) A (3) I
  (2) B (4) D

71　Which structure controls involuntary activities such as breathing and heartbeat?
  (1) A (3) C
  (2) B (4) G

72 Which two structures secrete substances that control the men-
    strual cycle?
    (1) *A* and *F*   (3) *C* and *D*
    (2) *B* and *H*   (4) *E* and *I*

73 Which letter indicates the location of nephrons in the diagram
    below?

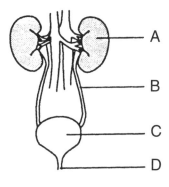

    (1) *A*   (3) *C*
    (2) *B*   (4) *D*

74 Which sequence represents the direction of flow of carbon
    dioxide as it passes out of the respiratory system into the
    external environment?
    1   alveoli → trachea → bronchioles → bronchi → pharynx →
        nasal cavity
    2   alveoli → bronchi → pharynx → bronchioles → trachea →
        nasal cavity
    3   alveoli → pharynx → trachea → bronchioles → bronchi →
        nasal cavity
    4   alveoli → bronchioles → bronchi → trachea → pharynx →
        nasal cavity

75 An inflammation of the region labeled
    A in the diagram at the right is
    known as

    1   meningitis
    2   arthritis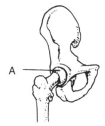
    3   bronchitis
    4   tendinitis

76 Which substances produced in the body are directly responsi-
    ble for the rejection of a transplanted organ?
    1 antigens   3 antibodies
    2 histamines   4 excretions

**Base your answers to questions 77 through 79 on the diagram below
and on your knowledge of biology.**

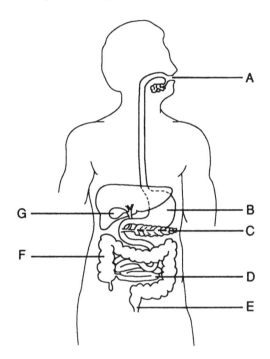

77 Which letter indicates the organ that secretes hydrochloric
    acid and protease?
    (1) A   (3) E
    (2) B   (4) D

78 Which letter indicates the organ that produces insulin and
    glucagon?
    (1) E   (3) C
    (2) B   (4) F

79 A painful condition resulting from the formation of small
    stone-like deposits of cholesterol may be treated by surgically
    removing structure
    (1) *G*   (3) *F*
    (2) *E*   (4) *D*

GROUP 3 — REPRODUCTION AND DEVELOPMENT

If you choose this group, be sure to answer questions 80–89.

**Base your answers to questions 80 through 83 on the diagram below and on
your knowledge of biology. The diagram shows stages in the life cycle of a
unicellular flagellated green alga.**

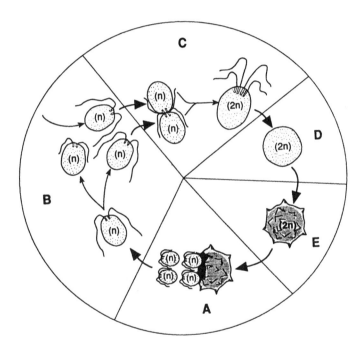

80 The process that takes place at stage *B* normally produces
    cells with
    1   the same chromosome number as the parent cell
    2   fewer chromosomes than the parent cell
    3   pairs of homologous chromosomes
    4   a polyploid number of chromosomes

81 Fertilization involving like gametes takes place at stage
    (1) *A*   (3) *C*
    (2) *B*   (4) *E*

82 The process that most likely takes place between stages *E* and *A* is
    1 mitosis   3 fertilization
    2 meiosis   4 cleavage

83 A specialized structure that provides protection from harsh
    environmental conditions is represented at stage
    (1) *E*   (3) *C*
    (2) *B*   (4) *D*

Base your answers to questions 84 through 86 on the graph below and
on your knowledge of biology. The graph shows the different concentrations of female reproductive hormones during the menstrual cycle
of humans.

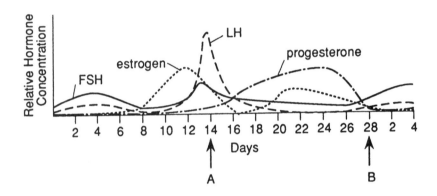

84 Which event normally occurs at *A*?
    1 ovulation
    2 embryo implantation
    3 differentiation
    4 follicle formation

85 Which process usually begins at *B*?
    1 fertilization
    2 embryo development
    3 corpus luteum development
    4 menstruation

86 Which is a correct inference about an event that occurs prior to day 14?
1 A high level of estrogen may stimulate the production of LH.
2 A high level of LH may stimulate the production of FSH.
3 A low level of FSH inhibits the production of estrogen.
4 A low level of progesterone inhibits the production of estrogen.

87 The yolk of a developing bird embryo functions as a
1 moist respiratory membrane
2 storage site for waste
3 food source
4 fluid environment

88 In humans, the fertilization of two eggs at the same time usually results in
1 chromosome abnormalities
2 gene mutations
3 identical twins
4 fraternal twins

89 In chicken eggs, the embryonic membrane known as the allantois functions in the
1 release of oxygen to the atmosphere
2 storage of nitrogenous wastes
3 absorption of nitrogen for use in protein synthesis
4 transport of carbon dioxide directly to the embryo

GROUP 4 — MODERN GENETICS

If you choose this group, be sure to answer questions 90–99.

Base your answers to questions 90 through 92 on the chart below and on your knowledge of biology. The chart represents the inheritance of Tay-Sachs disease in a family.

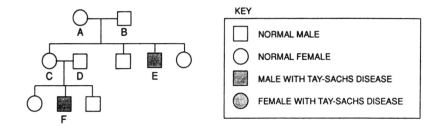

KEY

☐ NORMAL MALE

◯ NORMAL FEMALE

▨ MALE WITH TAY-SACHS DISEASE

◉ FEMALE WITH TAY-SACHS DISEASE

90 What are the genotypes of individuals *A* and *B* with regard to Tay-Sachs disease?
  1 One must be homozygous dominant and the other must be homozygous recessive.
  2 One must be homozygous dominant and the other must be heterozygous.
  3 Both must be homozygous.
  4 Both must be heterozygous.

91 If individuals *C* and *D* have another child, what is the chance this child will exhibit Tay-Sachs disease?
  (1) 0%   (3) 50%
  (2) 25%   (4) 100%

92 Which statement is true about individuals *E* and *F*?
  1 They are unable to metabolize glucose.
  2 They are unable to metabolize phenylalanine because they lack a specific enzyme.
  3 They have an accumulation of excess fatty material in their nerve tissue.
  4 They have an abnormal chromosome number.

93 Which event is *not* part of the process of DNA replication?
  1 Nitrogenous base pairs are formed.
  2 Hydrogen bonds are broken.
  3 A double-stranded molecule unwinds.
  4 Ribosomes are synthesized.

94 Deoxyribonucleic acid molecules serve as a template for the synthesis of molecules of

1 amino acids
2 carbohydrates
3 messenger RNA
4 lipids

95 Which procedure is usually used to help determine whether a child will be born with Down's syndrome?

1 amniocentesis
2 cloning
3 microdissection of sperm cells and egg cells
4 analysis of urine samples from the mother

Base your answers to questions 96 through 99 on the information below and on your knowledge of biology.

> For many generations, a particular species of snail has lived in an isolated pond. Some members of the species have light-colored shells and some have dark-colored shells. During this time, the species has been producing large numbers of offspring through random mating, and no migration has occurred.

96 Which additional condition must be present if the gene frequencies of these snails are to remain constant?

1 asexual reproduction
2 lack of mutations
3 genetic variation
4 common ancestry

97 A change in the environment of the pond caused the light-colored shells to become an important survival trait, and the number of light-colored snails increased. This situation will most likely cause

1 the addition of a fifth nitrogenous base to the DNA of the snails
2 a change in the frequency of the genes for shell color
3 an increase in the number of ribosomes in the cells of the snail
4 the extinction of this species of snail

98 The total of all the inheritable genes found in these snails is referred to as a

1 pedigree
2 karyotype
3 phenotypic ratio
4 gene pool

99 All of the snails of this species living in the pond may be classified as

1   a population   3   a community
2   an ecosystem   4   a biome

GROUP 5 — ECOLOGY

If you choose this group, be sure to answer questions 100–109.
Base your answers to questions 100 and 101 on the diagram below and on your knowledge of biology.

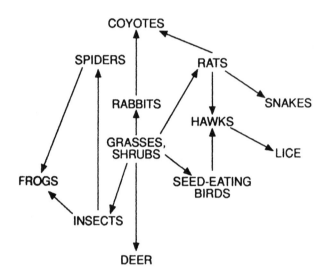

100 Which organisms would contain the greatest amount of available energy?

1   rabbits and deer   3   lice
2   grasses and shrubs   4   hawks

101 The primary consumers include

1   rabbits and snakes
2   insects and seed-eating birds
3   rats and frogs
4   spiders and coyotes

102 The diagram below represents the feeding areas during summer and fall of two populations in the same ecosystem. Both populations feed on oak trees.

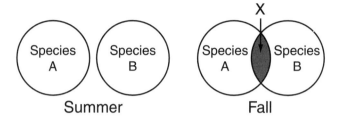

The portion of the diagram labeled X most likely indicates that
1 these populations compete for food in the fall, but not in the summer
2 the species are separated by a geographic barrier in the fall
3 the supply of oxygen is greater in the summer than in the fall
4 random mating occurs between these species in the summer

103 One reason a marine organism may have trouble surviving in a freshwater habitat is that
1 there are more carnivores in freshwater habitats
2 salt water holds more nitrogen than fresh water
3 more photosynthesis occurs in fresh water than in salt water
4 water balance is affected by salt concentration

104   The chart below illustrates some methods of pest control.

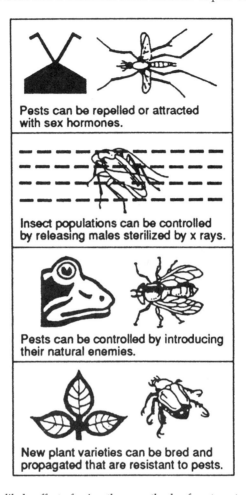

Pests can be repelled or attracted with sex hormones.

Insect populations can be controlled by releasing males sterilized by x rays.

Pests can be controlled by introducing their natural enemies.

New plant varieties can be bred and propagated that are resistant to pests.

One likely effect of using these methods of pest control will be to
1   prevent the extinction of endangered species
2   increase water pollution
3   reduce pesticide contamination of the environment
4   harm the atmosphere

Base your answers to questions 105 through 107 on the sequence of diagrams below and on your knowledge of biology.

1840

1870

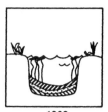

1900

1930

1960

1990

105 This sequence of diagrams best illustrates
   1   ecological succession
   2   organic evolution
   3   the effects of acid rain
   4   a food chain

106 If no human intervention or natural disaster occurs, by the year 2050 this area will most likely be a
   1   lake   3   desert
   2   swamp   4   forest

107 The natural increase in the amount of vegetation from 1840 to 1930 is related to the
   1   decreasing water depth
   2   increasing amount of sunlight
   3   presence of bottom-feeding fish
   4   use of the pond for fishing

108 In the nitrogen cycle, plants use nitrogen compounds to produce
   1   glucose   3   lipids
   2   starch   4   proteins

109 A flea in the fur of a mouse benefits at the mouse's expense. This type of relationship is known as

1 commensalism   3 saprophytism
2 parasitism   4 mutualism

PART III: This part consists of five groups. Choose three of these five groups. For those questions that are followed by four choices, record the answers in the space provided on your answer sheet. For all other questions in this part, record your answers in accordance with the directions given in the question. [15]

GROUP 1

If you choose this group, be sure to answer questions 110–114.
Base your answers to questions 110 through 114 on the reading passage below and on your knowledge of biology.

Viruses

Most viruses are little more than strands of genetic material surrounded by a protein coat. Given the opportunity to enter a living cell, a virus springs into action and is reproduced.

Researchers have long known that viruses reproduce by using some of the cell's enzymes and protein-making structures. However, the precise details of the process remain unclear. Microbiologists have recently enabled viruses to reproduce outside a living cell, in a test-tube medium containing crushed human cells, salts, ATP, amino acids, and nucleotides.

In the test tube, the viral genetic material was replicated and new viral proteins were synthesized. These new proteins were then organized into coats around the newly formed genetic material. Complete viruses were formed, demonstrating that a virus can be active outside the cell if given the right environment.

110 When a virus enters a human cell, it may

1 control photosynthesis
2 copy the DNA of the cell
3 reproduce
4 enlarge

111 Microbiologists were able to grow viruses in a test tube containing

1 crushed human cells   3 glucose
2 nutrient agar   4 ammonia

Directions (112–114): Write your answers to questions 112 through 114 in the space provided on the separate answer sheet. Your answers must be written in ink.

112 Using one or more complete sentences, describe a possible reason that the microbiologists added ATP to the test-tube medium.

113 Using one or more complete sentences, explain the function of the new viral proteins.

114 Using one or more complete sentences, state a valid conclusion that can be drawn from this research about viruses.

GROUP 2

If you choose this group, be sure to answer questions 115–119.

Base your answers to questions 115 through 119 on the information below and on your knowledge of biology.

To measure glucose use in a human, a blood sample was taken from a vein, and the amount of glucose in the sample was determined. A glucose solution was then ingested by the person being tested. Blood samples were taken periodically for 5 hours and tested to determine the amount of glucose present. Results from the tests were used to construct the data table below.

Data Table

Time (hours)	Glucose (mg/100 dL)
0	80
0.5	170
1	120
2	90
3	80
4	70
5	70

Directions (115–116): Using the information in the data table, construct a line graph on the grid provided, following the directions below.

115 Mark an appropriate scale on each of the labeled axes.

116 Plot the data from the data table. Surround each point with a small circle and connect the points.

Example:

Blood Glucose Levels

Glucose (mg/100 dL)

Time (hours)

117 Using one or more complete sentences, give a possible explanation for the drop in the glucose level between 0.5 and 1 hour after the glucose was ingested.

118 Using one or more complete sentences, state a function of glucose in the human body.

119 Based on the information given, how much glucose would most likely be present in 100 deciliters (dL) of the blood 1.5 hours after the glucose was ingested?
   (1) 90 mg   (3) 120 mg
   (2) 105 mg   (4) 170 mg

GROUP 3

If you choose this group, be sure to answer questions 120–124.

Directions (120–121): Write your answers to questions 120 and 121 in the space provided on the separate answer sheet. Your answers must be written in ink.

120 Forty bean seeds were planted in 40 different pots containing soil of the same composition and moisture level. All seeds were of the same age and plant species. The pots were divided into four groups of 10, and each group was kept at a different temperature: 5°C, 10°C, 15°C, and 20°C, respectively, for a period of 30 days. All other environmental conditions were kept constant.

Using one or more complete sentences, state a problem being investigated in this experimental setup.

121   Choose one of the labeled animal cell parts from the diagram below. In the space provided, write the letter of the part you have chosen and, using one or more complete sentences, identify the part and state one of its functions.

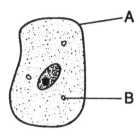

122   Twenty-five geranium plants were placed in each of four closed containers and then exposed to the light conditions shown in the data table below. All other environmental conditions were held constant for a period of 2 days. At the beginning of the investigation, the quantity of CO_2 present in each closed container was 250 cubic centimeters. The data table shows the amount of CO_2 remaining in each container at the end of 2 days.

Data Table

Container	Color of Light	CO_2 (cm^3)
1	blue	75
2	red	50
3	green	200
4	orange	150

The variable in this investigation was the
1   type of plant
2   color of light
3   amount of CO_2 in each container at the beginning of the investigation
4   number of days needed to complete the investigation

123 In the diagram below, the view of the insect specimen can best be described as
1 a ventral view, with the posterior end to the right of the page
2 an external view showing the ventral side of the abdomen
3 a dorsal view, with the anterior end to the left of the page
4 an internal view showing the dorsal side of the head region

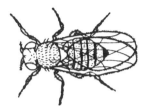

124 In addition to an indicator and proper safety equipment, which pieces of equipment shown below should be used to test for the presence of glucose in apple juice?

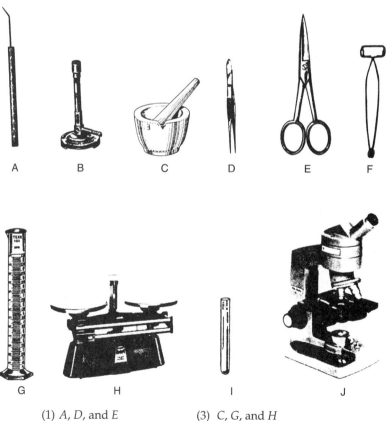

(1) *A*, *D*, and *E*   (3) *C*, *G*, and *H*
(2) *B*, *F*, and *I*   (4) *A*, *B*, and *J*

GROUP 4

If you choose this group, be sure to answer questions 125–129.

Base your answers to questions 125 through 129 on the information below and on your knowledge of biology.

A human was fed a meal containing measured amounts of proteins, starch, and fats. Eight hours later, a 10-milliliter sample fluid was removed from the human's small intestine for analysis.

Note that question 125 has only three choices.

125 Based on the relative amounts of nutrients present, which graph best represents the results of the analysis?

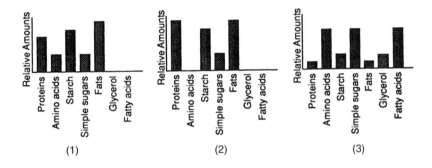

126 Which piece of equipment should be used to accurately measure the 10-milliliter sample for analysis?
   1 triple-beam balance   3 large test tube
   2 graduated cylinder   4 metric ruler

127 Which indicators could be used to test for the presence of some of the substances in the fluid sample?
   (1) Benedict's solution and Lugol's iodine
   (2) bromthymol blue solution and pH paper
   (3) Fehling's solution and bromthymol blue solution
   (4) pH paper and Lugol's iodine

Directions (128–129): Write your answers to questions 128 and 129 in the space provided on the separate answer sheet. Your answers must be written in ink.

128 Using one or more complete sentences, describe *one* safety precaution that a technician should use while analyzing the sample of intestinal fluid.

129 Using one or more complete sentences, describe *one* way that the results of the analysis would be different if the human was fed a single boiled potato instead of the meal containing measured amounts of proteins, starch, and fats.

GROUP 5

If you choose this group, be sure to answer questions 130–134.

Base your answers to questions 130 through 134 on the photograph below and on your knowledge of biology. The photograph shows onion root-tip tissue viewed under the high-power objective of a compound light microscope.

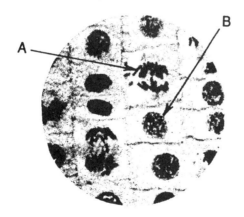

130 The photograph illustrates stages in the process of
   1 meiosis in root tips
   2 mitotic cell division in plants
   3 water conduction in onions
   4 chlorophyll production in chloroplasts

131 Identify the structure indicated by arrow *A*.

132 Identify the structure indicated by arrow *B*.

133 Using one or more complete sentences, describe one adjust-ment that could be made to the microscope to make the field of view brighter.

134 When viewed with a compound light microscope, which letter would best illustrate that the microscope inverts and reverses an image?
    (1) **A**   (3) **F**
    (2) **W**   (4) **D**

ANSWER KEY
EXAM TWO

PART I

1. 1
2. 3
3. 4
4. 1
5. 2
6. 2
7. 3
8. 1
9. 4
10. 3
11. 2
12. 1
13. 4
14. 2
15. 1
16. 4
17. 2
18. 3
19. 3
20. 4
21. 3
22. 1
23. 2
24. 4
25. 4
26. 2
27. 1
28. 3
29. 3
30. 4
31. 2
32. 2
33. 1
34. 4
35. 3
36. 3
37. 2
38. 2
39. 1
40. 3
41. 2

42. 4
43. 2
44. 3
45. 2
46. 4
47. 1
48. 1
49. 3
50. 3
51. 1
52. 1
53. 2
54. 1
55. 4
56. 3
57. 4
58. 3
59. 4

PART II

60. 1
61. 2
62. 1
63. 2
64. 3
65. 4
66. 2
67. 4
68. 3
69. 2
70. 2
71. 3
72. 2
73. 1
74. 4
75. 2
76. 3
77. 2
78. 3
79. 1
80. 1
81. 3

82. 2
83. 1
84. 1
85. 4
86. 1
87. 3
88. 4
89. 2
90. 4
91. 2
92. 3
93. 4
94. 3
95. 1
96. 2
97. 2
98. 4
99. 1
100. 2
101. 2
102. 1
103. 4
104. 3
105. 1
106. 4
107. 1
108. 4
109. 2

PART III

110. 3
111. 1

The answers here represent sample responses. Other complete-sentence responses are acceptable.

112. Microbiologists probably added ATP to the test-tube medium as an energy source.

113. The new proteins were used to form protective coats around the newly formed genetic material.

114. A virus can be active outside a cell if given the proper environment.

115–116.

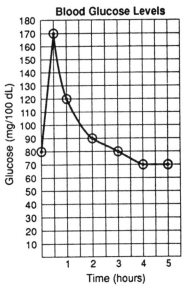

Blood Glucose Levels

117. The glucose was stored or used by the cells of the body. -OR- The glucose level dropped because body cells absorbed the glucose from the blood.

118. In the human body, glucose is used as an energy source.

119. 2

120. This experimental setup was used to investigate the effect of temperature on plant growth.

121. Part A is the plasma (cell) membrane. The plasma membrane regulates the transport of materials into and out of the cell. Part B is the vacuole. Vacuoles store materials for the cell.

122. 2
123. 3
124. 2
125. 3
126. 2
127. 1

128. While analyzing the intestinal fluid, a technician should wear goggles.

129. If the human was fed only a boiled potato, the results of the graph would be different. -OR- Not as many nutrients would be detected in the analysis.

130. 2

131. chromosome

132. nucleus or nuclear membrane

133. The diaphragm (or the mirror) could be adjusted. -OR- The objective could be switched to low power.

134. 3

The University of the State of New York

REGENTS HIGH SCHOOL EXAMINATION

BIOLOGY

Exam One

ANSWER PAPER

Part I Score (Use table below)	....
Part II Score	....
Part III Score	....
Total Score	....

Rater's Initials: ....

Pupil .... Sex: ☐ Male ☐ Female

Teacher .... School ....

All of your answers should be recorded on this answer paper.

Part I (65 credits)

1	1 2 3 4	21	1 2 3 4	41	1 2 3 4
2	1 2 3 4	22	1 2 3 4	42	1 2 3 4
3	1 2 3 4	23	1 2 3 4	43	1 2 3 4
4	1 2 3 4	24	1 2 3 4	44	1 2 3 4
5	1 2 3 4	25	1 2 3 4	45	1 2 3 4
6	1 2 3 4	26	1 2 3 4	46	1 2 3 4
7	1 2 3 4	27	1 2 3 4	47	1 2 3 4
8	1 2 3 4	28	1 2 3 4	48	1 2 3 4
9	1 2 3 4	29	1 2 3 4	49	1 2 3 4
10	1 2 3 4	30	1 2 3 4	50	1 2 3 4
11	1 2 3 4	31	1 2 3 4	51	1 2 3 4
12	1 2 3 4	32	1 2 3 4	52	1 2 3 4
13	1 2 3 4	33	1 2 3 4	53	1 2 3 4
14	1 2 3 4	34	1 2 3 4	54	1 2 3 4
15	1 2 3 4	35	1 2 3 4	55	1 2 3 4
16	1 2 3 4	36	1 2 3 4	56	1 2 3 4
17	1 2 3 4	37	1 2 3 4	57	1 2 3 4
18	1 2 3 4	38	1 2 3 4	58	1 2 3 4
19	1 2 3 4	39	1 2 3 4	59	1 2 3 4
20	1 2 3 4	40	1 2 3 4		

PART I CREDITS

Directions to Teacher:

In the table below, draw a circle around the number of right answers and the adjacent number of credits. Then write the number of credits (not the number right) in the space provided above.

No. Right	Credits	No. Right	Credits
59	65	29	35
58	64	28	34
57	63	27	33
56	62	26	32
55	61	25	31
54	60	24	30
53	59	23	29
52	58	22	28
51	57	21	27
50	56	20	26
49	55	19	25
48	54	18	24
47	53	17	23
46	52	16	22
45	51	15	21
44	50	14	20
43	49	13	18
42	48	12	17
41	47	11	15
40	46	10	14
39	45	9	13
38	44	8	11
37	43	7	10
36	42	6	8
35	41	5	7
34	40	4	6
33	39	3	4
32	38	2	3
31	37	1	1
30	36	0	0

No. right ....

Part II (20 credits)

Answer the questions in only two of the five groups in this part. Be sure to mark the answers to the groups of questions you choose in accordance with the instructions on the front page of the test booklet. Leave blank the three groups of questions you do not choose to answer.

Group 1
Biochemistry

60	1	2	3	4
61	1	2	3	4
62	1	2	3	4
63	1	2	3	4
64	1	2	3	4
65	1	2	3	4
66	1	2	3	4
67	1	2	3	
68	1	2	3	
69	1	2	3	4

Group 3
Reproduction and
Development

80	1	2	3	4
81	1	2	3	4
82	1	2	3	4
83	1	2	3	4
84	1	2	3	4
85	1	2	3	4
86	1	2	3	4
87	1	2	3	4
88	1	2	3	4
89	1	2	3	4

Group 5
Ecology

100	1	2	3	4
101	1	2	3	4
102	1	2	3	4
103	1	2	3	4
104	1	2	3	4
105	1	2	3	4
106	1	2	3	4
107	1	2	3	4
108	1	2	3	4
109	1	2	3	4

Group 2
Human Physiology

70	1	2	3	4
71	1	2	3	4
72	1	2	3	4
73	1	2	3	4
74	1	2	3	4
75	1	2	3	4
76	1	2	3	4
77	1	2	3	4
78	1	2	3	4
79	1	2	3	4

Group 4
Modern Genetics

90	1	2	3	4
91	1	2	3	4
92	1	2	3	4
93	1	2	3	4
94	1	2	3	4
95	1	2	3	4
96	1	2	3	4
97	1	2	3	4
98	1	2	3	4
99	1	2	3	4

Part III (15 credits)

Answer the questions in only three of the five groups in this part. Leave blank the groups of questions you do not choose to answer.

Group 1

110 1 2 3 4

111 1 2 3 4

112 1 2 3 4

113 1 2 3 4

114 1 2 3 4

Group 2

115 1 2 3 4

116 1 2 3 4

117 1 2 3 4

118 1 2 3 4

119 1 2 3 4

Group 3

120 _____

121 _____

122 _____

123 1 2 3 4

124 1 2 3 4

Group 4

125 1 2 3 4

126 1 2 3 4

127 1 2 3 4

128 _____

_____

_____

_____

129 _____

_____

_____

_____

Group 5

130–132

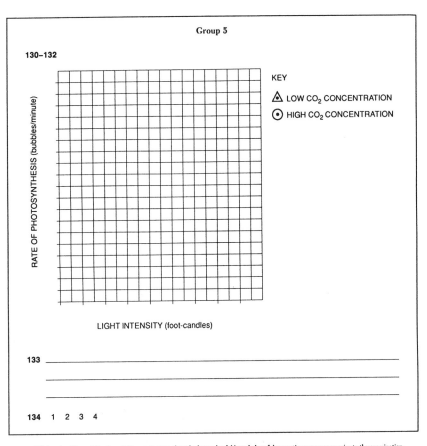

RATE OF PHOTOSYNTHESIS (bubbles/minute)

LIGHT INTENSITY (foot-candles)

KEY

△ LOW CO_2 CONCENTRATION

⊙ HIGH CO_2 CONCENTRATION

133 _____

_____

_____

134   1   2   3   4

The University of the State of New York

REGENTS HIGH SCHOOL EXAMINATION

BIOLOGY

Exam Two

ANSWER PAPER

Part I Score	....
(Use table below)	
Part II Score	....
Part III Score	....
Total Score	....

Rater's Initials: ....

Pupil .... Sex: ☐ Male ☐ Female

Teacher .... School ....

All of your answers should be recorded on this answer paper.

Part I (65 credits)

1	1 2 3 4	21	1 2 3 4	41	1 2 3 4
2	1 2 3 4	22	1 2 3 4	42	1 2 3 4
3	1 2 3 4	23	1 2 3 4	43	1 2 3 4
4	1 2 3 4	24	1 2 3 4	44	1 2 3 4
5	1 2 3 4	25	1 2 3 4	45	1 2 3 4
6	1 2 3 4	26	1 2 3 4	46	1 2 3 4
7	1 2 3 4	27	1 2 3 4	47	1 2 3 4
8	1 2 3 4	28	1 2 3 4	48	1 2 3 4
9	1 2 3 4	29	1 2 3 4	49	1 2 3 4
10	1 2 3 4	30	1 2 3 4	50	1 2 3 4
11	1 2 3 4	31	1 2 3 4	51	1 2 3 4
12	1 2 3 4	32	1 2 3 4	52	1 2 3 4
13	1 2 3 4	33	1 2 3 4	53	1 2 3 4
14	1 2 3 4	34	1 2 3 4	54	1 2 3 4
15	1 2 3 4	35	1 2 3 4	55	1 2 3 4
16	1 2 3 4	36	1 2 3 4	56	1 2 3 4
17	1 2 3 4	37	1 2 3 4	57	1 2 3 4
18	1 2 3 4	38	1 2 3 4	58	1 2 3 4
19	1 2 3 4	39	1 2 3 4	59	1 2 3 4
20	1 2 3 4	40	1 2 3 4		

PART I CREDITS

Directions to Teacher:

In the table below, draw a circle around the number of right answers and the adjacent number of credits. Then write the number of credits (not the number right) in the space provided above.

No. Right	Credits	No. Right	Credits
59	65	29	35
58	64	28	34
57	63	27	33
56	62	26	32
55	61	25	31
54	60	24	30
53	59	23	29
52	58	22	28
51	57	21	27
50	56	20	26
49	55	19	25
48	54	18	24
47	53	17	23
46	52	16	22
45	51	15	21
44	50	14	20
43	49	13	18
42	48	12	17
41	47	11	15
40	46	10	14
39	45	9	13
38	44	8	11
37	43	7	10
36	42	6	8
35	41	5	7
34	40	4	6
33	39	3	4
32	38	2	3
31	37	1	1
30	36	0	0

No. right ....

Part II (20 credits)

Answer the questions in only two of the five groups in this part. Be sure to mark the answers to the groups of questions you choose in accordance with the instructions on the front page of the test booklet. Leave blank the three groups of questions you do not choose to answer.

Group 1 **Biochemistry**	**Group 3** **Reproduction and** **Development**	**Group 5** **Ecology**

Group 1
Biochemistry

60 1 2 3 4
61 1 2 3 4
62 1 2 3 4
63 1 2 3 4
64 1 2 3 4
65 1 2 3 4
66 1 2 3 4
67 1 2 3
68 1 2 3
69 1 2 3 4

Group 3
Reproduction and
Development

80 1 2 3 4
81 1 2 3 4
82 1 2 3 4
83 1 2 3 4
84 1 2 3 4
85 1 2 3 4
86 1 2 3 4
87 1 2 3 4
88 1 2 3 4
89 1 2 3 4

Group 5
Ecology

100 1 2 3 4
101 1 2 3 4
102 1 2 3 4
103 1 2 3 4
104 1 2 3 4
105 1 2 3 4
106 1 2 3 4
107 1 2 3 4
108 1 2 3 4
109 1 2 3 4

Group 2
Human Physiology

70 1 2 3 4
71 1 2 3 4
72 1 2 3 4
73 1 2 3 4
74 1 2 3 4
75 1 2 3 4
76 1 2 3 4
77 1 2 3 4
78 1 2 3 4
79 1 2 3 4

Group 4
Modern Genetics

90 1 2 3 4
91 1 2 3 4
92 1 2 3 4
93 1 2 3 4
94 1 2 3 4
95 1 2 3 4
96 1 2 3 4
97 1 2 3 4
98 1 2 3 4
99 1 2 3 4

Answer the questions in only three of the five groups in this part. Leave blank the groups of questions you do not choose to answer.

Group 1

110 1 2 3 4

111 1 2 3 4

112 _____

_____

_____

113 _____

_____

_____

114 _____

_____

_____

Group 2

115–116

Blood Glucose Levels

Glucose (mg/100 dL)

Time (hours)

117 _____

_____

_____

118 _____

_____

_____

119 1 2 3 4

Group 3

120 _____
_____
_____
_____
_____

121 _____
_____
_____
_____

122   1   2   3   4
123   1   2   3   4
124   1   2   3   4

Group 4

125   1   2   3   4
126   1   2   3   4
127   1   2   3   4
128 _____
_____
_____
_____

129 _____
_____
_____
_____

Group 5

130 1 2 3 4

131 _____

132 _____

133 _____

_____

_____

_____

134 1 2 3 4

I do hereby affirm, at the close of this examination, that I had no unlawful knowledge of the questions or answers prior to the examination, and that I have neither given nor received assistance in answering any of the questions during the examination.

_____
Signature

Index

Bronchioles, 53
Bronchitis, 54
Bronchus, in human respiratory system, 53
Bryophytes, 33–34
Budding, 91
Bulbs, vegetative propagation in, 92

Cambium, 37
Capillary, 54, 59, 60
Carbohydrates, 3–6
Carbon, 2–8
Carbon fixation reaction, 30
Cardiac muscle, 79
Carnivore, 149, 150
Cartilage, 78–79
Cell, 15–20
    in animals, 19
    eukaryotic, 15
    measuring length of, 162
    in plants, 18–19
    prokaryotic, 15, 19
Cell plate, 90
Cell theory, 15
Cellular respiration, 21–26. *See also*
        Aerobic respiration;
        Anaerobic respiration
    shorthand reaction of, 22
Cellulose, 6
Central nervous system, 72. *See also*
        Nervous system
Centrioles, 18, 19, 89
Centromere, 88
Cerebellum, 72
Cerebral palsy, 73
Cerebrum, 72
Chemical equation, 2
Chemical reactions, 2, 8–12. *See also*
        Enzymes
Chemical symbols, 1
Chick embryos, development of,
        104–105
Chloroplasts, 19
Chorion, 104, 105
Chromatids, sister, 88
Chromosomes, 119
    mutations of, 126
Chyme, 49
Cilia, 18

Circulatory system
    closed vs. open, 57
    in humans, 58–62
        blood, 61–62. *See also* Blood
        disorders of, 64–65
        heart, 58, 60
        pulmonary, 60–61
Classification. *See* Taxonomy
Cleavage, in embryonic development, 102
Cleavage furrow, 90
Climax community, in ecological succession, 152
Codons, 124
Coenzymes, 9
Cofactors, 9
Cohesion, and ability of water to rise in plants, 34
Color blindness, 115–116
Commensalism, 151
Community, ecological, 148–149
Compounds, 2
Constipation, 50
Consumers, in ecology, 21, 148, 149, 150
Coronary thrombosis, 64
Cotyledons, 37
Crop, in earthworm, 46
Crossing-over, in meiosis, 94
Cuticle of leaf, 27, 28
Cytokinesis, 90
Cytokinins, 38
Cyton, 69
Cytoplasm, 15
Cytosine, 120

Darwin, Charles, 131–132. *See also*
        Evolution
Deamination, 68
Deciduous forest, temperate, 146
Decomposers, in ecology, 148, 149, 150
Dehydration synthesis, 4–5, 7
Dendrites, 69
Deoxyribonucleic acid. *See* DNA
Deoxyribose, 120
Dermis, 68
Deserts, 146
Diabetes, 76, 77
Diarrhea, 50
Diffusion, 51, 52, 55

Digestion, 44
Digestive system, in humans, 47–50
    disorders of, 50–51
    large intestine, 50
    mouth, 48
    pancreas, 49–50
    small intestine, 49
    stomach, 48–49
Dipeptides, 6–7
Disaccharides, 3, 4–5
DNA, 8, 119–122
    base pairing in, 121
    double-stranded, 121
    recombinant, 126
    replication of, 121–122
    single-stranded, 120
    vs. RNA, 123
Double fertilization, 36–37
Double helix, 119. *See also* DNA

Earthworm
    circulatory system in, 57
    digestive system in, 46
    excretory system in, 65
    locomotion in, 78
    nervous system in, 70
Ecology, 145–155
    biosphere, 145–147
    community, 148–149
    ecological succession, 151–152
    ecosystems, 147–148
    food chain, 149–150
    and humans, 152–153
    nitrogen cycle, 148
    symbiotic relationships, 150–151
    water cycle, 148
Ecosystem, 147–148
Ectoderm, in embryonic development,
        103, 104
Effector neurons, 71
Egestion, 44
Elements, 1–2
    essential, 2
Embryo, development of, 101–105
    blastula, 103
    in chicks, 104–105
    cleavage, 102
    differentiation, 104
    gastrula, 103–104

Embryology, as evidence of evolution, 133
Emphysema, 54
Endocrine system, 74–77
    adrenal glands, 76
    disorders of, 77
    negative feedback in, 74–75
    hypothalamus, 75
    pancreas, 75–76
    parathyroid glands, 77
    pituitary gland, 75
    sex hormones, 77
    thyroid, 76–77
Endocytosis, 56
Endoderm, in embryonic develop-
        ment, 103, 104
Endoplasmic reticulum, 17
Endoskeleton, 78
Endosperm, 36
Environment. *See* Ecology
Enzyme specificity, 9
Enzyme-substrate complex, 8–9
Enzymes, 8–11
    denatured, 10
    saturated, 11
Epidermis, 68
    lower, of leaf, 27, 28
Epiglottis, 53
Esophagus, 48
Estrogen, 77, 99
Ethylenes, 38
Euglena, 18
    locomotion in, 78
Eukaryotes, 15, 142
Evolution, 131–137
    Darwin's theory of, 131–132
    evidence for, 132–133
    fast vs. slow, 134–135
    heterotroph hypothesis, 135–136
    Lamarck's theory of, 132
    speciation and, 133–134
Excretion, 65–68
    in earthworms, 65
    in humans, 66–68. *See also* Excretory
        system, in humans
    in insects, 66
Excretory system, in humans, 66–68
    disorders of, 68
    nephrons, 66–67
    skin, 67–68

Exoskeleton, 78
Expiration, 54

Fallopian tube, 99, 100
Fauna, 145
Feces, 50
Fehling's solution, 162
Fermentation, 24
Fertilization, 101–102
    double, 36–37
Fight-or-flight response, 76
Filament, 36
Filtrate, 67
Fission, binary, 91
Flagella, 18
Flora, 145
Fluid-mosaic model, 16–17, 56
Follicle-stimulating hormone, 75, 99
Food chain, 149–150
Food vacuole, in *Amoeba*, 44
Fossils, as evidence of evolution, 132
Fructose, 3–4
Fungi, classification of, 141

Gallstones, 51
Gametes, 96
Gametogenesis. *See* Meiosis
Ganglia, 70
Gastric caeca, in grasshopper, 47
Gastrovascular cavity, 44
Gastrula, 103–104
Gastrulation, 103
Gene-chromosome theory, 114
Genetic engineering, 126–127
Genetic screening, 127
Genetics, 109–117. *See also* DNA; RNA
    alleles, definition of, 109
    codons, 124
    detection of defects, 127–128
    disorders due to, 128
    dominant vs. recessive, 109–110
    F2 generation, 112–113
    gene-chromosome theory, 114
    genes, definition of, 109, 125
    genotype, definition of, 110
    homozygous vs. heterozygous, 110
    law of dominance, 110–111, 114
    law of independent assortment,
        113–114
    law of segregation, 112–113, 114

mutations, 125–126
non-Mendelian, 115
one gene–one polypeptide hypothe-
    sis, 125
parent and filial generations, 110
phenotype, definition of, 110
proteins and the genetic code,
    122–124
Punnett squares, 111–112
sex determination, 102, 115
sex linkage, 115–116
Genotype, definition of, 110
Geographic isolation, 133
Germ layers, in embryonic develop-
    ment, 103–104
Gibberellins, 39
Gills, 52
Gizzard, in earthworm, 46
Glomerulus, 66, 67
Glucagon, 75
Glucose, 3–4, 22–23
Glycogen, 6, 76
Glycolysis, 22–23
Goiter, 77
Golgi bodies, 17
Gonads, 93–94
Gout, 68
Gradualism, 134–135
Grafting, 92
Grana, 28
Grasshopper
    circulatory system in, 57
    digestion in, 46–47
    locomotion in, 78
    nervous system in, 70
    respiration in, 52
Grasslands, 146
Gravitropism, 38
Growth-stimulating hormone, 75
Guanine, 120
Guard cells, of leaf, 27, 28

Heart, human, 58
Hemophilia, 115
Herbivore, 149, 150
Heterotrophs, 21, 43, 149, 150
Heterotroph hypothesis, 135–136
Homeostasis, 73
Homologous structures, 133
Hormones, 74

Hybridization, 126
Hydra, 45
Hydrolysis, 5, 22
Hypocotyl, 37
Hypothalamus, 75

Immune system, in humans, 62–64
Immunity, 64
Inbreeding, 126
Indicators, 162
Induced fit, 9
Ingestion, 44
Inorganic compounds, 3
Inspiration, 54
Insulin, 75
Interneurons, 71
Intestines, in human digestive system,
    49, 50
Iodine, 161
Iodine solution, 162
Islet of Langerhans, 75

Karyotyping, 127–128
Kidney failure, 68
Kidneys, 66
Krebs cycle, 23

Lactic acid, 24, 25
Lamarck, and theory of evolution, 132
Large intestine, in human digestive
    system, 50
Larynx, in human respiratory sys-
    tem, 53
Law of dominance, 110–111, 114
Law of independent assortment, 113–114
Law of segregation, 112–113, 114
Leaf, anatomy of, 27–28
Leukemia, 65
Lichens, as pioneer organisms in eco-
    logical succession, 151–152
Ligaments, 79
Linnaeus, Carolus, binomial classifica-
    tion system of, 142
Lipase, 49
Lipids, 7
Liver, 68
Lock-and-key theory, 9
Locomotion, 77–80. See also Skeletal
    system
    in earthworms, 78

in grasshoppers, 78
in unicellular organisms, 78
in vertebrates, 78
Lugol's solution, 162
Lungs, 52, 68
Luteal surge, 99
Luteinizing hormone, 75, 99
Lymph, 63
Lymph node, 63–64
Lymph vessels, 63
Lymphocytes, 62
Lysosomes, 18

Magnification, 160–161
Malpighian tubules, 66
Marsupials, embryo development in, 105
Medulla, 72
Meiosis, 93–98
    first division, 94–96, 97
    second division, 96, 97
    vs. mitosis, 98
Mendel, Gregor, 109. See also Genetics
Meningitis, 73
Menstrual cycle, 99–100
    corpus luteum stage, 100
    follicle stage, 99–100
Meristems, 37
Mesoderm, in embryonic develop-
    ment, 103, 104
Messenger RNA, 123
Metaphase
    in meiosis
        first division, 95
        second division, 96
    in mitosis, 89, 91
Metaphase plate, 89
Methylene blue, 161
Microdissection instrument, 161
Microscope
    compound light, 160–161
    dissecting, 161
    electron, 161
Mitochondria, 17–18
Mitosis, 87–91
    mnemonic for, 90–91
    stages of, 88–90
    vs. meiosis, 98
Monera, classification of, 142
Monohybrid cross, 110
Monosaccharides, 3–4

Morula, 102
Motor neurons, 71
Mouth, in human digestive system, 48
Muscles, 79
Mutation, genetic, 125–126
Mutualism, 151
Myelin sheath, 72

NADPH, 29
Natural selection, 131–132
Negative feedback system, 74–75
Nephridia, 65
Nephrons, 66
Nerve net, 70
Nervous system, 69–73
    in animals, 70
    in humans, 71–73
        disorders of, 73
        parts of, 72–73
Neuron, 69
    communication in, 71–72
    types of, 71
Neurotransmitter, 69
Nondisjunction, 126
Nose, in human respiratory sys-
        tem, 52–53
Nucleic acids, 7–8
Nucleotides, 119–120
Nucleus, 15, 17, 19
Nutrition, 43–51
    in complex animals, 46–47
    in humans, 47–50. See also Digestive
        system, in humans
    in simple animals, 44–45
    in unicellular animals, 44

Omnivore, 149, 150
Oogenesis, 97
Oral cavity, in human digestive sys-
        tem, 48
Oral groove, in *Paramecium*, 44
Organelles, 15, 16–18, 19
Organic catalysts, 8
Organic compounds, 3
Osmosis, 55
Ova, 99
Ovaries, 94, 99
Oviduct, 99, 100
Ovulation, 100
Oxidation of glucose, 22–23

Oxidative phosphorylation, 23

Palisade layer of leaf, 27, 28
Pancreas, 49–50, 75
Pancreatic duct, 50
Paramecium, 18
    locomotion in, 78
    nutrition and, 44
Parasitism, 151
Parathormone, 77
Parathyroid glands, 77
Passive transport, 55
Pepsin, 48–49
Periodic table of elements, 1
Peripheral nervous system, 72
Peristalsis, 48
Permeability, selective, of plasma
        membrane, 55
pH, and enzymatic reactions, 10–11
pH paper, 162
Phagocytes, 62
Phagocytosis, 44, 56
Pharynx, in human respiratory sys-
        tem, 53
Phenotype, definition of, 110
Phenylketonuria, 128
Phloem, 34
Phosphoglyceraldehyde (PGAL), 30
Photolysis, 30
Photons, 29
Photosynthesis, 4, 27–32
    dark reaction, 30
    light reaction, 29–30
Phototropism, 38
Pinocytosis, 56
Pioneer organisms, in ecological suc-
        cession, 151–152
Pistil, 35, 36
Pituitary gland, 75
Placenta, 105
Plants, 33–41
    classification of, 33–35
    embryonic development in, 37
    flowering, 35–36
    growth in, 37
    respiration in, 51
    roots of, 35
    tropism in, 38
Plasma, 60
Plasma membrane, 16–17, 19, 55

Platelets, 62
Polar bodies, 98
Polio, 73
Pollination, 36
Polypeptides, 6–7, 124
Polysaccharides, 3, 5–6
Population growth, 153
"Primordial soup," 135–136
Producers, in ecology, 21, 148–149, 150
Products, 2
Progesterone, 77, 99, 100
Prokaryotes, 15, 142
Prophase
    in meiosis
        first division, 94–95
        second division, 96
    in mitosis, 88–89, 91
Proteases, 49
Protein, 7
    synthesis of, 123–124
Pseudopodia, in *Amoeba*, 44
Puberty, 101
Pulmonary artery, 60
Pulmonary circulation, 60–61
Pulmonary veins, 61
Punctuated equilibrium, 134–135
Punnett squares, 111–112
    and sex linkage, 116
Pyruvic acid, 23

Rain forests, tropical, 146
Reactants, 2
Recombinant DNA, 126
Red blood cells, 62
Reflex arc, 71–72
Regeneration, 93
Regulation, 69–77. *See also* Endocrine
        system; Nervous system
Reproduction, 87–108. *See also* Meiosis;
        Mitosis
    asexual, 91–93
    human, 98–101. *See also* Embryo,
        development of
        female, 99. *See also* Menstrual cycle
        male, 101
Reproductive isolation, 133–134
Respiration, 51–54
    in animals, 51–52
    in humans, 52–54. *See also*
        Respiratory system, in humans

in microorganisms, 51
in plants, 51
Respiration, cellular. *See* Aerobic respi-
        ration; Anaerobic respiration
Respiratory system, in humans, 52–54
    breathing, mechanics of, 54
    disorders of, 54
Ribonucleic acid. *See* RNA
Ribosomal RNA, 123
Ribosomes, 17
RNA, 8, 122–124
    types of, 123
    vs. DNA, 123
Roots, plant, 35
Runners, vegetative propagation in, 92

Salivary amylase, 48
Salivary glands
    in grasshoppers, 47
    in humans, 48
Saprophyte, 149
Schwann's cells, 72
Scientific method, 157–160
    experimental controls, 159
    generalization, 159
    hypothesis, 157
    results, 158
    variables, 157
Scrotum, 101
Sensory neurons, 71
Setae, 78
Sex determination, 102, 115
Sex hormones, 77
Sex linkage, 115–116
Sickle cell anemia, 128
Sister chromatids, 88
Skeletal muscle, 79
Skeletal system, 78–80
    bones and joints, 79
    diseases of, 80
    muscles, 79
Skin, 67–68
Small intestine, in human digestive
        system, 49
Smooth (visceral) muscle, 79
Somatic nervous system, 73
Speciation, 133–134
Spermatogenesis, 97
Spinal cord, 72
Spindle fibers, 89

Spiracles, 52
Spongy layer of leaf, 27, 28
Sporulation, 91–92
Staining, 161
Stamen, 35, 36
Starch, 6
Stomach, in human digestive system, 48–49
Stomates of leaf, 27, 28
Striations, 79
Stroke, 73
Stroma, 28
Subcutaneous tissue, 68
Substrates, concentration of, and enzymatic reactions, 12
Sugars, 3–6
Sweat glands, 67, 68
Symbiotic relationships, 150–151
Synapse, 69
Synapsis, in meiosis, 94
Systemic circulation, 58–59

Taiga, 146
Target cells, 74
Taxonomy, 139–142
    of animals, 141–142
    binomial classification, 142
    of fungi, 141
    kingdoms, 140–142
Tay-Sachs disease, 128
Telophase
    in meiosis
        first division, 96
        second division, 96
    in mitosis, 89, 91
Temperature, and enzymatic reactions, 9–10
Tendonitis, 80
Tendons, 79
Terminal branches, 69
Testes, 94, 101
Testosterone, 77, 101
Tetrads, in meiosis, 94, 95
Thigmotropism, 38
Thrombosis, coronary, 64

Thylakoids, 28
Thymine, 120
Thyroid, 76–77
Thyroid-stimulating hormone, 75
Thyroxin, 76
Trachea, in human respiratory system, 53
Tracheal tubes, 52
Tracheophytes, 33, 34
Transfer RNA, 123
Transport, 54–65. *See also* Circulatory system; Immune system, in humans
    active, 55–56
    in animals, 57
    passive, 55
Triglycerides, 7
Tropical rain forests, 146
Tropisms, 38
Tubers, vegetative propagation in, 92
Tundra, 146

Ulcers, 50
Ultracentrifuge, 161
Uracil, 122
Ureter, 67
Urethra, 67

Vacuoles, 18
Vegetative propagation, 92
Veins, 60
Ventral nerve cord, 70
Ventricles, in human heart, 58
Venules, 60
Vertebrates, respiration in, 52
Villi, 50

White blood cells, 62

Xylem, 34

Yolk sac, 104, 105

Zygote, 101

ABOUT THE AUTHOR

Kim Magloire received a biology and Science and Human Affairs degree from Princeton University. She is now completing graduate work at Columbia University. As a teacher for The Princeton Review, Kim has prepared hundreds of students for a variety of standardized tests, including the Biology Regents exam.

Kim Magloire is also the publisher of *SciTech Magazine,* a publication that includes a wide range of articles to motivate students to learn about science, math, and technology. She is also the founder of the SciTech Youth Foundation, a non-profit organization that inspires interest in the sciences by hosting a variety of events for high school students. To contact the author about this book or *SciTech Magazine* call 212-288-0914 or send e-mail to km@interport.net.

NOTES:

NOTES:

NOTES:

NOTES:

NOTES:

NOTES:

NOTES:

NOTES:

NOTES:

NOTES:

FIND US...

International

Hong Kong
4/F Sun Hung Kai Centre
30 Harbour Road, Wan Chai,
Hong Kong
Tel: (011)85-2-517-3016

Japan
Fuji Building 40, 15-14
Sakuragaokacho, Shibuya Ku,
Tokyo 150, Japan
Tel: (011)81-3-3463-1343

Korea
Tae Young Bldg, 944-24,
Daechi- Dong, Kangnam-Ku
The Princeton Review- ANC
Seoul, Korea 135-280,
South Korea
Tel: (011)82-2-554-7763

Mexico City
PR Mex S De RL De Cv
Guanajuato 228 Col. Roma
06700 Mexico D.F., Mexico
Tel: 525-564-9468

Montreal
666 Sherbrooke St.
West, Suite 202
Montreal, QC H3A 1E7 Canada
Tel: (514) 499-0870

Pakistan
1 Bawa Park - 90 Upper Mall
Lahore, Pakistan
Tel: (011)92-42-571-2315

Spain
Pza. Castilla, 3 - 5° A, 28046
Madrid, Spain
Tel: (011)341-323-4212

Taiwan
155 Chung Hsiao East Road
Section 4 - 4th Floor,
Taipei R.O.C., Taiwan
Tel: (011)886-2-751-1243

Thailand
Building One, 99 Wireless Road
Bangkok, Thailand 10330
Tel: (662) 256-7080

Toronto
1240 Bay Street, Suite 300
Toronto M5R 2A7 Canada
Tel: (800) 495-7737
Tel: (716) 839-4391

Vancouver
4212 University Way NE,
Suite 204
Seattle, WA 98105
Tel: (206) 548-1100

National (U.S.)
We have over 60 offices around the U.S. and
run courses in over 400 sites. For courses and locations
within the U.S. call 1 (800) 2/Review and you will be
routed to the nearest office.

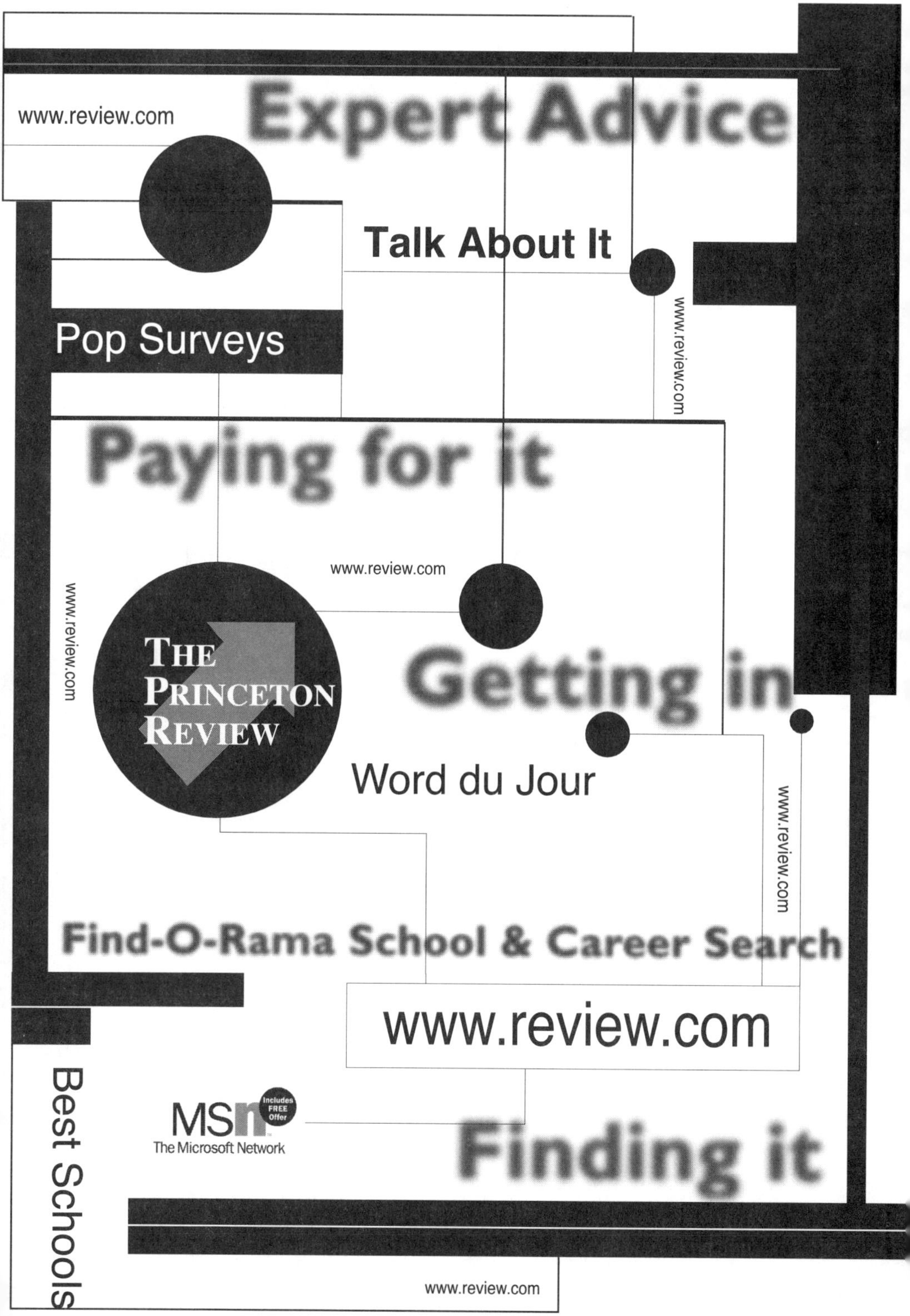

www.review.com

Expert Advice

Talk About It

www.review.com

Pop Surveys

Paying for it

www.review.com

www.review.com

THE
PRINCETON
REVIEW

Getting in

Word du Jour

www.review.com

Find-O-Rama School & Career Search

www.review.com

MSn
The Microsoft Network
Includes FREE Offer

Finding it

Best Schools

Free!

Did you know that The Microsoft Network gives you one free month?

Call us at 1-800-FREE MSN. We'll send you a free CD to get you going.

Then, you can explore the World Wide Web for one month, free. Exchange e-mail with your family and friends. Play games, book airline tickets, handle finances, go car shopping, explore old hobbies and discover new ones. There's one big, useful online world out there. And for one month, it's a free world.

Call **1-800-FREE MSN,** Dept. 3197, for offer details or visit us at **www.msn.com**. Some restrictions apply.

MSN.

Microsoft· Where do you want to go today?®   The Microsoft Network